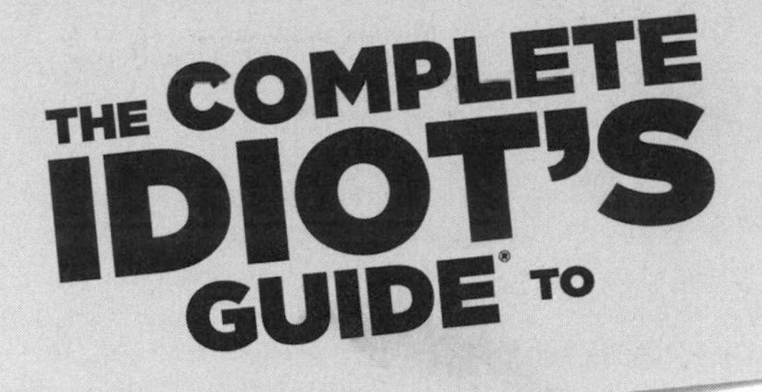

The TOEFL®

by Elizabeth Rollins

A member of Penguin Group (USA) Inc.

ALPHA BOOKS

Published by Penguin Group (USA) Inc.

Penguin Group (USA) Inc., 375 Hudson Street, New York, New York 10014, USA • Penguin Group (Canada), 90 Eglinton Avenue East, Suite 700, Toronto, Ontario M4P 2Y3, Canada (a division of Pearson Penguin Canada Inc.) • Penguin Books Ltd., 80 Strand, London WC2R 0RL, England • Penguin Ireland, 25 St. Stephen's Green, Dublin 2, Ireland (a division of Penguin Books Ltd.) • Penguin Group (Australia), 250 Camberwell Road, Camberwell, Victoria 3124, Australia (a division of Pearson Australia Group Pty. Ltd.) • Penguin Books India Pvt. Ltd., 11 Community Centre, Panchsheel Park, New Delhi—110 017, India • Penguin Group (NZ), 67 Apollo Drive, Rosedale, North Shore, Auckland 1311, New Zealand (a division of Pearson New Zealand Ltd.) • Penguin Books (South Africa) (Pty.) Ltd., 24 Sturdee Avenue, Rosebank, Johannesburg 2196, South Africa • Penguin Books Ltd., Registered Offices: 80 Strand, London WC2R 0RL, England

International Standard Book Number: 978-1-61564-306-6
Library of Congress Catalog Card Number: 2013933132

15 14 13 8 7 6 5 4 3 2 1

Interpretation of the printing code: The rightmost number of the first series of numbers is the year of the book's printing; the rightmost number of the second series of numbers is the number of the book's printing. For example, a printing code of 13-1 shows that the first printing occurred in 2013.

Printed in the United States of America

Publisher: *Mike Sanders*
Executive Managing Editor: *Billy Fields*
Executive Acquisitions Editor: *Lori Cates Hand*
Development Editor: *Kayla Dugger*
Production Editor: *Jana M. Stefanciosa*

Cover Designer: *William Thomas*
Book Designers: *William Thomas, Rebecca Batchelor*
Indexer: *Tonya Heard*
Layout: *Ayanna Lacey*
Proofreader: *Laura Caddell*

Contents

Appendixes

Introduction

Are you ready to take the TOEFL? If you're planning to apply to an academic program that requires the TOEFL, this book is the place to start. The TOEFL is a standardized test, which means everyone who takes it is scored by the same criteria, no matter how long they have studied English or how much experience they have speaking, reading, listening, and writing it. This gives the programs to which you apply the amount of information they need to assess your ability to do well in an academic or university setting.

The TOEFL can be challenging, even for people who are fluent in everyday English. Because of the way the test is written and scored, you need to understand exactly how to approach listening, reading, speaking, and writing on the test to score your best. Whether you're confident in your ability to study and pass the test—or if you think you may need more preparation before you take the exam—this book explains exactly what skills you need to have and how to use them to do your best on the test, without spending time on anything you don't need for the exam.

This book is written to take you calmly and logically through the basics of the TOEFL and to show you how to conquer each of the sections of the exam. There are no shortcuts or secret tricks to taking the TOEFL, but this book will lead you through the best ways to use what you already know to score as high as possible. This book contains practice sections and full-length tests modeled after the TOEFL so you will be able to practice what you've learned and be ready to take the TOEFL with confidence. *The Complete Idiot's Guide to the TOEFL* is the first step in conquering the exam.

How This Book Is Organized

To use this book, start at the beginning and work your way through. You may know some of the things outlined in the first part already, especially if you've already registered for or taken the TOEFL. You also may be stronger in some sections of the test than others. While it may be tempting to read through the how-to chapters of the book and not do the practice questions, or focus only on the sections you struggle in, don't skip any portion of the book. You will get the maximum benefit from this book only if you work through each section in order, paying special attention to the practice sections and the answer keys and explanations. For ease of use, this book is divided into seven parts:

Part 1, Taking the Test, talks about TOEFL basics, including what the TOEFL is and how the TOEFL is written. This part tells you what you need to know to register and prep for the exam. It also gives you a countdown to prepping for exam day, including what to study when and how to take care of yourself physically and mentally so you can be at your best for the exam and avoid test anxiety.

Part 2, TOEFL Reading, discusses the TOEFL Reading section. It looks at how to read the specific kinds of passages that appear in this section of the TOEFL, as well as how to answer the multiple-choice questions asked about each passage. This part also contains practice passages and questions, along with an answer key and explanations for the answers.

Part 3, TOEFL Listening, covers the TOEFL Listening section. It discusses how to listen to the two specific kinds of lectures that appear in this section of the TOEFL, as well as how to answer the multiple-choice questions asked about each lecture. This part also contains practice lectures and questions, along with an answer key and explanations for the answers.

Part 4, TOEFL Speaking, discusses the TOEFL Speaking section. It explores the kinds of lectures and passages used as prompts for the Speaking questions, as well as how you should format your responses to these prompts. You can also find practice questions and a scoring guide in this part.

Part 5, TOEFL Writing, covers the TOEFL Writing section. It looks at the two types of writing prompts and how to approach them, as well as how to format your responses to these prompts. You can also find practice questions and a scoring guide in this part.

Part 6, Vocabulary and Fluency for All Sections of the TOEFL, covers concepts that will help you with all sections of the TOEFL, including vocabulary, grammar, idioms, and fluency.

Part 7, Full-Length Practice Tests, includes two practice tests you can take to prepare for the TOEFL, along with the answer keys and explanations for each test.

Extra

Throughout the book, you'll find especially helpful tips and information set off in sidebars. There are four types of sidebars, each providing something extra you can really use:

DEFINITION

These clarify and define words, giving you a better understanding of important terms related to the TOEFL.

WARNING

These sidebars provide advice to help you steer clear of trouble when studying for and taking the TOEFL.

PRACTICE TIP

These tips help you practice more efficiently and intelligently for the different sections on the TOEFL.

EXAM TIP

These sidebars give you information and techniques to help you score your best on the actual exam.

But Wait! There's More!

Have you logged on to idiotsguides.com lately? If you haven't, go there now! We've included audio files for the Listening and Speaking sections in the practice tests you'll want to check out, all online. Point your browser to idiotsguides.com/toefl, and enjoy!

Acknowledgments

This book would not have been possible without the support and encouragement of everyone I've worked with teaching TOEFL throughout the years, especially my students, who were always so open and eager to learn.

Special thanks to Lori Cates Hand and Kayla Dugger for their patience, good humor, and common sense.

Special Thanks to the Technical Reviewer

The Complete Idiot's Guide to the TOEFL was reviewed by an expert who double-checked the accuracy of what you'll learn here, to help us ensure that this book gives you everything you need to know about the TOEFL. Special thanks are extended to Jeff Burnham.

Jeff Burnham has taught English to speakers of other languages at the postsecondary level for more than 15 years, including courses on all skill areas, and has taught TOEFL preparation courses. He is currently coordinator and assistant professor in the ESOL program at Central Campus of the Ivy Tech Community College of Indiana. Jeff has a Master's degree in linguistics from the University of Utah.

Trademarks

Part 1
Taking the Test

This part provides basic information about the TOEFL.

Chapter 1 discusses what the TOEFL is, who writes it, what it tests, how it differs from the TOEIC, how the TOEFL is administered and scored, and how to register for the TOEFL.

Chapter 2 contains best practices for preparing for and taking the TOEFL and includes information on preparing for the questions, preparing physically to take the exam, and staying emotionally neutral and focused during the exam. It also has a discussion of test anxiety and ways you can surmount it.

Chapter 1

What Is the TOEFL?

In This Chapter

- What the TOEFL is
- How the TOEFL is scored
- What to do with your TOEFL score after the test

Congratulations! You're taking the TOEFL! That's great news, because it means you've decided to advance your education by applying to attend a university or graduate school in the United States. You're ready to move to a new country, expand your knowledge, meet new people, and get a whole different view of the world.

There's just one obstacle standing in your way: this test. You may be afraid of taking the TOEFL, or simply annoyed you have to do it. Either way, this book is going to make your life significantly easier by teaching you everything you need to know to take the TOEFL with confidence.

Stop! If you could not read the previous two paragraphs easily and fluidly, you are not ready to take the TOEFL, or to study in an all-English environment in the United States. Keep studying English, read everything you can find in English, and find conversation partners to help you with your comprehension and speaking—then revisit this book in a few months.

About the TOEFL

The TOEFL is the Test of English as a Foreign Language. It tests your proficiency at English in a university setting. It is designed to discover if you have the ability to communicate in English well enough to succeed at an English-speaking university.

The TOEFL tests your ability to understand readings and lectures on academic subjects such as history, science, and the humanities. It also tests your comprehension of readings and conversations that occur in a university setting on topics such as study skills and living in university housing, as well as your ability to speak and write on academic and university life topics.

What Does the TOEFL Test?

The TOEFL tests four areas: reading, listening, speaking, and writing.

WARNING

You may be able to read, write, listen to, and speak English in your daily life, but these tasks are very specific on the TOEFL. They don't resemble what you do on a daily basis. Be sure you understand exactly how you should answer the questions to score as well as you can in each section.

The Reading section consists of 3 or 4 passages with 12 to 15 multiple-choice questions for each passage, for a total of 36 to 56 questions. You have 60 to 80 minutes to complete this section.

The Listening section consists of audio lectures and conversations. You are asked 4 to 8 questions per lecture or conversation, for a total of 34 to 51 questions. You have 60 to 90 minutes to complete this section.

There is a 10-minute break after the Listening section.

The Speaking section consists of six different passages, some of which are combined with audio lectures. You must formulate a response to each passage and speak your response into the computer to record it. You have 20 minutes to complete this section.

The Writing section consists of two prompts: one a passage and listening task, and one a question prompt. You must write a response to each of these prompts. You have 50 minutes to complete this section.

Who Writes the TOEFL?

The TOEFL is written by the Educational Testing Service (ETS). The ETS writes the TOEFL, the SAT, and a number of other standardized tests used for entrance into American universities. Because the ETS writes these tests in specific ways, it is possible to learn the patterns used to write the test and increase your chances of answering questions correctly.

Multiple-choice questions in particular are written so incorrect answer choices are tempting for consistent reasons. Once you can recognize a trap answer in a few questions, you will be able to recognize tempting-but-incorrect answer choices in more questions. The Speaking and Writing sections require writing essays, and these are scored in predictable ways (which I'll discuss later, in Parts 4 and 5).

Who Takes the TOEFL?

Anyone applying to a U.S. university program at either an undergraduate or graduate level needs to take the TOEFL, unless they are coming from an English-speaking secondary school or undergraduate program in an English-speaking country. Universities assume people who have graduated from English-speaking programs in English-speaking countries communicate in English well enough to succeed in an undergraduate or graduate program conducted in English.

This means people taking the TOEFL have all sorts of different backgrounds and proficiency levels in English. They may have been speaking English their whole lives and have strong fluency that simply hasn't been documented in an academic program or by an official test. Or they may have started studying English only recently and have no real indicator of how well they speak and understand it. Most people are in between those two extremes. With the TOEFL, university programs have an objective measure of whether or not test-takers will be able to do well in an academic program conducted entirely in English.

Do you really need to take the TOEFL? It depends. If you already have a degree from an English-speaking university or secondary school program in an English-speaking country, you may not need to take the TOEFL. Some programs may not require the TOEFL for English speakers who have not graduated from English-language programs. But some programs may require the TOEFL even if the applicant has graduated from an English-language program in an English-speaking program.

Before you take the TOEFL (or decide not to take the TOEFL), check with the programs to which you're applying to find out if they require it as part of your application. You can call or email the contact listed for the application process to find out for sure whether you need to take the TOEFL to apply to that program. If you are applying to more than one program, you may need to submit a TOEFL score to some of the programs and not others, so check with each program individually to determine if you need to submit a TOEFL score or not.

PRACTICE TIP

Think carefully about when you should take the TOEFL. If you are confident about your score (based on taking a practice test), you can take the test later on relative to when you need to submit your application. If, however, you're not so confident about your score, you should schedule the TOEFL early enough that you have time to study, but also early enough that if you need to retake it you still have time to meet your application deadlines. You will need to study before taking it a second time, of course, so calculate the amount of time you can and will need to spend studying before taking it a second time.

The TOEFL vs. the TOEIC

The TOEFL is not the only test of English ability. The Test of English for International Communication (TOEIC) also tests proficiency in reading, writing, speaking, and listening in English.

The TOEIC is a computer-based test consisting of 200 multiple-choice questions given in two sections, the Listening Comprehension section and the Reading Comprehension section. It has a similar format (multiple-choice questions and essays, given on a computer) as the TOEFL.

Like the TOEFL, the TOEIC is given in designated test centers around the world, and is scheduled at the convenience of the test-taker. Official score reports are sent to the test-taker, who may include a TOEIC score on a résumé or in job applications.

The TOEFL and TOEIC are similar tests in that they both test the test-taker's ability to read, listen, and write English. They are both administered on the computer at the test-taker's convenience at a designated test center. Also, they both have scores available within several days of taking the test.

The important difference between the TOEFL and the TOEIC is the TOEFL tests English in an academic or university setting, while the TOEIC tests English used in a business setting. Those who take the TOEIC do so primarily to have an objective measure of their English proficiency for their résumés to prove to employers or potential employers that they are proficient in English.

If you are applying to academic programs in the United States, you should take the TOEFL. If you are not planning to attend a college or university in the United States and just want proof that you speak English well enough to succeed at a job requiring English fluency, you should take the TOEIC.

PRACTICE TIP

The TOEIC is for business English, while the TOEFL is for academic English. If you are not applying to an academic program, you should consider taking the TOEIC instead of the TOEFL.

How Is the TOEFL Administered?

The TOEFL is administered in two versions: the iBT, or computer-based version, and the pencil-and-paper version.

iBT is short for "internet-based test" and refers to the computerized version of the test. It is a computer-based test, not an adaptive test, which means that the questions are delivered through the internet, but you may skip around inside each section and go back to previous questions. The test questions do not increase or decrease in difficulty depending on how you're doing. Instead, you see the same questions no matter how you're doing.

EXAM TIP

When you begin a new section on the TOEFL, take advantage of the fact that you can move around in the test to look at all the questions first, briefly, then go back and start at the beginning of the section. This way, you'll know what's coming in the rest of the section.

The pencil-and-paper version of the TOEFL is only given where the internet is not available or reliable. It is less convenient than the iBT version because it is only offered six times per year. Also, it is different in scoring, in that a person's score is converted to take into account that some tests are more difficult than others. The converted score corrects the differences in difficulty.

The iBT version is given 30 to 40 times a year at over 4,500 different locations around the world, so if you have the option, you should take the iBT version of the test instead of the pencil-and-paper version.

All the scores and format guidelines mentioned throughout this book are based on the iBT version of the test because it is the most common.

How Is the TOEFL Scored?

Each section is scored on a scale from 0 to 30 for a total of 0 to 120 on the entire exam. There is no set passing score; instead, the schools to which you apply look at your TOEFL score as part of your application. A higher score indicates stronger fluency. If you do not answer one question each in the Reading and Listening sections, write one response in the Writing section, and speak one response in the Speaking section, you will not receive a score for the TOEFL.

The multiple-choice questions on the TOEFL are scored by the computer, and the essay responses on the Writing section and spoken responses on the Speaking section are scored by trained human raters.

Logistics of the TOEFL

The TOEFL takes around four and a half hours to complete, from the time you arrive at the test center until the time you are done with the exam. You may not use notes, dictionaries, or any other aids during the test. You may take notes during the test with a pencil and paper provided to you at the test center, but you must turn in these notes when you are finished taking the test. During the 10-minute break between the Listening and Speaking sections, you may not leave the test center.

Registering for the TOEFL

The simplest way to register to take the TOEFL is online at ets.org/toefl. When you register, you need to have your official identification with you so you can enter your name exactly as it's spelled on your ID. You also need a credit card, electronic check, or TOEFL payment voucher to pay for the test. More information about everything you need to register is available at ets.org/toefl.

Score Reports and Sending Your Score to Schools

Your score will be reported online two weeks after you take the TOEFL. You may print your score for that posting, but you will also receive an official score report through the postal mail. You may send your score to up to four institutions as part of your registration fee, and you can decide which institutions to send to up to the day before you take the TOEFL. If you would like to send your score to institutions after you take the exam, you may do so for a fee.

EXAM TIP

Deciding whether or not to send a score report to a school is a decision you should make based on how confident you are about taking the TOEFL. If you are confident that you will score well, you can save money by designating which schools to send your score to before the exam administration. However, if you are not as confident about your score, you should not have your score sent automatically. If you earn a score you are happy with, you can send your score to institutions later by paying an extra fee.

In the next chapter, I discuss the best practices for taking standardized tests in general and for sections of the TOEFL in particular.

The Least You Need to Know

- If you can read this entire book, you can take the TOEFL.
- The TOEFL tests your proficiency at English in a university setting.
- Each section of the TOEFL is scored on a scale from 0 to 30 for a total of 0 to 120 on the entire exam.
- You can register for the TOEFL at ets.org/toefl.

Chapter 2

Test-Taking Basics

In This Chapter

- General best practices for standardized tests
- Preparing for specific sections of the TOEFL
- Combating test anxiety
- Dealing with a bad score

Maybe you have been dreading taking the TOEFL ever since you discovered that you needed to take it to apply to the program you want to attend. That's natural. Most people do not enjoy taking standardized tests at all, and feel a significant amount of anxiety at taking them. Even those who have grown up in the American school system—which gives standardized tests frequently, even to young children—dread taking tests.

The good news is that by familiarizing yourself with standardized test-taking practices both in general and specific to the TOEFL, you will be able to study for the TOEFL more effectively. You will also have a better experience on your actual test day, because you will be more prepared, less anxious, and more focused on what you know and how to demonstrate your knowledge on the test. So think of this chapter as an investment in the whole TOEFL studying experience, the TOEFL-taking experience, and your entire application process to your chosen programs.

Best Practices for Taking Standardized Tests

Those who help teach techniques to succeed at taking standardized tests know that all standardized tests have certain things in common, no matter what the subject of the test, and even across formats. And those things can be learned. Following are some general best practices for standardized tests.

Practice, Practice, Practice

The single best thing you can do to prepare for any standardized test is to give yourself the gift of enough time to prepare and practice so you're familiar with the kinds of questions you'll see on the test. It is extremely tempting to close your eyes and hope for the best, but this will not work if you haven't put in the preparation time in the weeks before the test. Spending time familiarizing yourself with the test format and question formats will give you the best possible chance to earn an excellent score on the test, no matter what the test is.

PRACTICE TIP

Do you have a friend or schoolmate who is also studying for the TOEFL? It may be easier to get into the habit of practicing every day if you can study with someone else. Pick a time of day that you can both work on TOEFL practice and study together.

Yes, studying can be a bit tedious. That's why it's key to make a study plan, so you don't end up trying to cram it all in the week before the test and hoping your brain can keep up with all the questions you're trying to throw at it. If you do a little bit every day, you'll make progress and be prepared. Make a schedule for yourself that includes 30 to 90 minutes each day of study time.

As you practice, focus your time on assessing your own performance. Instead of answering a bunch of questions, do one practice section. Then spend twice as much time reviewing the section and noting where you got the correct answer and how you arrived at that answer. Spend even more time on the questions you got incorrect until you are sure that you understand why you answered them incorrectly and what process you should have used to arrive at the correct answer.

All the time you spend learning the process of how to get to the correct answer will pay off on the day of the test. By then you will be an expert not only in how to approach each type of question you will see on the test, but you will also know what problems you are most likely to have with each specific question type. This will allow you to relax when you are in the test center, because you will know how to answer any question the test asks and will guard against making your typical mistakes.

Mental Prep

Like almost everything else in life, the key to success on standardized tests, including the TOEFL, is being mentally prepared. Even if you've adequately practiced each type of question you'll see, if you aren't mentally ready to take the test, you won't do your best. Do not leave your test score to chance. Do some mental prep before you go in to take the test.

First, it's important to know what you're going to be doing. Make sure you know exactly where the test center is located. And don't just look at a map—go to the test center a few days before the test to make sure you know how to get there and where you'll park your car or get off public transportation. If you're taking the test on a weekend, do your practice run on a weekend; if you're taking it during the week, do your practice trip during the week. Once you've figured out how long it will take you to get to the test center and deal with any obstacles you'll encounter, allow yourself 20 minutes on top of that to get to the test center.

Second, while most of your practice will be done one section at a time so you can thoroughly assess your process of answering the questions, you'll need to practice doing one full test all at one sitting to know how to pace yourself mentally for the actual exam. If you allow yourself to become mentally fatigued, even if you are able answer the questions, you won't do as well as you can. So make sure you've had the experience of answering all four sections (with a short break between the second and third sections) at least once so you can pace yourself when you're in the actual exam. In Part 7, I provide two full-length practice tests you can use to prepare yourself.

EXAM TIP

Some test centers are busier than others. When you do your practice run to the test center, go inside if you have the chance to see how many people are there and how loud it is. Then you'll be prepared for the noise level and the number of other test-takers there on your exam day, and you won't be intimidated.

One other thing to consider is that there will be other people in the test center taking tests while you are taking yours. Do not allow yourself to think about these other people. Some of them may be taking the TOEFL, but others will be taking other standardized tests issued by the ETS and other testing companies.

If you allow yourself to pay attention to other test-takers, you can get anxious for no reason. For example, you and another test-taker could start a section at the same time, and the other test-taker might finish before you do. If you allow yourself to worry about that and wonder if you're not doing as well as that other test-taker, you will not perform as well as you can on your own test. (And the other test-taker may not be taking the TOEFL, so their test sections may be shorter.)

Remember that you are there to do as well as *you* can, and nothing anyone else does at the test center has any effect on you. Even if everyone there was taking the TOEFL, what are the chances that any of them are applying to all the same programs you are? Very slim. So the other test-takers in the center are not your competition.

Physical Prep

It is important to manage your physical condition leading up to and while taking the test so your mind can be clear and you can focus on the test and not on how you're feeling. Make a plan for the days before the exam so you can feel good physically going into the test.

Study for the last time two days before the exam. Take the day before the test off to give yourself a mental and physical break from studying. Do normal but fun things on that day so you're not stressing your body. Also, be sure to drink enough water the day before the exam.

The evening before the exam, lay out everything you'll need the next day. This includes your clothes (with an extra layer in case the test center is cold), but also anything you need to take to the test—your entrance ticket, directions to the center, and money or tickets for parking or public transportation. Also make sure to pack a snack to eat before the test or during the break. It should be something filling that will give you good energy, like nuts, cheese, a banana or other fruit, or a granola bar. Also pack water to drink. And lip balm (it's surprising how distracting it can be to need lip balm and not have any).

The night before the exam, go to bed at your usual time. Even if your test is scheduled for early the next morning, you will probably not fall asleep early, and could lie in bed worrying about the test if you try to go to bed too early. So go to bed at the same time as usual and follow your usual routine. Make sure you have your alarm set to give you adequate time to get up and to the test center in the morning (don't forget to build in an extra 20 minutes from the time it took during your practice run to the test center). Ask someone else, such as a parent or friend, to make sure you're awake on time so you have a backup in case your alarm doesn't go off or you sleep through it.

The morning of the test, get up, do your usual routine to get ready, and eat breakfast. Eat something filling that will stay with you for several hours but won't make you sleepy. If you normally drink coffee or tea in the morning, drink those, but not more than usual. Too much coffee or tea can make you jittery and nervous during the test or give you a stomachache, and it can make you need to use the restroom at inopportune times. So make sure you're at your normal level of caffeination for optimal brain functioning, but no more.

When you leave your house, remember to bring the bag containing this book, your entrance ticket, anything you need for transportation, a sweater, food, water, and lip balm. Take the same route to the test center that you did during your practice run.

When you get to the test center, check in and have a seat where they tell you to. See how you feel, and eat or drink if you need to. Otherwise, get out this book and review a section or two to warm up your mind while you're waiting for your test appointment. When they call you in for your appointment, you may be asked to put your bag in a locker or other secure site.

PRACTICE TIP

Once you have your official test scheduled, try to study for the TOEFL at the same time of day that your test is scheduled for. That way you'll be in the habit of thinking about TOEFL questions at that time of day.

During your break after the first two sections, use the restroom and eat a snack to keep your energy up for the second half of the test. Do some light exercises (bend your knees, jog in place, and so on) to get your blood flowing. Then go back in for the second half and give it your best.

TOEFL-Specific Basics

In addition to the general tips mentioned previously, there are some things you can do to prepare specifically for the Reading, Listening, Speaking, and Writing sections on the TOEFL. It is important to remember that even if you listen to English frequently and can speak it in normal conversation, the TOEFL is testing your listening and speaking abilities in a specific, structured environment.

Again, practice with the formats of the questions is key. If you're not used to listening to TOEFL passages, you will have a hard time responding to them in a way that scores well on the exam. So spend a little time doing specific prep for the kind of listening and speaking you'll need to do on the TOEFL, and you'll feel much better on the day of the exam—and you'll score better, too.

Reading Prep

The Reading section on the TOEFL asks you to read passages on academic topics. If you are currently in an academic program conducted in English you may have good practice with reading these sorts of passages. If you are not, you can prepare by reading article-length passages (of around 700 words) on academic topics. Good sources for these passages are news magazines such as *Time* and *The Economist*.

As you prepare, practice reading the passages quickly to get the main idea and to determine the structure of the passage. Once you've read through quickly the first time, read through again more slowly to check your comprehension and to pick up details you may have missed the first time.

Listening Prep

The Listening section of the TOEFL asks you to listen to lectures on academic or school-related topics. The most difficult aspect of this section for most test-takers is that they are purely listening and can't see the speakers' lips or faces to get cues from them. This means they need to recognize nearly every word to understand the meaning.

Understanding the structure of the passages (which I'll talk about in Part 3 of this book) will help enormously, but it is also helpful to practice listening to academic topics without being able to see the speakers while they speak. You can do this by accessing videos on academic topics on the internet. Play the video, but do not watch the screen; instead, listen to what the speaker says and try to understand the meaning based only on what you hear. After a few minutes, stop and write down the main points of what you heard. Then replay the lecture (again without watching the video). Did you miss anything? Finally, replay the video a third time, this time watching the speaker in the video, to pick up any nuances you may have missed.

Speaking Prep

The Speaking section of the TOEFL asks you to speak in a structured way in a specific format. The topics you will be asked to speak on are either academic subjects based on written and spoken lectures or topics related to university life, such as living in student housing, taking student transportation, and managing homework demands. While you may be very good at casual conversations with other people in English, the structure of the TOEFL Speaking section does not reward conversational skills but rather structured skills that are more similar to public speaking skills.

To practice for the Speaking section, find passages on academic topics on the internet and practice reading and summarizing them, then speaking about the passages. Give yourself 60 seconds to speak a summary of the passage, using your phone or a computer to record your summary. Once you've summarized the passage, go back and read it again carefully. Then listen to the recording of your summary and assess how well you summarized the passage and how fluent you were in your speaking. The more you practice this, the more easily you will be able to do it on the actual exam.

Writing Prep

The Writing section on the TOEFL asks you to write response essays to two different types of prompts. The tricky part is that you have a limited amount of time in which to write. If you are currently in an academic program conducted in English, you may have practice in writing essays in English, although you may not be used to writing under time pressure. If you are not currently in an academic program, you will need to practice writing quickly and efficiently.

To practice for the integrated writing task portion, find a topic from a newspaper or magazine article and time yourself for 20 minutes while you type in a summary of the important points of the article. To prepare for the independent writing task, pick any issue with two sides (go to school versus working, cats versus dogs, science versus humanities, beach versus mountains) and time yourself for 30 minutes while you type in an essay arguing for one side. The more you practice, the more efficient and fluid you'll become at writing quickly on demand.

Dealing with Test Anxiety

Some people become so anxious about taking standardized tests that they develop full-blown test anxiety. If you're one of them, I have some ways you can alleviate your anxiety.

First, practice. (Of course!) Not only will you get better at answering the questions, you'll also become more bored with the questions. And the more bored you are, the less anxious you'll be.

Follow the plan earlier in the chapter for physical management on the day before and day of the test, so you can feel as physically good as possible.

And give yourself a break. It's completely normal to feel test anxiety. If you spend time making yourself feel bad or guilty about being anxious, you'll become even more anxious and scared. Instead, just accept that you're a person who gets anxious but that you can work through it.

Spend time learning to relax, too. Start at your toes and focus on relaxing from there up to your feet, then your ankles, all the way to your scalp. If you can relax your body, you will feel less anxious.

Start thinking of any anxious feelings you perceive as "getting ready" feelings and use them to help you become more alert and focused on the exam. This way you'll use any natural anxiety to help you instead of to make you feel worse.

What If I Get a Bad Score?

By the time you've finished working through the exercises and taking the practice tests in this book, you will know whether you are prepared to take the TOEFL. If you're prepared to take it, you can expect to score about as well as you have been doing on your practice tests. Occasionally, however, something happens during the actual exam—you have a bad day, you just can't focus on some questions, you're faced with distractions you can't overcome. If this is the case, and you didn't do as well as you wanted to, don't panic. You may still have scored better than you think.

EXAM TIP

If you do not score as well as you wanted to the first time you take the TOEFL, you might be tempted to give up. Don't. The TOEFL tests the learned skills of reading, listening, speaking, and writing. With practice, you *will* get better, so the next time you take the test you will score better.

If, however, you get a bad score, you can take the TOEFL again. You will need to pay for the exam a second time and go through the same studying process. But there is always another chance. You can do this, even if it takes more than one try.

Just know that "bad score" is a relative term. How high you need to score depends on what field of study you're going into and what specific programs you're applying to, as well as the rest of your application. Remember that there is no passing score on the TOEFL, so your score may not be as bad as you think it is.

Will I Survive Taking the TOEFL?

If you can read and do all the exercises in this book, then you will survive taking the TOEFL. It may seem daunting, but remember that it is only a few hours. In addition, if you are not happy with the score you receive, you can always study hard for a few more weeks or months and then retake it to get a higher score. So taking the test isn't your only chance to get into the program you want to be accepted to.

Another thing to think about is that people with all ranges of English fluency take this test. It's likely that you fall somewhere in the middle. And simply by reading this entire book and working through all the exercises and taking the practice tests, you are improving your ability—and therefore the score you earn—above what it was before you opened this book. This is one case in which hard work definitely pays off.

The Least You Need to Know

- Prepare mentally and physically for the TOEFL in addition to practicing questions.
- The TOEFL uses a specific formula, so you should become familiar with each type of question.
- You can get past test anxiety by learning to relax and using excess energy to help you focus.
- If you get a bad score, you have the option of taking the TOEFL again.

Part 2
TOEFL Reading

This part guides you through the TOEFL Reading section, helping you assess your reading level so you know what to focus on when you practice.

Chapter 3 covers the specific ways the Reading section presents passages and how to read those passages for structure and content. This chapter also includes a special focus on taking good notes in preparation to answer the multiple-choice questions about each passage and choosing the correct answer to each type of question.

Chapter 4 consists of Reading section passages and questions formatted to be as close as possible to passages and questions on the real TOEFL. Once you've answered the questions, check your answers and the explanations for those answers in Chapter 5.

Chapter 3

Acing the Reading Section

In This Chapter

- What reading skills the TOEFL tests
- What skills get good scores in the Reading section
- How to approach the Reading section
- The different types of Reading section questions

If you're reading this and understanding it, you can read in English. But that doesn't mean you'll score well on the TOEFL Reading section.

The Reading section tests very specific ways of reading very specific types of written passages. And it tests your comprehension by asking multiple-choice questions about what you read. Not exactly like reading in real life, is it? But this chapter will lead you through reading the passages, what you need to get out of the passages before you go to the questions, and exactly what each type of question is asking and how to answer it.

TOEFL Reading Basics

The Reading section of the TOEFL consists of 3 or 4 passages of approximately 700 words each, on academic topics such as history, the humanities, and science. Each passage has 12 to 15 multiple-choice questions with 4 answer choices each. There are a total of 36 to 56 questions, and you have 60 to 80 minutes to complete this section.

The Reading section is the first section of the TOEFL, which has its advantages. One advantage of having Reading as the first section is that if you are a little nervous about taking the test, you can focus on the passages and then use the techniques I talk about later in this chapter to go through the multiple-choice questions. This section of the TOEFL has more content and requires less pinpoint focus than the Speaking and Writing sections. Another advantage is that you base your answers on what's in the passage, not on your opinion or other thoughts about the topic, so it's a good section to work on while your brain is still warming up.

The structure of the passages in the Reading section is straightforward, and there are few rhetorical devices. This is not like reading beautiful literature. However, because the passages cover academic topics, they may be filled with scientific terms or other jargon you may not be familiar with. This is important to know because it affects your entire reading strategy. You know you will need to decipher unfamiliar words or concepts by using the context of the passage. Use the structural elements of the passage to help you figure out what a sentence is saying so you can understand unfamiliar words.

And remember that the passage *must* give you a definition of any uncommon words, scientific concepts, or technical jargon. You are asked to answer the questions based only on the information given in the passage, so the passage has to give you any information you'll need—which means it needs to define unfamiliar terms, but also give enough context so you can understand the subjects they discuss.

PRACTICE TIP

While you are reading practice passages, write down the words you do not understand and look them up. Take note of which words are technical and scientific, and which are nontechnical words you should add to your vocabulary study list.

Knowing that everything you need to answer the questions correctly is in the passage is the first step to scoring well in the Reading section. But reading the passage is only the beginning. Next, I talk about what skills will help you get a good score in the Reading section.

Skills That Score Points in the Reading Section

The skills rewarded with good scores in the Reading section are as follows:

Reading efficiently. You will have 3 or 4 passages to read, each one approximately 700 words. You'll need to read each passage at least once for general comprehension, and then reread parts to find the answers to specific questions. That means you need to be able to read efficiently and with focus to get through the passages in a logical manner with enough time.

Understanding written text. Seven hundred words is a lot, and some of those words can be difficult. To understand the entire passage, pay attention to the main idea of the passage to keep yourself on track.

Deciphering words in context. Because the passages are on academic topics, it is unlikely that you will be familiar with all of the words and concepts mentioned. This means you need to use the words and sentences around a word you don't know—the context—to determine what it means.

Summarizing an argument. You will be asked about the main idea and author's main points in the passage, so make sure you have practiced summarizing the main ideas of longer passages before you take the TOEFL.

Writing notes. You should take notes on what you read in the passage so you can understand the logic of the entire passage, and to use as a map for when you need to go back and look for details. You could take these notes in your native language, but it makes more sense to take them in English so you can use them to answer the questions. You'll turn in your notes at the end of the exam, but they won't be used as part of your grade.

Looking for details in the text. Some of the questions will ask you about details in the passage, so you will have to be able to go back to the passage and find the details you need. This will be easier if you take good notes about the passage so you know which paragraphs talk about what topics.

WARNING

Don't make the mistake of thinking that because you can read a magazine or book in English you can read the Reading section passages on the TOEFL. Part of the trick to the Reading section is being able to read dense material under time pressure. Without practice, you could run out of time on the exam.

If you can develop these skills, your score on the Reading section will reflect your hard work. Resist the temptation to try to memorize what you read. If you notice, the previous skills focus on reading rapidly and for general understanding and then going back to find details. There is no need to memorize or have detailed recall of the passages.

Key Issues in the Reading Section

The following are five key issues to pay attention to in the Reading section:

Issue 1: Understand what type of question you're answering. There are 10 question types. (See the "Question Types" section later in this chapter for more detail.) By the time you take the test, you should have practiced enough to know exactly how to approach each type of question—even if you can't name it. As you practice, make part of your routine identifying the type of question and how you answer it. Don't just blindly take each practice question as it comes. By working consciously through the questions, you will know exactly what to do with each question on the Reading section of the real test.

Issue 2: Organization is everything. Figuring out how the passages are organized is key to understanding what the passages are saying as well as finding the information you need to answer each question asked about the passage. The passages will contain language that helps you understand the organization, so learn to recognize these words to help you figure out how the passage is structured.

Issue 3: Be a smart notetaker. You'll score better if you can take good notes on the passages. However, that doesn't mean your notes all have to be in words. Because the main purpose of taking notes on the passage is to draw a map of the passage so you can go back to find the specific passages you need for the detail questions, you can use signs, symbols, and drawings if they make the structure clear to you. Remember that you'll be turning in your notes at the end of the exam, but they won't be scored with your exam.

Issue 4: Watch your time. It can be tempting to spend as much time as possible reading a passage for full comprehension and recall. But with 3 or 4 passages and 12 to 15 questions per passage, you simply don't have time to do that. Look at how much time you're allotted, as well as how many passages you have and the number of questions in each passage. Write down in your notes a rough guide of how much time you can spend on each passage and its questions. Stick to that guide so you don't run out of time.

EXAM TIP

Practice drawing maps of passages to get used to summarizing the main points. Having a plan in mind to deal with the passages in the Reading section will help you be less nervous when exam time comes.

Issue 5: Skip around in the questions. Some of the questions are simpler to answer than others, so you should answer the most direct ones first. You've already read the passage for the general idea and drawn your map, so answer questions about the main topic and general ideas first. Then answer the questions that require context but not a full understanding of the details, such as the vocabulary and insert-word/sentence questions. After you've answered these questions, go back and answer the questions that require more digging and careful elimination.

Strategy for the Reading Section

The Reading section, as I previously mentioned, is not just a test to see if you can read anything in English. The Reading section tests your ability to read in English on specific topics and in a specific format. The key to doing well in this section and answering the questions effectively is getting an accurate picture of what each passage is about and knowing how to find detailed information in the passage. This part of the chapter focuses on knowing the passage (you can find information about the different types of questions and strategies to answer them later in the chapter).

What follows is the three-step process you should follow when you begin a passage in the Reading section of the TOEFL.

Step 1: Identify How the Passage Is Organized

Each passage is approximately 700 words long, so don't just begin reading and hope for the best. Instead, scan the passage visually and see how it's organized. How many paragraphs does it have? How long are the paragraphs? How dense or general is the language in the paragraphs?

Also note whether there are *transition words* at the beginnings and endings of paragraphs. You should have an idea of whether the passage is presenting an argument that builds progressively, or whether the author is stating a point and then backing it up with paragraphs of supporting details that are distinct from one another.

DEFINITION

Transition words are words or short phrases that connect one idea to another. Examples of transition words include *next, therefore, first,* and *in conclusion.* I discuss transition words more in Chapter 18.

Make some notes on your paper about the organization of the passage. Numbering the paragraphs and leaving spaces for a couple of words on each paragraph is one way to do this. Another way is to draw boxes, one for each paragraph, so you can write down a few words of description for each paragraph in its box. Do whatever makes sense to you visually and helps you understand how the passage is organized.

Step 2: Identify the Main Idea

Now it's time to actually read the passage. Read through it at a comfortable pace so you understand the sentences. Don't worry if you don't know every single word. Some of them will be explained by the text, especially if they are scientific words or other jargon. If they're simply words you don't happen to know that aren't specific terms, you can figure them out by using the context of the rest of the sentence and paragraph.

As you read, keep in mind the structure of the passage, and as you finish a paragraph, write down a few words about what the paragraph was about in your notes. Remember that your notes are set up to correspond with the structure of the passage, so you should be able to write next to the number of the paragraph or inside the box you drew for that paragraph.

Once you get to the end of the passage, think about the main idea of the passage. Write it down someplace in your notes in a few words. You will be asked a question about the main idea of the passage, so if you have it written down in your notes, that question will be very simple to answer.

Step 3: Identify the Purpose of the Passage

You've already identified the main idea of the passage, so now it's time to identify the purpose of the passage. They may sound like the same thing, but the main idea and purpose are not the same. The main idea is the topic of the passage, but the purpose is more than that. It answers the question, "What does the author want me to do?"

By determining what the author wants you to do, you know the purpose of the passage. Is it merely informing you about a subject? Is it trying to convince you of a point of view? Is it explaining one perspective on a topic and then advocating for a different perspective? Is it calling for more research on a topic?

Once you determine what the author wants you to do based on what you've read, write that down in your notes. You may not be asked directly what the purpose of the passage is, but you will probably be asked about the author's viewpoint, and having it written down will help you answer the question directly without having to go back and read the whole thing again.

PRACTICE TIP

Approach passages by determining their structure and using that structure to help you understand them. It's a skill that will not only help you on the TOEFL, but will help you in the program you're applying to. You may have to do a significant amount of reading, so knowing how to read efficiently helps.

When you study practice passages, use the three steps outlined previously, in order, for each passage. Once you've done this a few times, it will become second nature, and you'll do it automatically when you get to the passages on the actual TOEFL exam. Doing these three steps with the passages puts you in the perfect position to begin answering questions, so let me talk about the question types now.

Question Types

Now that you've prepped the passage, you're ready to roll with the actual questions. The following are the different types of questions you can be asked in the Reading section, and how to answer each one. Note that there are only 10 question types, and a minimum of 12 questions per passage, so you will see more than one of some types of questions in each passage, and you may not see all 10 types on any one passage. So learn them all, but know that you'll see some question types more frequently than others.

Fact

A fact question asks you, not surprisingly, about a fact in the passage. It can be about the main idea of the passage or the purpose of the passage. If it is, you're in luck, because you already have them written down in your notes.

It could also ask you about a specific detail, though. Remember when you drew a map of the passage to tell you what information was where so you could go back and find details? Now is the time to use your map.

Here's how to answer a fact question:

1. Read the question.
2. Go back to the map in your notes and see where this fact is likely to be in the passage.
3. Go to the passage and find the fact.
4. Look at the answer choices for the question. Eliminate the ones that don't say what the fact in the passage said.
5. Choose the answer choice that's left. It should match what the fact in the passage said.

EXAM TIP

You don't need to remember what a question type is called to be able to answer it. Focus on the process to answer each question, not the name of the question type.

Negative Fact

A negative-fact question is just like a fact question, except it asks you which answer choice is *not* contained in the passage. That little three-letter word is vital, so pay special attention and remember to choose the answer choice you can't find in the passage, not the ones you can.

Here's how to answer a negative-fact question:

1. Read the question.
2. Go back to the map in your notes and see where this fact is likely to be in the passage.
3. Go to the passage and find the fact.
4. Look at the answer choices for the question. Eliminate the ones that *do* say what the fact in the passage said.
5. Choose the answer choice that's left. It will be something that is not in the passage at all, is misrepresented, or is the opposite of what was in the passage.

Inference

An inference question is just like a fact question, except a fact question has an answer choice that is directly, 100 percent in the passage. An inference question requires you to use your imagination very slightly to connect some ideas in the passage to find the answer.

This means your process for answering an inference question is exactly the same as answering a fact question, except that after you eliminate the incorrect answer choices, the one that's left will go along with the passage but will not be directly stated in the passage.

Here's how to answer an inference question:

1. Read the question.
2. Go back to the map in your notes and see where this fact is likely to be in the passage.
3. Go to the passage and find the fact.
4. Look at the answer choices of the question. Eliminate the ones that *don't* say what the fact in the passage said.
5. Choose the answer choice that's left. It should match what the fact in the passage implied or got close to saying.

Simplify Information

Simplify-information questions always ask the same thing in the same format. There is a sentence highlighted in the passage, and the question below it says the following:

> Which of the following best expresses the essential information in the highlighted sentence? Incorrect answer choices change the meaning in important ways or leave out essential information.

Simplify-information questions basically ask you to paraphrase the highlighted sentence.

Here's how to answer a simplify-information question:

1. Read the highlighted sentence in the passage.
2. Paraphrase it in your head and write down that paraphrase in your notes.
3. Go to the answer choices and carefully eliminate the ones that don't match your paraphrase.
4. Choose the answer choice that's left. Incorrect answers will contain too many elements or not enough elements, or will say the opposite of what the sentence says.

Summarize Information

The summarize-information question asks you to summarize the entire passage in three sentences. You are given six sentences and asked to choose three of them and arrange them in the correct order by dragging and dropping the sentences.

Here's how to answer a summarize-information question:

1. Read the question and look at the answer choices.
2. Go back to your map and notes on the passage and use them to remember what the passage said.

3. Go back to the answer choices and eliminate any that misrepresent information in the passage, based on your notes.
4. If you need to review details presented in some of the answer choices, use your map to go back to the passage and reread sections.
5. Arrange the three sentences that best summarize the passage in the correct order. Recheck your map to make sure they are in the correct order.

WARNING

Summarizing-information questions don't look like the other types of questions, which can make students afraid of them. Since you already have a map of the passage, they won't take as much time as they look like they'll take. Just attack them, using your map, and you'll be able to answer them.

Vocabulary

A vocabulary question asks you, very simply, what a word in the passage means. The format of the question is always the same:

The word *blank* in the passage is closest in meaning to

word

word

word

word

These questions are extremely straightforward. The only thing to watch out for is that sometimes there are answer choices that are possible meanings of the word in the question or that sound like they could mean what the word in the question means. If you do not go back and look at that word in the actual passage to see what it means in the passage, you can be tricked into picking the wrong answer choice.

Here's how to answer a vocabulary question:

1. Find the word in the passage (it will be highlighted).
2. Read the word in the sentence in the passage.
3. Come up with your own synonym for the word in the sentence in the passage.
4. Go back to the question and find the answer choice that matches the synonym you came up with that fits in the sentence in the passage.

Table

A table question contains a table or chart with empty spaces and several sentences or phrases below the table. You are asked to drag and drop the sentences into the table in a way that makes sense. (These questions may be worth more points than questions with four mutually exclusive answer choices.) You may need to arrange the sentences chronologically, or in categories.

Here's how to answer a table question:

1. Read the question and the description of that table and the information it contains.
2. Determine what the structure of the table is and how many answer choices can go in each space.
3. Go through the answer choices one at a time, dragging and dropping them into the table in the proper location.

Insert Word/Sentence

An insert-word/sentence question consists of the passage with four black squares inserted at different locations in the passage, and a word or sentence. You need to determine where the word or sentence would make the most sense if inserted into the sentence, and choose that answer choice. The squares are there to help you keep your place in the passage.

Here's how to answer an insert-word/sentence question:

1. Reread the section of the passage with the black squares.
2. Read the word or sentence to be inserted.
3. Figure out where that word or sentence would make sense.
4. Look at the answer choices and pick the one that matches with what you decided.

Reference

A reference question is very similar to a vocabulary question, except that it asks what a word or phrase refers to, instead of what a word means. Otherwise, the format is very similar. The format of the question looks like this:

The phrase *phrase phrase phrase* in the passage refers to

word

word

word

word

Here's how to answer a reference question:

1. Find the word or phrase in the passage (it will be highlighted).
2. Read the word or phrase in the passage and find what it refers to. This might be in the same sentence or in a previous sentence.
3. Go back to the question and find the answer choice that matches the thing you found in the passage that the word or phrase refers to.

PRACTICE TIP

Because vocabulary and reference questions look so similar, make sure you pay attention to whether you're looking for a synonym for the highlighted word, or what the word refers to.

Rhetorical Purpose

A rhetorical-purpose question asks you why the author mentions something in the passage. Questions are phrased like these examples:

> Why does the author mention *X* in the third paragraph?
>
> The author discusses *X* in order to …
>
> The author mentions *X* as an example of …

These questions do not focus on details in the passage, but instead on how the phrases and sentences relate to each other.

Here's how to answer a rhetorical-purpose question:

1. Read the question and find the highlighted phrase in the passage.
2. Read the phrase, as well as the sentences before and after it.
3. Determine what the phrase does and how it holds together the sentences around it—either connecting or contrasting them.
4. Look at the answer choices and eliminate the ones that don't do what you determined the phrase did in the passage.

Now you should be ready to try some of the practice sections in the next chapter.

The Least You Need to Know

- The TOEFL tests you on how you read very specific academic passages.
- Understand the structure of each passage, and draw yourself a map of it to help ensure you know what the passage says.
- Use your map and find details in the passage to answer the questions.
- Study the 10 different types of Reading questions on the TOEFL so you'll know how to answer them.

Chapter 4

Reading Practice Sections

Work through these practice sections carefully, using the techniques and tips from Chapter 3. Give yourself 20 minutes for each section. When you finish a section, check the answers and explanations in Chapter 5 and review them carefully.

Practice Section 1

Read the following passage, then answer the questions.

Sustainable Fisheries Certification

In 1997, multinational corporate giant Unilever joined with the World Wildlife Fund (WWF) to create the Marine Stewardship Council (MSC), an organization created to set standards for sustainable, environmentally sound practices for the fishing industry. These standards, based on the United Nations' Code of Conduct for Responsible Fishing, were voluntary for fisheries and fish suppliers, but full compliance with the standards earned any supplier MSC certification, which assured buyers that the seafood was caught and handled responsibly. Seafood with MSC certification earns higher prices on the wholesale and retail markets, so achieving MSC certification is worth it for producers. The cost of making the changes required to become MSC certified ranges from $50,000 to $500,000 for each fishing boat operator or processor, and can take up to two years to complete the rigorous process. Despite this, becoming MSC certified makes sense for operators and processors because of the higher prices their products command.

There are two standards managed by the MSC: the environmental standard for sustainable fishing and the chain of custody standard for seafood traceability. The environmental standard contains three practices: 1) sustainable fish stocks, 2) minimizing environmental impact, and 3) effective management. Each of these 3 practices is supported by approximately 10 more detailed criteria.

Sustainable fish stocks are important so that the seafood population continues to thrive. Overfishing of certain species threatens their existence, so to prevent extinction, the MSC requires boat operators and fisheries to prove that they are fishing numbers of each species that allow for repopulation. The standard states that "The fishing activity must be at a level which is sustainable for the fish population. Any certified fishery must operate so that fishing can continue indefinitely and is not overexploiting the resources." This means that fisheries may not be able to supply the full demand for every species from the market, but they are committed to ensuring the continuation of these species in the long run.

Minimizing environmental impact means that fisheries commit to leave the ecosystems and neighborhoods in which they operate undamaged by their operations. The standard states, "Fishing operations should be managed to maintain the structure, productivity, function and diversity of the ecosystem on which the fishery depends." If fisheries are damaging the ecosystems in which they operate, even if they are not overfishing they are harming the fish and the rest of the environment.

The effective management requirement is designed to prevent fisheries from receiving MSC certification once and then not responding to changes in the environment, local laws and policies, or fish populations. The standard states, "The fishery must meet all local, national and international laws and must have a management system in place to respond to changing circumstances and maintain sustainability." This requires fisheries to think about possible changes that can occur and how they will respond to those changes in a way that keeps them in compliance with MSC certification standards.

The chain of custody standard is designed to ensure that fish that is labeled with the MSC certification was caught at a certified fishery, and that noncertified fish does not enter the MSC-certified system. This standard establishes processes to check origin and chain of custody at all steps in the chain.

The actual MSC certification process relies on independent agencies, certified by the MSC, that audit fishing boat, fishery, and processing plant practices and chains of custody to guarantee that seafood is managed according to procedure from the time it is caught to the time it is sold to consumers. Because of the structure of the fishing industry, with many small, independent boat owners fishing and selling to various processors and suppliers, this chain of command can be complex and confusing. In addition, there is room for abuse of the system, with unscrupulous dealers selling frozen and thawed seafood as fresh, or lying about the location of origin or fishing practices they participate in. Using this network of agencies, the MSC ensures that misrepresentation of product is caught and "counterfeit" seafood is not given MSC certification.

By establishing these two standards and intelligently using various agencies with different levels of access and authority, the MSC has ensured that the path to certification for suppliers is clear and achievable. It has also provided consumers with a way to know that the seafood they buy to consume is as safe and environmentally sound as possible.

1. The word *rigorous* in the passage is closest in meaning to

(A) dead

(B) difficult

(C) ancient

(D) renewable

In 1997, multinational corporate giant Unilever joined with the World Wildlife Fund (WWF) to create the Marine Stewardship Council (MSC), an organization created to set standards for sustainable, environmentally sound practices for the fishing industry. These standards, based on the United Nations' Code of Conduct for Responsible Fishing, were voluntary for fisheries and fish suppliers, but full compliance with the standards earned any supplier MSC certification, which assured buyers that the seafood was caught and handled responsibly. Seafood with MSC certification earns higher prices on the wholesale and retail markets, so achieving MSC certification is worth it for producers. The cost of making the changes required to become MSC certified ranges from $50,000 to $500,000 for each fishing boat operator or processor, and can take up to two years to complete the rigorous process. Despite this, becoming MSC certified makes sense for operators and processors because of the higher prices their products command.

There are two standards managed by the MSC: the environmental standard for sustainable fishing and the chain of custody standard for seafood traceability. The environmental standard contains three practices: 1) sustainable fish stocks, 2) minimizing environmental impact, and 3) effective management. Each of these 3 practices is supported by approximately 10 more detailed criteria.

Sustainable fish stocks are important so that the seafood population continues to thrive. Overfishing of certain species threatens their existence, so to prevent extinction, the MSC requires boat operators and fisheries to prove that they are fishing numbers of each species that allow for repopulation. The standard states that "The fishing activity must be at a level which is sustainable for the fish population. Any certified fishery must operate so that fishing can continue indefinitely and is not overexploiting the resources." This means that fisheries may not be able to supply the full demand for every species from the market, but they are committed to ensuring the continuation of these species in the long run.

Minimizing environmental impact means that fisheries commit to leave the ecosystems and neighborhoods in which they operate undamaged by their operations. The standard states, "Fishing operations should be managed to maintain the structure, productivity, function, and diversity of the ecosystem on which the fishery depends." If fisheries are damaging the ecosystems in which they operate, even if they are not overfishing they are harming the fish and the rest of the environment.

The effective management requirement is designed to prevent fisheries from receiving MSC certification once and then not responding to changes in the environment, local laws and policies, or fish populations. The standard states, "The fishery must meet all local, national, and international laws and must have a management system in place to respond to changing circumstances and maintain sustainability." This requires fisheries to think about possible changes that can occur and how they will respond to those changes in a way that keeps them in compliance with MSC certification standards.

The chain of custody standard is designed to ensure that fish that is labeled with the MSC certification was caught at a certified fishery, and that noncertified fish does not enter the MSC-certified system. This standard establishes processes to check origin and chain of custody at all steps in the chain.

The actual MSC certification process relies on independent agencies, certified by the MSC, that audit fishing boat, fishery, and processing plant practices and chains of custody to guarantee that seafood is managed according to procedure from the time it is caught to the time it is sold to consumers. Because of the structure of the fishing industry, with many small, independent boat owners fishing and selling to various processors and suppliers, this chain of command can be complex and confusing. In addition, there is room for abuse of the system, with unscrupulous dealers selling frozen and thawed seafood as fresh, or lying about the location of origin or fishing practices they participate in. Using this network of agencies, the MSC ensures that misrepresentation of product is caught and "counterfeit" seafood is not given MSC certification.

By establishing these two standards and intelligently using various agencies with different levels of access and authority, the MSC has ensured that the path to certification for suppliers is clear and achievable. It has also provided consumers with a way to know that the seafood they buy to consume is as safe and environmentally sound as possible.

2. The word *indefinitely* in the passage is closest in meaning to
   (A) earlier than expected
   (B) after a certain date
   (C) at no specific time
   (D) without authorization
3. The word *them* in the passage refers to
   (A) fisheries
   (B) fish
   (C) changes
   (D) MSC
4. The MSC is concerned with sustainable fish stocks because it wants to
   (A) bill fisheries more for overfished species
   (B) breed new species of fish
   (C) guarantee delivery of species ordered by retailers
   (D) preserve fish species from extinction
5. The MSC uses a network of independent agencies to help enforce certification because
   (A) it cannot finance certification processes alone
   (B) certification is too difficult for the MSC to earn without help
   (C) no single agency can be responsible for standards as stringent as the MSC's standards
   (D) the chain of suppliers is too complex for one agency alone to monitor

In 1997, multinational corporate giant Unilever joined with the World Wildlife Fund (WWF) to create the Marine Stewardship Council (MSC), an organization created to set standards for sustainable, environmentally sound practices for the fishing industry. These standards, based on the United Nations' Code of Conduct for Responsible Fishing, were voluntary for fisheries and fish suppliers, but full compliance with the standards earned any supplier MSC certification, which assured buyers that the seafood was caught and handled responsibly. Seafood with MSC certification earns higher prices on the wholesale and retail markets, so achieving MSC certification is worth it for producers. The cost of making the changes required to become MSC certified ranges from $50,000 to $500,000 for each fishing boat operator or processor, and can take up to two years to complete the rigorous process. Despite this, becoming MSC certified makes sense for operators and processors because of the higher prices their products command.

There are two standards managed by the MSC: the environmental standard for sustainable fishing and the chain of custody standard for seafood traceability. The environmental standard contains three practices: 1) sustainable fish stocks, 2) minimizing environmental impact, and 3) effective management. Each of these 3 practices is supported by approximately 10 more detailed criteria.

Sustainable fish stocks are important so that the seafood population continues to thrive. Overfishing of certain species threatens their existence, so to prevent extinction, the MSC requires boat operators and fisheries to prove that they are fishing numbers of each species that allow for repopulation. The standard states that "The fishing activity must be at a level which is sustainable for the fish population. Any certified fishery must operate so that fishing can continue indefinitely and is not overexploiting the resources." This means that fisheries may not be able to supply the full demand for every species from the market, but they are committed to ensuring the continuation of these species in the long run.

Minimizing environmental impact means that fisheries commit to leave the ecosystems and neighborhoods in which they operate undamaged by their operations. The standard states, "Fishing operations should be managed to maintain the structure, productivity, function, and diversity of the ecosystem on which the fishery depends." If fisheries are damaging the ecosystems in which they operate, even if they are not overfishing they are harming the fish and the rest of the environment.

The effective management requirement is designed to prevent fisheries from receiving MSC certification once and then not responding to changes in the environment, local laws and policies, or fish populations. The standard states, "The fishery must meet all local, national, and international laws and must have a management system in place to respond to changing circumstances and maintain sustainability." This requires fisheries to think about possible changes that can occur and how they will respond to those changes in a way that keeps them in compliance with MSC certification standards.

The chain of custody standard is designed to ensure that fish that is labeled with the MSC certification was caught at a certified fishery, and that noncertified fish does not enter the MSC-certified system. This standard establishes processes to check origin and chain of custody at all steps in the chain.

The actual MSC certification process relies on independent agencies, certified by the MSC, that audit fishing boat, fishery, and processing plant practices and chains of custody to guarantee that seafood is managed according to procedure from the time it is caught to the time it is sold to consumers. Because of the structure of the fishing industry, with many small, independent boat owners fishing and selling to various processors and suppliers, this chain of command can be complex and confusing. In addition, there is room for abuse of the system, with unscrupulous dealers selling frozen and thawed seafood as fresh, or lying about the location of origin or fishing practices they participate in. Using this network of agencies, the MSC ensures that misrepresentation of product is caught and "counterfeit" seafood is not given MSC certification.

By establishing these two standards and intelligently using various agencies with different levels of access and authority, the MSC has ensured that the path to certification for suppliers is clear and achievable. It has also provided consumers with a way to know that the seafood they buy to consume is as safe and environmentally sound as possible.

6. The phrase *This standard* in the passage refers to
   (A) the chain of custody standard
   (B) the fisheries standard
   (C) the environmental standard
   (D) the sustainable standard
7. According to the passage, making changes that will lead to MSC certification for a fishery can be
   (A) unknown
   (B) expensive
   (C) impossible
   (D) antagonistic
8. You can infer from the passage that
   (A) most fisheries already conform to MSC certification standards
   (B) concern for MSC certification standards is largely politically motivated
   (C) it is easier for fisheries to catch seafood that does not conform to MSC certification standards
   (D) conforming to MSC certification standards will cause more damage to the environment than initially thought
9. You can infer that the author of the passage
   (A) does not oppose using MSC certification standards to certify fisheries
   (B) intends to become MSC certified in the future
   (C) is associated with the MSC or one of its associated agencies or organizations
   (D) thinks fisheries should be forced to comply with MSC certification standards
10. The passage suggests all of the following EXCEPT
   (A) obtaining MSC certification can be a costly, lengthy process
   (B) the benefits of obtaining MSC certification are intangible
   (C) fisheries are only part of the seafood supply chain
   (D) sustainable fishing practices benefit fish populations

In 1997, multinational corporate giant Unilever joined with the World Wildlife Fund (WWF) to create the Marine Stewardship Council (MSC), an organization created to set standards for sustainable, environmentally sound practices for the fishing industry. These standards, based on the United Nations' Code of Conduct for Responsible Fishing, were voluntary for fisheries and fish suppliers, but full compliance with the standards earned any supplier MSC certification, which assured buyers that the seafood was caught and handled responsibly. Seafood with

MSC certification earns higher prices on the wholesale and retail markets, so achieving MSC certification is worth it for producers. The cost of making the changes required to become MSC certified ranges from $50,000 to $500,000 for each fishing boat operator or processor, and can take up to two years to complete the rigorous process. Despite this, becoming MSC certified makes sense for operators and processors because of the higher prices their products command.

There are two standards managed by the MSC: the environmental standard for sustainable fishing and the chain of custody standard for seafood traceability. The environmental standard contains three practices: 1) sustainable fish stocks, 2) minimizing environmental impact, and 3) effective management. Each of these 3 practices is supported by approximately 10 more detailed criteria.

Sustainable fish stocks are important so that the seafood population continues to thrive. Overfishing of certain species threatens their existence, so to prevent extinction, the MSC requires boat operators and fisheries to prove that they are fishing numbers of each species that allow for repopulation. The standard states that "The fishing activity must be at a level which is sustainable for the fish population. Any certified fishery must operate so that fishing can continue indefinitely and is not overexploiting the resources." This means that fisheries may not be able to supply the full demand for every species from the market, but they are committed to ensuring the continuation of these species in the long run.

Minimizing environmental impact means that fisheries commit to leave the ecosystems and neighborhoods in which they operate undamaged by their operations. The standard states, "Fishing operations should be managed to maintain the structure, productivity, function, and diversity of the ecosystem on which the fishery depends." If fisheries are damaging the ecosystems in which they operate, even if they are not overfishing they are harming the fish and the rest of the environment.

The effective management requirement is designed to prevent fisheries from receiving MSC certification once and then not responding to changes in the environment, local laws and policies, or fish populations. The standard states, "The fishery must meet all local, national, and international laws and must have a management system in place to respond to changing circumstances and maintain sustainability." This requires fisheries to think about possible changes that can occur and how they will respond to those changes in a way that keeps them in compliance with MSC certification standards.

The chain of custody standard is designed to ensure that fish that is labeled with the MSC certification was caught at a certified fishery, and that noncertified fish does not enter the MSC-certified system. This standard establishes processes to check origin and chain of custody at all steps in the chain.

The actual MSC certification process relies on independent agencies, certified by the MSC, that audit fishing boat, fishery, and processing plant practices and chains of custody to guarantee that seafood is managed according to procedure from the time it is caught to the time it is sold to consumers. Because of the structure of the fishing industry, with many small, independent boat owners fishing and selling to various processors and suppliers, this chain of command can be complex and confusing. In addition, there is room for abuse of the system, with unscrupulous dealers selling frozen and thawed seafood as fresh, or lying about the location of origin or fishing practices they participate in. Using this network of agencies, the MSC ensures that misrepresentation of product is caught and "counterfeit" seafood is not given MSC certification.

By establishing these two standards and intelligently using various agencies with different levels of access and authority, the MSC has ensured that the path to certification for suppliers is clear and achievable. It has also provided consumers with a way to know that the seafood they buy to consume is as safe and environmentally sound as possible.

11. Which of the following choices best expresses the essential meaning of the highlighted sentence in the passage? Incorrect choices will change the meaning or leave out important details.

    (A) If too many of one type of fish are caught, that type of fish can go extinct, so the MSC asks people who catch fish to prove that they aren't catching so many of any one type that that type can't reproduce.

    (B) If too many of one type of fish are caught, the MSC cannot certify people who catch that type of fish because there won't be enough fish left to reproduce.

    (C) If too many of one type of fish are caught, none of them can be certified by the MSC because no one can be certain that the fish that repopulate are caught in a responsible way.

    (D) If too many of one type of fish are caught, boat operators and fisheries may end up putting themselves out of business because they won't have any fish left to catch.

12. The author discusses fraudulent activities in the supply chain in the seventh paragraph in order to

    (A) give reasons that support the MSC's use of multiple agencies to help with certification

    (B) show examples of crimes committed by MSC-certified fisheries

    (C) explain how fisheries can get around the standards set by the MSC while not violating them directly

    (D) question the usefulness of MSC certification entirely

Practice Section 2

Read the following passage, then answer the questions.

Milgram Experiment

In the 1960s, Yale University psychologist Stanley Milgram conducted a series of experiments designed to test subjects' obedience to authority figures. His experiment was inspired by hearing Nazi war criminal Adolph Eichmann claim that he was just following orders when he killed millions of people in the Holocaust. Milgram was asking the question, "Could it be that Eichmann and his million accomplices in the Holocaust were just following orders? Could we call them all accomplices?"

Milgram designed his experiment to put the subjects in the position of having to inflict harm on another person. The subjects were told they were helping with a learning experiment and that there were different volunteer subjects ("learners") in another room that needed to be helped in their learning tasks. The subjects were seated at a panel that appeared to allow them to administer electric shocks by flipping the switches on the panel. The switches were labeled from 30 volts ("slight shock") up to 450 volts ("XXX"). The subjects were told that the learners in the other room were hooked up to the panel so that when the subject flipped a switch, the learner was given the shock. There were no other subjects in the experiment, and no "learners." Any words or noises the subjects heard that were attributed to the learners were actually generated by the experimenters.

Experimenters gave the subjects a list of words and asked them to read the words out loud to the learners. If the learners repeated the words in order (the task the subjects were told was the purpose of the experiment), the subject proceeded to the next list of words. If the learner repeated the words incorrectly or out of order, the subject was told to give the learner a shock. The subject was to start with the 30-volt shock for the first mistake, and proceed in order for each subsequent mistake. The subject could hear increasingly strong buzzing sounds as the shocks were delivered.

The subjects began the experiment with lists of words that were easy to recite back in order, and the learners ran through a few sets before making a mistake. After the first few mistakes and shocks, however, the learners began to exclaim and say things like "That hurts!" upon being shocked, and their accuracy at reciting the words suffered. Each time a learner failed to recite back a list correctly, the subject was required to give a progressively greater shock. With each progressively greater shock, the learner cried out in pain more strongly, and asked to be let out of the experiment and for the subject to stop. After the subject administered shocks at the 300-volt level, the learner banged on the wall and demanded to be let out. Above the 300 level, the learner did not respond to the lists of words or to the shocks. Although the learners were not actually being shocked or hurt, the subjects did not know this, and thought they were administering shocks to another person who was begging for them to stop or who had possibly expired from the shocks.

When subjects asked the experimenter if they should and could stop the experiment, the experimenter told them to continue, using phrases such as "Please continue" and "The experiment requires that you continue" and "You have no other choice; you must go on." Stanley Milgram had predicted that no more than 3 percent of subjects would continue the experiment to administering the maximum level of shocks. However, in the end, 65 percent of subjects continued to administer shocks up to the lethal 450-volt level. At the end of the session, the experiment was explained to the subject with the intention of letting the subject know what the experiment was actually testing.

Milgram speculated that several factors contributed to such a high percentage of subjects being willing to inflict pain on another human for no reason: the presence of the authority figure experimenter, the assumption that the experimenter was an expert, the fact that the experiment was taking place at a reputable university, and the apparent selection of teacher and learner randomly. What the experiment showed was that we cannot predict our own behavior until we are in a situation. As Milgram said, "Often it is not so much the kind of person a man is as the kind of situation in which he finds himself that determines how he will act."

1. The word *inflict* in the passage is closest in meaning to
   (A) make sick
   (B) cause
   (C) ask
   (D) provide help
2. The word *subsequent* in the passage is closest in meaning to
   (A) absent
   (B) worse
   (C) following
   (D) previous
3. Which of the following questions about Milgram's experiment is NOT answered in the third paragraph?
   (A) What happened if the learner repeated the list out of order?
   (B) How strong was the first shock the subjects gave?
   (C) Could the subjects hear the learners being shocked?
   (D) How many words were on the list the subjects read?

In the 1960s, Yale University psychologist Stanley Milgram conducted a series of experiments designed to test subjects' obedience to authority figures. His experiment was inspired by hearing Nazi war criminal Adolph Eichmann claim that he was just following orders when he killed millions of people in the Holocaust. Milgram was asking the question, "Could it be that Eichmann and his million accomplices in the Holocaust were just following orders? Could we call them all accomplices?"

Milgram designed his experiment to put the subjects in the position of having to inflict harm on another person. The subjects were told they were helping with a learning experiment and that there were different volunteer subjects ("learners") in another room that needed to be helped in their learning tasks. The subjects were seated at a panel that appeared to allow them to administer electric shocks by flipping the switches on the panel. The switches were labeled from 30 volts ("slight shock") up to 450 volts ("XXX"). The subjects were told that the learners in the other room were hooked up to the panel so that when the subject flipped a switch, the learner was given the shock. There were no other subjects in the experiment, and no "learners." Any words or noises the subjects heard that were attributed to the learners were actually generated by the experimenters.

Experimenters gave the subjects a list of words and asked them to read the words out loud to the learners. If the learners repeated the words in order (the task the subjects were told was the purpose of the experiment), the subject proceeded to the next list of words. If the learner repeated the words incorrectly or out of order, the subject was told to give the learner a shock. The subject was to start with the 30-volt shock for the first mistake, and proceed in order for each subsequent mistake. The subject could hear increasingly strong buzzing sounds as the shocks were delivered.

The subjects began the experiment with lists of words that were easy to recite back in order, and the learners ran through a few sets before making a mistake. After the first few mistakes and shocks, however, the learners began to exclaim and say things like "That hurts!" upon being shocked, and their accuracy at reciting the words suffered. Each time a learner failed to recite back a list correctly, the subject was required to give a progressively greater shock. With each progressively greater shock, the learner cried out in pain more strongly, and asked to be let out of the experiment and for the subject to stop. After the subject administered shocks at the 300-volt level, the learner banged on the wall and demanded to be let out. Above the 300 level, the learner did not respond to the lists of words or to the shocks. Although the learners were not actually being shocked or hurt, the subjects did not know this, and thought they were administering shocks to another person who was begging for them to stop or who had possibly expired from the shocks.

When subjects asked the experimenter if they should and could stop the experiment, the experimenter told them to continue, using phrases such as "Please continue" and "The experiment requires that you continue" and "You have no other choice; you must go on." Stanley Milgram had predicted that no more than 3 percent of subjects would continue the experiment to administering the maximum level of shocks. However, in the end, 65 percent of subjects continued to administer shocks up to the lethal 450-volt level. At the end of the session, the experiment was explained to the subject with the intention of letting the subject know what the experiment was actually testing.

Milgram speculated that several factors contributed to such a high percentage of subjects being willing to inflict pain on another human for no reason: the presence of the authority figure experimenter, the assumption that the experimenter was an expert, the fact that the experiment was taking place at a reputable university, and the apparent selection of teacher and learner randomly. What the experiment showed was that we cannot predict our own behavior until we are in a situation. As Milgram said, "Often it is not so much the kind of person a man is as the kind of situation in which he finds himself that determines how he will act."

4. The phrase *them all* in the passage refers to
   (A) Milgram
   (B) Eichmann
   (C) Eichmann's accomplices
   (D) the experiments
5. Which of the following can you infer from the passage?
   (A) The subjects did not know that the learners were not also volunteers.
   (B) The subjects did not know that they had volunteered for an experiment.
   (C) The learners were volunteers, as were the subjects.
   (D) The learners did not know that they were going to be shocked.
6. Which of the following can you infer from the fifth paragraph?
   (A) At least some of the experimenters were uneasy about using subjects who did not understand the real purpose of the experiment.
   (B) At least some of the subjects of the experiment were aware of what the experiment was testing before they started the experiment.
   (C) At least some of the learners who were subjected to the highest level of shocks were physically injured.
   (D) At least some of the subjects who asked if they could stop may have continued to the end of the experiment.

In the 1960s, Yale University psychologist Stanley Milgram conducted a series of experiments designed to test subjects' obedience to authority figures. His experiment was inspired by hearing Nazi war criminal Adolph Eichmann claim that he was just following orders when he killed millions of people in the Holocaust. Milgram was asking the question, "Could it be that Eichmann and his million accomplices in the Holocaust were just following orders? Could we call them all accomplices?"

Milgram designed his experiment to put the subjects in the position of having to inflict harm on another person. The subjects were told they were helping with a learning experiment and that there were different volunteer subjects ("learners") in another room that needed to be helped in their learning tasks. The subjects were seated at a panel that appeared to allow them to administer electric shocks by flipping the switches on the panel. The switches were labeled from 30 volts ("slight shock") up to 450 volts ("XXX"). The subjects were told that the learners in the other room were hooked up to the panel so that when the subject flipped a switch, the learner was given the shock. There were no other subjects in the experiment, and no "learners." Any words or noises the subjects heard that were attributed to the learners were actually generated by the experimenters.

Experimenters gave the subjects a list of words and asked them to read the words out loud to the learners. If the learners repeated the words in order (the task the subjects were told was the purpose of the experiment), the subject proceeded to the next list of words. If the learner repeated the words incorrectly or out of order, the subject was told to give the learner a shock. The subject was to start with the 30-volt shock for the first mistake, and proceed in order for each subsequent mistake. The subject could hear increasingly strong buzzing sounds as the shocks were delivered.

The subjects began the experiment with lists of words that were easy to recite back in order, and the learners ran through a few sets before making a mistake. After the first few mistakes and shocks, however, the learners began to exclaim and say things like "That hurts!" upon being shocked, and their accuracy at reciting the words suffered. Each time a learner failed to recite back a list correctly, the subject was required to give a progressively greater shock. With each progressively greater shock, the learner cried out in pain more strongly, and asked to be let out of the experiment and for the subject to stop. After the subject administered shocks at the 300-volt level, the learner banged on the wall and demanded to be let out. Above the 300 level, the learner did not respond to the lists of words or to the shocks. Although the learners were not actually being shocked or hurt, the subjects did not know this, and thought they were administering shocks to another person who was begging for them to stop or who had possibly expired from the shocks.

When subjects asked the experimenter if they should and could stop the experiment, the experimenter told them to continue, using phrases such as "Please continue" and "The experiment requires that you continue" and "You have no other choice; you must go on." Stanley Milgram had predicted that no more than 3 percent of subjects would continue the experiment to administering the maximum level of shocks. However, in the end, 65 percent of subjects continued to administer shocks up to the lethal 450-volt level. At the end of the session, the experiment was explained to the subject with the intention of letting the subject know what the experiment was actually testing.

Milgram speculated that several factors contributed to such a high percentage of subjects being willing to inflict pain on another human for no reason: the presence of the authority figure experimenter, the assumption that the experimenter was an expert, the fact that the experiment was taking place at a reputable university, and the apparent selection of teacher and learner randomly. What the experiment showed was that we cannot predict our own behavior until we are in a situation. As Milgram said, "Often it is not so much the kind of person a man is as the kind of situation in which he finds himself that determines how he will act."

7. Which of the following best expresses the essential information in the highlighted sentences? Incorrect answer choices change the meaning in important ways or leave out essential information.

   (A) Although Milgram thought few subjects would inflict the maximum amount of pain on the learners, 65 percent of them gave the highest shock.

   (B) Although Milgram did not predict that this would happen, most subjects used 65 percent of the maximum available shock level.

   (C) Although the subjects did not want to, 65 percent of them gave the learners the highest shock possible.

   (D) Although the learners did not want to be shocked, 65 percent of them made enough mistakes to be shocked at the highest level the subjects were able to inflict.

8. The word *recite* in the passage is closest in meaning to

   (A) write

   (B) pass

   (C) bill

   (D) say

9. Sum up the passage by choosing three of the six sentences below and putting them in the correct order following the introductory sentence. The incorrect sentences express information that was not in the passage or are minor ideas in the passage. This question is worth 2 points.

   Stanley Milgram conducted an experiment in the 1960s to determine how likely the average person was to obey authority against their morals.

   *

   *

   *

   1. The subjects were told to ask the learners to repeat lists of words and give them progressively more painful electric shocks when they made mistakes.
   2. The subjects were recruited with ads posted around the campus of Yale University, and subjects were paid for participating in the experiment.
   3. The subjects of the experiment were told they would be teaching learners in another room, but the learners were just experimenters pretending to be learners.
   4. Even though the subjects felt uncomfortable with hurting the learners, more than half of them continued giving the shocks up to the most painful level available.
   5. Milgram designed the experiment after he heard a quote from Adolph Eichmann that Eichmann and his followers were simply following orders.
   6. The subjects were forced to watch the learners through a window as they administered the electric shocks.

10. The passage implies that at least some of the subjects

    (A) were familiar with adult learning theory

    (B) did not want to continue to administer shocks to the learners

    (C) had heard of Adolph Eichmann and his followers

    (D) understood the medical effects of administering electric shocks to the human body

Milgram designed his experiment to put the subjects in the position of having to inflict harm on another person. The subjects were told they were helping with a learning experiment and that there were different volunteer subjects ("learners") in another room that needed to be helped in their learning tasks. The subjects were seated at a panel that appeared to allow them to administer electric shocks by flipping the switches on the panel. The switches were labeled from 30 volts ("slight shock") up to 450 volts ("XXX"). The subjects were told that the learners in the other room were hooked up to the panel so that when the subject flipped a switch, the learner was given the shock. There were no other subjects in the experiment, and no "learners." Any words or noises the subjects heard that were attributed to the learners were actually generated by the experimenters.

11. The phrase *another person* in the second paragraph refers to

    (A) Milgram

    (B) another subject in another room

    (C) an unseen person pretending to be a learner

    (D) the subject himself

12. The author of the passage mentions the labels on the switches of the control panels the subjects were seated at in order to

    (A) make it clear to the subjects that they were required to flip the switches

    (B) show that the subjects were given descriptions of the shocks that they could understand

    (C) demonstrate that the experimenters did not trust the subjects

    (D) separate the technical voltage definitions from the real-life strength of the shocks

Practice Section 3

Read the following passage, then answer the questions.

Nickel Mining

Nickel (Ni), a precious metal with unique resistance to high temperatures, corrosion, and other extreme conditions, is occasionally used alone but is more often combined with another metal or metals to form an alloy used for different industrial applications. Different combinations of nickel and other metals can be combined to form alloys with specific characteristics.

One common nickel-based alloy is stainless steel, which generally contains 10 percent nickel and 90 percent iron. Alloys containing lower percentages of nickel resist stress and extreme temperatures more poorly compared to alloys with higher percentages of nickel. Alloys with higher percentages of nickel are called super-alloys, and may have nickel percentages as high as 70 percent, along with other substances that give them very specific performance features. Substances commonly combined with nickel to make super-alloys are chromium, iron, and cobalt. Super-alloys are used for chemical processing, the aerospace industry, various medical applications, and power plants.

It is vital that nickel mined for use in super-alloys is as pure as possible, because the parts manufactured from super-alloys are generally responsible for the proper functioning of the larger unit, or "safety-critical." For this reason, mined nickel is refined specifically until it reaches the proper level of purity to be combined in a super-alloy for safety-critical parts. This extremely pure nickel is called high-purity nickel, and is extremely valuable because only a small portion of the nickel mined worldwide is ever refined to the required state of purity to be labeled high-purity nickel.

Nickel is extracted from ore by roasting at high temperatures. This achieves up to a 75 percent purity level, which is enough for the many alloys creating stainless steel. For more resistant alloys, however, the nickel must be refined further. The most common nickel-refining process is a three-step procedure of flotation, smelting, and something called the Sherritt-Gordon process, in which the nickel is treated with hydrogen sulfide (which removes any copper) and then a solvent that separates the nickel from any cobalt. This procedure can achieve 99 percent purity, which is enough for most industrial applications, but is still not high-purity nickel.

High-purity nickel is further refined using the Mond process. The Mond process can achieve 99.99 percent purity to create high-purity nickel. Named after its creator, the Mond process has been in use for over a century and involves several steps of refining. The first involves changing the nickel to nickel carbonyl by combining the nickel with carbon monoxide at a very specific temperature. Then the nickel carbonyl is put through a chamber filled with nickel pellets and stirred until it decomposes and sticks to the pellets, or heated to a temperature of 230 degrees Celsius at which it turns into a fine, pure powder called carbonyl nickel, or high-purity nickel.

Because the refining process to create high-purity nickel requires so many steps and such specific conditions, it is not performed in many locations. This means that high-purity nickel is quite expensive, and the producers of high-purity nickel have significant control over the market price. This creates a unique industry situation, and the two main producers of high-purity nickel have been investigated by authorities in several countries to determine if they have been colluding on price or exercising undue control over prices through the duopoly in the industry. While these two producers have never been found guilty of specifically preventing others from entering the high-purity nickel market, the amount of capital and access to nickel—which is mined in finite amounts which are bought by existing nickel refiners—required to enter the market is prohibitive. As a result, the two producers of high-purity nickel have been barred by legal authorities from merging or collaborating under antimonopoly laws. However, they are still the only major producers of high-purity nickel, and therefore have strong influence over the price to buyers.

The ultimate outcome of the structure of the high-purity nickel industry is that super-alloys for safety-critical parts are extremely expensive to create and use. This requires producers of safety-critical parts to maintain production processes with low error rates and high efficiency.

1. The word *stress* in the passage is closest in meaning to

    (A) pressure

    (B) anger

    (C) nickel

    (D) cobalt

2. The word *refined* in the passage is closest in meaning to

    (A) paid

    (B) mined

    (C) combined

    (D) purified

3. The phrase *This procedure* in the passage refers to

    (A) the alloy process

    (B) the Sherritt-Gordon process

    (C) the Mond process

    (D) the carbonyl nickel process

4. Super-alloys are different from alloys in that super-alloys

    (A) contain higher percentages of nickel

    (B) contain higher percentages of stainless steel

    (C) require longer mining times

    (D) do not contain nickel

5. Part of the Sherritt-Gordon process involves
   (A) mining the nickel
   (B) removing copper from the nickel
   (C) creating a super-alloy
   (D) achieving 99.9 percent purity
6. In the second paragraph, the author implies that
   (A) super-alloys resist stress and extreme temperatures better than regular alloys do
   (B) super-alloys contain iron just as stainless steel does
   (C) super-alloys contain cobalt instead of iron
   (D) stainless steel is a super-alloy with stress-resistant characteristics
7. The author implies which of the following about the Mond process?
   (A) The Mond process and Sherritt-Gordon process are interchangeable.
   (B) The Mond process achieves lower purity than the Sherritt-Gordon process does.
   (C) The Mond process must be started immediately after mining the nickel to be effective.
   (D) The Mond process achieves higher purity than the Sherritt-Gordon process does.
8. Which of the following is NOT implied in the passage?
   (A) Nickel not refined and made into super-alloys is made into stainless steel.
   (B) Nickel must be refined before it can be combined into a super-alloy.
   (C) The Mond process produces high-purity nickel.
   (D) The Sherritt-Gordon process is not sufficient to refine nickel enough to make safety-critical parts.

High-purity nickel is further refined using the Mond process. The Mond process can achieve 99.99 percent purity to create high-purity nickel. Named after its creator, the Mond process has been in use for over a century and involves several steps of refining. The first involves changing the nickel to nickel carbonyl by combining the nickel with carbon monoxide at a very specific temperature. Then the nickel carbonyl is put through a chamber filled with nickel pellets and stirred until it decomposes and sticks to the pellets, or heated to a temperature of 230 degrees Celsius at which it turns into a fine, pure powder called carbonyl nickel, or high-purity nickel.

9. The phrase *its creator* in the paragraph above refers to
   (A) the creator of nickel
   (B) the creator of the Mond process
   (C) the creator of the smelting process
   (D) the creator of the alloy process

10. The author mentions the cost of refining high-purity nickel in the sixth paragraph in order to
    - (A) speculate why safety-critical parts are so expensive to manufacture
    - (B) propose a solution to the revenue problems the producers of high-purity nickel face
    - (C) question why producers can't lower prices to the market
    - (D) explain why the two producers of high-purity nickel have such influence over the price of high-purity nickel

Nickel is extracted from ore by roasting at high temperatures.• This achieves up to a 75 percent purity level, which is enough for many alloys creating stainless steel. •For more resistant alloys, however, the nickel must be refined further. •The most common nickel-refining process is a three-step procedure of flotation, smelting, and something called the Sherritt-Gordon process, in which the nickel is treated with hydrogen sulfide (which removes any copper) and then a solvent that separates the nickel from any cobalt. •This procedure can achieve 99 percent purity, which is enough for most industrial applications, but is still not high-purity nickel.

11. Look at the four bullets in the passage and indicate where the sentence below should be inserted.

    There are two processes used to refine nickel to a high-enough level of purity to be used in more resistant alloys.

    - (A) Nickel is extracted from ore by roasting at high temperatures.• There are two processes used to refine nickel to a high-enough level of purity to be used in more resistant alloys. This achieves up to a 75 percent purity level, which is enough for many alloys creating stainless steel. •For more resistant alloys, however, the nickel must be refined further. •The most common nickel-refining process is a three-step procedure of flotation, smelting, and something called the Sherritt-Gordon process, in which the nickel is treated with hydrogen sulfide (which removes any copper) and then a solvent that separates the nickel from any cobalt. •This procedure can achieve 99 percent purity, which is enough for most industrial applications, but is still not high-purity nickel.
    - (B) Nickel is extracted from ore by roasting at high temperatures.• This achieves up to a 75 percent purity level, which is enough for many alloys creating stainless steel. • There are two processes used to refine nickel to a high-enough level of purity to be used in more resistant alloys. For more resistant alloys, however, the nickel must be refined further. •The most common nickel-refining process is a three-step procedure of flotation, smelting, and something called the Sherritt-Gordon process, in which the nickel is treated with hydrogen sulfide (which removes any copper) and then a solvent that separates the nickel from any cobalt. •This procedure can achieve 99 percent purity, which is enough for most industrial applications, but is still not high-purity nickel.
    - (C) Nickel is extracted from ore by roasting at high temperatures.• This achieves up to a 75 percent purity level, which is enough for many alloys creating stainless steel. •For more resistant alloys, however, the nickel must be refined further. • There are two processes used to refine nickel to a high-enough level of purity to be used in more resistant alloys. The

most common nickel-refining process is a three-step procedure of flotation, smelting, and something called the Sherritt-Gordon process, in which the nickel is treated with hydrogen sulfide (which removes any copper) and then a solvent that separates the nickel from any cobalt. •This procedure can achieve 99 percent purity, which is enough for most industrial applications, but is still not high-purity nickel.

(D) Nickel is extracted from ore by roasting at high temperatures.• This achieves up to a 75 percent purity level, which is enough for many alloys creating stainless steel. •For more resistant alloys, however, the nickel must be refined further. •The most common nickel-refining process is a three-step procedure of flotation, smelting, and something called the Sherritt-Gordon process, in which the nickel is treated with hydrogen sulfide (which removes any copper) and then a solvent that separates the nickel from any cobalt. • There are two processes used to refine nickel to a high-enough level of purity to be used in more resistant alloys. This procedure can achieve 99 percent purity, which is enough for most industrial applications, but is still not high-purity nickel.

Because the refining process to create high-purity nickel requires so many steps and such specific conditions, it is not performed in many locations. This means that high-purity nickel is quite expensive, and the producers of high-purity nickel have significant control over the market price. This creates a unique industry situation, and the two main producers of high-purity nickel have been investigated by authorities in several countries to determine if they have been colluding on price or exercising undue control over prices through the duopoly in the industry. While these two producers have never been found guilty of specifically preventing others from entering the high-purity nickel market, the amount of capital and access to nickel—which is mined in finite amounts which are bought by existing nickel refiners—required to enter the market is prohibitive. As a result, the two producers of high-purity nickel have been barred by legal authorities from merging or collaborating under antimonopoly laws. However, they are still the only major producers of high-purity nickel, and therefore have strong influence over the price to buyers.

12. Which of the following best expresses the essential information in the highlighted sentence? Incorrect answer choices change the meaning in important ways or leave out essential information.

(A) The two companies that produce high-purity nickel have never been convicted of working together to keep other companies out of the nickel market, but nickel is still costly.

(B) The two companies that produce high-purity nickel have been convicted of working together to keep the costs of entering the high-purity nickel market so expensive that other companies cannot enter.

(C) The two companies that produce high-purity nickel have never been convicted of working to keep other companies from refining high-purity nickel, but it costs too much and is too difficult for other companies to get access to nickel for them to go into the business.

(D) The costs of starting a nickel-refining business are so high and it is so difficult to get access to nickel that it is difficult for companies to enter the market.

Practice Section 4

Read the following passage, then answer the questions.

Reverse Factoring

In many countries, access to capital markets and low-interest loans is limited to large corporations and government monopolies. Small businesses and suppliers do not have access to liquid cash, and run the risk of failing to fulfill orders because they do not have the capital to purchase supplies for the products they make. As a result of this credit crisis, a practice called factoring has become popular in many areas of the world.

In factoring, a bank or financial organization—called a factor—gives a supplier cash in exchange for the right to collect payment when the supplier delivers an order to a buyer. In effect, the factor is buying the supplier's Accounts Receivables at a discount off the face value of the accounts. The supplier benefits by receiving cash more quickly than it could from the buyer, but does not receive full payment for the accounts. The factor takes on a huge amount of risk by buying a supplier's Accounts Receivables, as each individual buyer must be researched to determine what the risk is of that buyer defaulting on payment. In some cases, these buyers are so small or obscure that risk cannot be determined, and a factor is buying a complete unknown. In this case, if a buyer defaults, the factor may go back to the supplier and ask for compensation for the default. Thus, factoring is risky for both the supplier and the factor.

In recent years, a new practice called reverse factoring has become increasingly popular because it shifts the anchor from supplier to buyer to virtually eliminate risk from the transaction. In reverse factoring, instead of buying a supplier's Accounts Receivables, a factor provides loans to a single large buyer's suppliers.

For example, a large corporation with an excellent credit rating and an extremely low chance of defaulting will have a list of suppliers. Many of these suppliers are small businesses without adequate access to liquid cash. When a factor contracts with the large buyer to supply payments to suppliers, the transaction works as follows: 1) the supplier signs an agreement to be entered into the factor's system, 2) the supplier delivers an order to the buyer, 3) the buyer approves the delivery and signs off with the factor, 4) the factor pays the supplier a percentage (usually 80 to 90 percent) of the price of the order immediately, 5) the buyer pays the factor for the order at whatever terms the agreement states, 6) the factor pays the supplier the remaining balance for the order. The factor takes a percentage of the transaction and charges interest to the buyer.

By originating the transaction with a large, risk-free buyer instead of a supplier, the risk is lowered significantly for all parties involved. The buyer carries no risk. The factor is only dependent on the buyer, who is unlikely to default, so the risk is minimal. The supplier knows the factor will pay promptly, so the supplier's risk is minimal.

In addition, all three parties benefit from this relationship over a traditional factoring relationship and over other nonstandard capital market arrangements. The factor earns a steady interest rate with very little risk, and by working with large buyers, has access to large volumes of business at one time. The buyers gain the ability to pay on better terms for lower interest than they would with traditional capital market structures. Suppliers get paid far more rapidly and at a far lower interest rate than they would be able to with a traditional factoring or capital market arrangement. Reverse factoring improves all parties' positions and liquidity.

By turning the traditional factoring relationship off balance and anchoring on a different party in the transaction, reverse factoring creates financial and relationship value where none existed, and increases stability for individual parties and across the transactional relationship.

1. The word *capital* in the passage is closest in meaning to

   (A) financial

   (B) principal

   (C) important

   (D) knowledgeable

2. The word *defaults* in the passage is closest in meaning to

   (A) does not ask

   (B) does not know

   (C) does not pay

   (D) does not loan

3. The phrase *all three parties* in the passage refers to

   (A) bank, factor, buyer

   (B) factor, bank, supplier

   (C) supplier, bank, product

   (D) factor, buyer, supplier

4. Factoring has increased as a practice in countries around the world because it

   (A) has a common language

   (B) attracts investors to foreign countries

   (C) solves a problem with credit

   (D) requires large amounts of land

5. One of the benefits of reverse factoring is that it

   (A) removes risk almost entirely from the transaction

   (B) does not involve an exchange of money

   (C) can be done on a boat or other sailing vessel

   (D) can be done by anyone, regardless of income

6. In reverse factoring, after the factor pays the supplier a percentage of the order amount

   (A) the supplier officially enters the factor's system

   (B) the buyer pays the factor for the order

   (C) the supplier delivers the order to the buyer

   (D) the factor contracts with the buyer

7. The word *liquid* in the passage is closest in meaning to
   (A) accessible
   (B) wet
   (C) complex
   (D) thin
8. Which of the following is NOT implied in the passage?
   (A) Reverse factoring helps both the supplier and the buyer with cash flow issues.
   (B) Reverse factoring reduces risk to the factor significantly.
   (C) Reverse factoring is only useful after a regular factoring relationship has been arranged with the factor.
   (D) Reverse factoring does not require suppliers to wait for payment from the factor for as long as they would have waited for it from the buyer.
9. Which of the following can you infer from the passage?
   (A) There are multiple ways to finance purchases from suppliers.
   (B) A factor must be prequalified to borrow money from a supplier.
   (C) Reverse factoring only works in European countries.
   (D) Small suppliers are more likely to have access to credit than small buyers.
10. In the sixth paragraph, the author mentions the benefits of reverse factoring to the factor in order to
    (A) prove that there is not a strong connection between a role in the reverse factoring transaction and the benefits received
    (B) show that the factor benefits more from reverse factoring than the supplier or the buyer
    (C) support the topic sentence of the paragraph that states that all three parties benefit from reverse factoring
    (D) connect the concept of factoring more closely with reverse factoring
11. In the last paragraph, the phrase *individual parties* refers to
    (A) individual buyers
    (B) individual suppliers, buyers, and factors
    (C) individual suppliers and factors
    (D) individual buyers and factors

In addition, all three parties benefit from this relationship over a traditional factoring relationship and over other nonstandard capital market arrangements. The factor earns a steady interest rate with very little risk, and by working with large buyers, has access to large volumes of business at one time. The buyers gain the ability to pay on better terms for lower interest than they would with traditional capital market structures. Suppliers get paid far more rapidly and at a far lower interest rate than they would be able to with a traditional factoring or capital market arrangement. Reverse factoring improves all parties' positions and liquidity.

12. Which of the following sentences best summarizes the highlighted section of the paragraph above?

    (A) The factor lends money at a higher rate than it could get otherwise, the supplier can pay later than it would otherwise, and the buyer receives its money more quickly than it would otherwise.

    (B) The factor lends money, the buyer pays money, and the supplier receives money.

    (C) The factor can get a high interest rate, and the buyer and supplier can get lower rates than they would otherwise.

    (D) The factor uses its money and gets a good interest rate with little risk, the buyer can extend payment without paying high interest rates, and the supplier gets paid more quickly at a lower rate.

Reading Practice Answer Keys and Explanations

Chapter 5

Here are the answer keys and explanations for the questions you just practiced in Chapter 4.

Practice Section 1 Answer Key

1. B
2. C
3. A
4. D
5. D
6. A
7. B
8. C
9. A
10. B
11. A
12. A

Practice Section 1 Explanations

1. The word *rigorous* in the passage is closest in meaning to

   (A) dead

   (B) difficult

   (C) ancient

   (D) renewable

   The answer is B. In the sentence, *rigorous* is used to describe the process of obtaining MSC certification, which is expensive and lengthy and requires significant change—therefore, it is difficult. Eliminate A, C, and D because they do not mean difficult.

2. The word *indefinitely* in the passage is closest in meaning to

   (A) earlier than expected

   (B) after a certain date

   (C) at no specific time

   (D) without authorization

   The answer is C. *Indefinitely* means without a definite time frame. Answers A and B specify a time, so eliminate them. *Indefinitely* has nothing to do with authorization, so eliminate D.

3. The word *them* in the passage refers to

   (A) fisheries

   (B) fish

   (C) changes

   (D) MSC

   The answer is A. What would be in compliance with MSC certification standards? Not the fish because they have no control over their status, so eliminate B. Changes cannot be in compliance, only the results of the changes, so eliminate C. Not the MSC itself, so eliminate D.

4. The MSC is concerned with sustainable fish stocks because it wants to

   (A) bill fisheries more for overfished species

   (B) breed new species of fish

   (C) guarantee delivery of species ordered by retailers

   (D) preserve fish species from extinction

   The answer is D. There is nothing in the passage about billing fisheries for overfished species, so eliminate A. The passage doesn't mention anything about new species, so eliminate B. C misrepresents the supply chain of fishing, so eliminate it.

5. The MSC uses a network of independent agencies to help enforce certification because

   (A) it cannot finance certification processes alone

   (B) certification is too difficult for the MSC to earn without help

   (C) no single agency can be responsible for standards as stringent as the MSC's standards

   (D) the chain of suppliers is too complex for one agency alone to monitor

   The answer is D. The passage states that the MSC used multiple agencies because the chain of command is so complex. There was nothing about financing certification processes, so eliminate A. The MSC gives the certification, it does not earn it—B is tempting but a misrepresentation of the passage, so eliminate it. C is too absolute and puts the reason for using agencies on the MSC's standards, not the complex supply chain, so eliminate it.

6. The phrase *This standard* in the passage refers to

   (A) the chain of custody standard

   (B) the fisheries standard

   (C) the environmental standard

   (D) the sustainable standard

   The answer is A. The phrase refers to "the chain of custody standard" in the previous sentence. Eliminate B, C, and D because they are not discussed in this paragraph.

7. According to the passage, making changes that will lead to MSC certification for a fishery can be

   (A) unknown

   (B) expensive

   (C) impossible

   (D) antagonistic

   The answer is B. The passage states that "The cost of making the changes required to become MSC certified ranges from $50,000 to $500,000 for each fishing boat operator or processor." It is not an unknown process, so eliminate A. It is also not impossible, so eliminate C. You do not have any information about whether it is an antagonistic process or not, so eliminate D.

8. You can infer from the passage that

   (A) most fisheries already conform to MSC certification standards

   (B) concern for MSC certification standards is largely politically motivated

   (C) it is easier for fisheries to catch seafood that does not conform to MSC certification standards

   (D) conforming to MSC certification standards will cause more damage to the environment than initially thought

   The answer is C. From the passage, you can infer that it is easier for fisheries to catch seafood that does not conform to MSC standards, or else the fisheries would already conform to the standards. If most fisheries already conformed to MSC certification standards, it wouldn't be so complicated for them to earn certification, so eliminate A. You have no information about motivation for MSC standards other than concern for the environment, so eliminate B. You can infer the opposite of D—that conforming to MSC standards will help, not hurt, the environment—so eliminate it.

9. You can infer that the author of the passage

   (A) does not oppose using MSC certification standards to certify fisheries

   (B) intends to become MSC certified in the future

   (C) is associated with the MSC or one of its associated agencies or organizations

   (D) thinks fisheries should be forced to comply with MSC certification standards

   The answer is A. The passage is neutral and informative in tone, so there is no indication that the author opposes or approves of MSC certification standards. There is no evidence that the author has anything to do with the fishing industry, so you cannot assume that the author intends to become certified in any capacity, so eliminate B. There is nothing to suggest that the author of the passage is associated with the MSC or anything related to it, so eliminate C. The passage is neutral in tone, so there is no evidence that the author feels fisheries should be forced to do anything, so eliminate D.

10. The passage suggests all of the following EXCEPT

    (A) obtaining MSC certification can be a costly, lengthy process

    (B) the benefits of obtaining MSC certification are intangible

    (C) fisheries are only part of the seafood supply chain

    (D) sustainable fishing practices benefit fish populations

    The answer is B. B contradicts the passage, which indicates benefits for fish populations, the environment, fisheries, and consumers from MSC certification. A is stated in the first paragraph, so eliminate it. C is implied by the discussion of the complex supply chain in the seventh paragraph, so eliminate it. D is addressed in the third paragraph, so eliminate it.

11. Which of the following choices best expresses the essential meaning of the highlighted sentence in the passage? Incorrect choices will change the meaning or leave out important details.

    (A) If too many of one type of fish are caught, that type of fish can go extinct, so the MSC asks people who catch fish to prove that they aren't catching so many of any one type that that type can't reproduce.

    (B) If too many of one type of fish are caught, the MSC cannot certify people who catch that type of fish because there won't be enough fish left to reproduce.

    (C) If too many of one type of fish are caught, none of them can be certified by the MSC because no one can be certain that the fish that repopulate are caught in a responsible way.

    (D) If too many of one type of fish are caught, boat operators and fisheries may end up putting themselves out of business because they won't have any fish left to catch.

    The answer is A. The highlighted sentence states that overfishing can cause extinction, so the MSC requires groups that fish to prove they are not taking too many fish of any one species. A represents that statement accurately. B does not place the responsibility on the individual fishers who catch too many fish, so it misrepresents the sentence—eliminate it. C says that the fish cannot be certified by the MSC, not the fisheries, so eliminate it. D skips over the idea of MSC certification entirely, so eliminate it.

12. The author discusses fraudulent activities in the supply chain in the seventh paragraph in order to

    (A) give reasons that support the MSC's use of multiple agencies to help with certification

    (B) show examples of crimes committed by MSC-certified fisheries

    (C) explain how fisheries can get around the standards set by the MSC while not violating them directly

    (D) question the usefulness of MSC certification entirely

    The answer is A. The fraudulent activities support the argument that the MSC needs help enforcing supply chain violations from other agencies. B is wrong because the purpose of the paragraph is not to focus on the crimes, but on the need for other agency involvement, so eliminate it. Eliminate C because the author is not suggesting that fisheries should get around MSC standards. The author does not question the MSC standards, so eliminate D.

Practice Section 2 Answer Key

1. B
2. C
3. D
4. C
5. A
6. D
7. A
8. D
9. 3, 1, 4
10. B
11. C
12. B

Practice Section 2 Explanations

1. The word *inflict* in the passage is closest in meaning to

   (A) make sick

   (B) cause

   (C) ask

   (D) provide help

   The answer is B. *Inflict* means "to cause." A is the meaning of *infect*, not *inflict*. C has nothing to do with the sentence, and D means the opposite—eliminate them both.

2. The word *subsequent* in the passage is closest in meaning to

   (A) absent

   (B) worse

   (C) following

   (D) previous

   The answer is C. The word *subsequent* in the passage means "coming next," which is closest in meaning to *following*. A makes no sense in the sentence, so eliminate it. B goes too far, so eliminate it. D is the opposite of the meaning, so eliminate it.

3. Which of the following questions about Milgram's experiment is NOT answered in the third paragraph?

   (A) What happened if the learner repeated the list out of order?

   (B) How strong was the first shock the subjects gave?

   (C) Could the subjects hear the learners being shocked?

   (D) How many words were on the list the subjects read?

   The answer is D. There is no information in the passage about the number of words on the list. The third paragraph tells you that the subjects gave the learner a shock, so eliminate A. It also tells you that the first shock was 30 volts, so eliminate B. The paragraph tells you that the subjects could hear the sound of the learner being shocked, so eliminate C.

4. The phrase *them all* in the passage refers to

   (A) Milgram

   (B) Eichmann

   (C) Eichmann's accomplices

   (D) the experiments

   The answer is C. The phrase *them all* refers back to the previous sentence, which mentions Eichmann's "million accomplices." The phrase cannot refer to Milgram or Eichmann, since they are each singular, so eliminate A and B. It does not refer to the experiments discussed in the passage, so eliminate D.

5. Which of the following can you infer from the passage?

   (A) The subjects did not know that the learners were not also volunteers.

   (B) The subjects did not know that they had volunteered for an experiment.

   (C) The learners were volunteers, as were the subjects.

   (D) The learners did not know that they were going to be shocked.

   The answer is A. The subjects thought the learners were other volunteers, not experimenters playing the role of learners. Eliminate B because the subjects did know that they had volunteered for the experiment. Eliminate C because the learners were not volunteers but were actually experimenters. Eliminate D because the learners were not actually shocked and were experimenters.

6. Which of the following can you infer from the fifth paragraph?

   (A) At least some of the experimenters were uneasy about using subjects who did not understand the real purpose of the experiment.

   (B) At least some of the subjects of the experiment were aware of what the experiment was testing before they started the experiment.

   (C) At least some of the learners who were subjected to the highest level of shocks were physically injured.

   (D) At least some of the subjects who asked if they could stop may have continued to the end of the experiment.

   The answer is D. Sixty five percent of the subjects continued to the end of the experiment, so it is likely that some of the subjects who asked if they could stop were in that 65 percent. Eliminate A because you do not have any information about how the experimenters felt about the subjects. Eliminate B because you are told that the subjects did not know what the experiment was actually testing until after they finished the experiment. Eliminate C because you know that no one was physically injured by shocks during the experiment.

7. Which of the following best expresses the essential information in the highlighted sentences? Incorrect answer choices change the meaning in important ways or leave out essential information.

   (A) Although Milgram thought few subjects would inflict the maximum amount of pain on the learners, 65 percent of them gave the highest shock.

   (B) Although Milgram did not predict that this would happen, most subjects used 65 percent of the maximum available shock level.

   (C) Although the subjects did not want to, 65 percent of them gave the learners the highest shock possible.

   (D) Although the learners did not want to be shocked, 65 percent of them made enough mistakes to be shocked at the highest level the subjects were able to inflict.

   The answer is A. This choice sums up the fact that Milgram predicted that not many subjects would inflict the maximum level of pain by shocking the learners, but that 65 percent of the subjects did give the highest shock. B misrepresents the 65 percent level as being the level of shock, not the percent of subjects giving the shock, so eliminate it. C does not mention Milgram's prediction, so eliminate it. D shifts the focus to the learners instead of the subjects and doesn't mention Milgram's prediction, so eliminate it.

8. The word *recite* in the passage is closest in meaning to

   (A) write

   (B) pass

   (C) bill

   (D) say

   The answer is D. The learners were supposed to say the list of words back to the subjects. A does not mean *say*, so eliminate it. B does not fit the meaning of the sentence, so eliminate it. C means *receipt*, not *recite*, so eliminate it.

9. Sum up the passage by choosing three of the six sentences below and putting them in the correct order following the introductory sentence. The incorrect sentences express information that was not in the passage or are minor ideas in the passage. This question is worth 2 points.

   Stanley Milgram conducted an experiment in the 1960s to determine how likely the average person was to obey authority against their morals.

   *

   *

   *

   1. The subjects were told to ask the learners to repeat lists of words and give them progressively more painful electric shocks when they made mistakes.
   2. The subjects were recruited with ads posted around the campus of Yale University, and subjects were paid for participating in the experiment.
   3. The subjects of the experiment were told they would be teaching learners in another room, but the learners were just experimenters pretending to be learners.
   4. Even though the subjects felt uncomfortable with hurting the learners, more than half of them continued giving the shocks up to the most painful level available.
   5. Milgram designed the experiment after he heard a quote from Adolph Eichmann that Eichmann and his followers were simply following orders.
   6. The subjects were forced to watch the learners through a window as they administered the electric shocks.

   The correct sequence is 3, 1, 4. This order summarizes the main points of the passage. Eliminate 2, as it gives information that was not mentioned in the passage. Eliminate 5, as it gives a minor detail from the passage. Eliminate 6, as it gives information contradicted in the passage.

10. The passage implies that at least some of the subjects

    (A) were familiar with adult learning theory

    (B) did not want to continue to administer shocks to the learners

    (C) had heard of Adolph Eichmann and his followers

    (D) understood the medical effects of administering electric shocks to the human body

    The answer is B. The passage states that some of the subjects asked the experimenters if they could stop. Eliminate A, as the passage says nothing about adult learning theory. Eliminate C, as you know that Milgram had heard of Eichmann, but you have no information about whether or not the subjects had heard of Eichmann. Eliminate D because there is no evidence in the passage that the subjects had any special medical knowledge relating to electrical shocks.

11. The phrase *another person* in the second paragraph refers to

    (A) Milgram

    (B) another subject in another room

    (C) an unseen person pretending to be a learner

    (D) the subject himself

    The answer is C. Eliminate A because the phrase does not refer to Milgram. Eliminate B because the subjects did not interact with each other. Eliminate D because the subject was not instructed to hurt himself.

12. The author of the passage mentions the labels on the switches of the control panels the subjects were seated at in order to

    (A) make it clear to the subjects that they were required to flip the switches

    (B) show that the subjects were given descriptions of the shocks that they could understand

    (C) demonstrate that the experimenters did not trust the subjects

    (D) separate the technical voltage definitions from the real-life strength of the shocks

    The answer is B. The descriptions on the switches were written so laypeople could understand them. Eliminate A because the descriptions did not mean that the subjects were required to flip the switches. Eliminate C because there is no evidence that the experimenters did not trust the subjects. Eliminate D because the technical labels and word labels corresponded.

Practice Section 3 Answer Key

1. A
2. D
3. B
4. A
5. B
6. A
7. D
8. A
9. B
10. D
11. C
12. C

Practice Section 3 Explanations

1. The word *stress* in the passage is closest in meaning to

   (A) pressure

   (B) anger

   (C) nickel

   (D) cobalt

   The answer is A. The sentence mentions "extreme temperature," so it must be something equally intense physically, and pressure is physically intense. Eliminate B because stress and anger are similar, but not in the context of metals. Eliminate C because alloys are not resistant to nickel. Eliminate D because cobalt is part of some alloys, not something alloys resist.

2. The word *refined* in the passage is closest in meaning to

   (A) paid

   (B) mined

   (C) combined

   (D) purified

   The answer is D. The sentence says this is done to reach the proper level of purity, so a good synonym is *purified*. Eliminate A because money is not mentioned in this part of the passage. Eliminate B because the nickel has already been mined at this point in the process. Eliminate C because it is not ready to be combined until it is already refined.

3. The phrase *This procedure* in the passage refers to

   (A) the alloy process

   (B) the Sherritt-Gordon process

   (C) the Mond process

   (D) the carbonyl nickel process

   The answer is B. The entire paragraph is about a refining process called the Sherritt-Gordon process, so eliminate A. The Mond process is not mentioned until the next paragraph, so eliminate C. Carbonyl nickel is a form of nickel, not a process, so eliminate D.

4. Super-alloys are different from alloys in that super-alloys

   (A) contain higher percentages of nickel

   (B) contain higher percentages of stainless steel

   (C) require longer mining times

   (D) do not contain nickel

   The answer is A. The passage states that "Alloys with higher percentages of nickel are called super-alloys." Eliminate B and D because they contradict the passage. Eliminate C because there is nothing about longer mining times in the passage.

5. Part of the Sherritt-Gordon process involves

   (A) mining the nickel

   (B) removing copper from the nickel

   (C) creating a super-alloy

   (D) achieving 99.9 percent purity

   The answer is B. The Sherritt-Gordon process takes place after the nickel is mined, so eliminate A. Creating a super-alloy takes place after the Sherritt-Gordon refining process, so eliminate C. The Mond process, not the Sherritt-Gordon process, involves achieving 99.9 percent purity, so eliminate D.

6. In the second paragraph, the author implies that

   (A) super-alloys resist stress and extreme temperatures better than regular alloys do

   (B) super-alloys contain iron just as stainless steel does

   (C) super-alloys contain cobalt instead of iron

   (D) stainless steel is a super-alloy with stress-resistant characteristics

   The answer is A. The paragraph states that alloys with higher percentages of nickel resist stress and extreme temperatures better than those with lower percentages, and

that super-alloys contain higher percentages of nickel than regular alloys do. Eliminate B because the paragraph does not say that super-alloys must contain iron. Eliminate C because the passage does not say that super-alloys contain cobalt instead of iron. Eliminate D because stainless steel is an alloy, not a super-alloy.

7. The author implies which of the following about the Mond process?

   (A) The Mond process and Sherritt-Gordon process are interchangeable.

   (B) The Mond process achieves lower purity than the Sherritt-Gordon process does.

   (C) The Mond process must be started immediately after mining the nickel to be effective.

   (D) The Mond process achieves higher purity than the Sherritt-Gordon process does.

   The answer is D. The Sherritt-Gordon process achieves 99 percent purity, while the Mond process achieves 99.9 percent purity, so eliminate A and B. There is no information about how soon after mining the Mond process can occur, so eliminate C.

8. Which of the following is NOT implied in the passage?

   (A) Nickel not refined and made into super-alloys is made into stainless steel.

   (B) Nickel must be refined before it can be combined into a super-alloy.

   (C) The Mond process produces high-purity nickel.

   (D) The Sherritt-Gordon process is not sufficient to refine nickel enough to make safety-critical parts.

   The answer is A. B is implied by the discussions of the Sherritt-Gordon and Mond processes happening before the nickel is made into super-alloys, so eliminate it. C is implied in the paragraph on the Mond process, so eliminate it. D is implied because safety-critical parts must be made from high-purity nickel—which can only be made from nickel refined by the Mond process, not the Sherritt-Gordon process—so eliminate it.

9. The phrase *its creator* in the paragraph above refers to

   (A) the creator of nickel

   (B) the creator of the Mond process

   (C) the creator of the smelting process

   (D) the creator of the alloy process

   The answer is B. The modifier refers to the thing directly after the comma, so the Mond process is named after the creator of the Mond process. Eliminate A, C, and D because they do not fit the meaning for the sentence.

10. The author mentions the cost of refining high-purity nickel in the sixth paragraph in order to

    (A) speculate why safety-critical parts are so expensive to manufacture

    (B) propose a solution to the revenue problems the producers of high-purity nickel face

    (C) question why producers can't lower prices to the market

    (D) explain why the two producers of high-purity nickel have such influence over the price of high-purity nickel

    The answer is D. Eliminate A because there is no mention of safety-critical parts in the sixth paragraph. Eliminate B because there are no revenue problems mentioned. Eliminate C because the paragraph does not discuss lowering prices to the market.

11. Look at the four bullets in the passage and indicate where the sentence below should be inserted.

    There are two processes used to refine nickel to a high-enough level of purity to be used in more resistant alloys.

    (A) Nickel is extracted from ore by roasting at high temperatures.• There are two processes used to refine nickel to a high-enough level of purity to be used in more resistant alloys. This achieves up to a 75 percent purity level, which is enough for many alloys creating stainless steel. •For more resistant alloys, however, the nickel must be refined further. •The most common nickel-refining process is a three-step procedure of flotation, smelting, and something called the Sherritt-Gordon process, in which the nickel is treated with hydrogen sulfide (which removes any copper) and then a solvent that separates the nickel from any cobalt. •This procedure can achieve 99 percent purity, which is enough for most industrial applications, but is still not high-purity nickel.

    (B) Nickel is extracted from ore by roasting at high temperatures.• This achieves up to a 75 percent purity level, which is enough for many alloys creating stainless steel. • There are two processes used to refine nickel to a high-enough level of purity to be used in more resistant alloys. For more resistant alloys, however, the nickel must be refined further. •The most common nickel-refining process is a three-step procedure of flotation, smelting, and something called the Sherritt-Gordon process, in which the nickel is treated with hydrogen sulfide (which removes any copper) and then a solvent that separates the nickel from any cobalt. •This procedure can achieve 99 percent purity, which is enough for most industrial applications, but is still not high-purity nickel.

    (C) Nickel is extracted from ore by roasting at high temperatures.• This achieves up to a 75 percent purity level, which is enough for many alloys creating stainless steel. •For more resistant alloys, however, the nickel must be refined further. • There are two processes used to refine nickel to a high-enough level of purity to be used in more resistant alloys. The most common nickel-refining process is a three-step procedure of flotation, smelting, and something called the Sherritt-Gordon process, in which the nickel is treated with hydrogen sulfide (which removes any copper) and then a solvent that separates the nickel from any cobalt. •This procedure can achieve 99 percent purity, which is enough for most industrial applications, but is still not high-purity nickel.

(D) Nickel is extracted from ore by roasting at high temperatures.• This achieves up to a 75 percent purity level, which is enough for many alloys creating stainless steel. •For more resistant alloys, however, the nickel must be refined further. •The most common nickel-refining process is a three-step procedure of flotation, smelting, and something called the Sherritt-Gordon process, in which the nickel is treated with hydrogen sulfide (which removes any copper) and then a solvent that separates the nickel from any cobalt. • There are two processes used to refine nickel to a high-enough level of purity to be used in more resistant alloys. This procedure can achieve 99 percent purity, which is enough for most industrial applications, but is still not high-purity nickel.

The answer is C. Inserting the sentence after the third square introduces the two different processes right before talking about the first process. Eliminate A because it makes no sense before the second sentence about 75 percent purity. Eliminate B because putting it in before the sentence discussing the need for further refining doesn't make sense logically. Eliminate D because it introduces the two processes in the middle of explaining the first process.

12. Which of the following best expresses the essential information in the highlighted sentence? Incorrect answer choices change the meaning in important ways or leave out essential information.

(A) The two companies that produce high-purity nickel have never been convicted of working together to keep other companies out of the nickel market, but nickel is still costly.

(B) The two companies that produce high-purity nickel have been convicted of working together to keep the costs of entering the high-purity nickel market so expensive that other companies cannot enter.

(C) The two companies that produce high-purity nickel have never been convicted of working to keep other companies from refining high-purity nickel, but it costs too much and is too difficult for other companies to get access to nickel for them to go into the business.

(D) The costs of starting a nickel-refining business are so high and it is so difficult to get access to nickel that it is difficult for companies to enter the market.

The answer is C. This covers the point that the two companies in the high-purity nickel market have never been convicted, but it is still difficult for other companies to enter the market because of the costs of entering and problems accessing nickel. Eliminate A because it ignores the problems of entering the market. Eliminate B because it says the opposite of what the highlighted sentence says. Eliminate D because it ignores the legal liability of the two companies already in the nickel market.

Practice Section 4 Answer Key

1. A
2. C
3. D
4. C
5. A
6. B
7. A
8. C
9. A
10. C
11. B
12. D

Practice Section 4 Explanations

1. The word *capital* in the passage is closest in meaning to

   (A) financial

   (B) principal

   (C) important

   (D) knowledgeable

   The answer is A. In the passage, the word *capital* refers to money, or financial markets. Eliminate B because it is a meaning of *capital* that doesn't apply in this context. Eliminate C and D because they do not make sense in the sentence.

2. The word *defaults* in the passage is closest in meaning to

   (A) does not ask

   (B) does not know

   (C) does not pay

   (D) does not loan

   The answer is C. The sentence indicates what happens when a buyer does not pay. Eliminate A and B because asking and knowing are not mentioned in the passage. Eliminate D because this is the opposite meaning of the sentence.

3. The phrase *all three parties* in the passage refers to

   (A) bank, factor, buyer

   (B) factor, bank, supplier

   (C) supplier, bank, product

   (D) factor, buyer, supplier

   The answer is D. The three parties to a reverse factoring arrangement are the factor (or bank), the buyer, and the supplier. The bank and factor are the same ting, so eliminate A and B. The product is not party to the arrangement, so eliminate C.

4. Factoring has increased as a practice in countries around the world because it

   (A) has a common language

   (B) attracts investors to foreign countries

   (C) solves a problem with credit

   (D) requires large amounts of land

   The answer is C. The passage discusses the problems with traditional factoring and then proposes reverse factoring as a solution to those problems. Eliminate A because there is no mention of a common language in the passage. Investors are not a problem addressed in the passage, so eliminate B. Reverse factoring has nothing to do with land, so eliminate D.

5. One of the benefits of reverse factoring is that it

   (A) removes risk almost entirely from the transaction

   (B) does not involve an exchange of money

   (C) can be done on a boat or other sailing vessel

   (D) can be done by anyone, regardless of income

   The answer is A. The passage discusses the lack of risk in reverse factoring. Reverse factoring involves an exchange of money, so eliminate B. Eliminate C because reverse factoring has nothing to do with boats. Eliminate D because reverse factoring can only be done by large, established buyers, banks, and suppliers, not private citizens.

6. In reverse factoring, after the factor pays the supplier a percentage of the order amount

   (A) the supplier officially enters the factor's system

   (B) the buyer pays the factor for the order

   (C) the supplier delivers the order to the buyer

   (D) the factor contracts with the buyer

   The answer is B. Eliminate A, C, and D because they take place before the factor pays the supplier.

7. The word *liquid* in the passage is closest in meaning to

   (A) accessible

   (B) wet

   (C) complex

   (D) thin

   The answer is A. In the sentence, *liquid* refers to cash that can be accessed to spend. Eliminate B because it is a meaning of *liquid* that does not apply in this context. Eliminate C and D because they do not make sense in the sentence.

8. Which of the following is NOT implied in the passage?

   (A) Reverse factoring helps both the supplier and the buyer with cash flow issues.

   (B) Reverse factoring reduces risk to the factor significantly.

   (C) Reverse factoring is only useful after a regular factoring relationship has been arranged with the factor.

   (D) Reverse factoring does not require suppliers to wait for payment from the factor for as long as they would have waited for it from the buyer.

   The answer is C. Reverse factoring takes the place of standard factoring, and does not rely on a previously established relationship. Eliminate A because the specific purpose of reverse factoring is to help both the supplier and the buyer with cash flow issues. By shifting the originator of the loans to a large buyer instead of small suppliers, reverse factoring reduces risk to the factor significantly, so eliminate B. Eliminate D because the purpose of reverse factoring is to shorten the wait time for payment to the suppliers while lengthening the time a buyer has to pay.

9. Which of the following can you infer from the passage?

   (A) There are multiple ways to finance purchases from suppliers.

   (B) A factor must be prequalified to borrow money from a supplier.

   (C) Reverse factoring only works in European countries.

   (D) Small suppliers are more likely to have access to credit than small buyers.

   The answer is A. The passage talks about traditional capital markets, factoring, and reverse factoring as only three methods of financing purchases. Eliminate B because the passage tells you the opposite—that a supplier must register with a factor in reverse factoring. Eliminate C because there is no information about where reverse factoring works. Eliminate D because there is nothing to support this assertion in the passage.

10. In the sixth paragraph, the author mentions the benefits of reverse factoring to the factor in order to

(A) prove that there is not a strong connection between a role in the reverse factoring transaction and the benefits received

(B) show that the factor benefits more from reverse factoring than the supplier or the buyer

(C) support the topic sentence of the paragraph that states that all three parties benefit from reverse factoring

(D) connect the concept of factoring more closely with reverse factoring

The answer is C. The topic sentence states that all three parties benefited from the arrangement, and the sentence with the benefits to the factor supports this. Eliminate A because the passage shows the opposite. Eliminate B because the sentence does not imply a hierarchy. Eliminate D because the paragraph draws no connection between factoring and reverse factoring.

11. In the last paragraph, the phrase *individual parties* refers to

(A) individual buyers

(B) individual suppliers, buyers, and factors

(C) individual suppliers and factors

(D) individual buyers and factors

The answer is B. Eliminate A, C, and D because none of these choices contains all three types of parties to a reverse factoring arrangement.

12. Which of the following sentences best summarizes the highlighted section of the paragraph above?

(A) The factor lends money at a higher rate than it could get otherwise, the supplier can pay later than it would otherwise, and the buyer receives its money more quickly than it would otherwise.

(B) The factor lends money, the buyer pays money, and the supplier receives money.

(C) The factor can get a high interest rate, and the buyer and supplier can get lower rates than they would otherwise.

(D) The factor uses its money and gets a good interest rate with little risk, the buyer can extend payment without paying high interest rates, and the supplier gets paid more quickly at a lower rate.

The answer is D. Eliminate A because it mixes up the buyer and supplier and is too simplistic. Eliminate B because it does not cover the benefits to each party. Eliminate C because it leaves out all benefits aside from interest rates.

Part 3

TOEFL Listening

This part takes you through the TOEFL Listening section, covering the differences between listening to English in regular conversation and listening to the lectures in the Listening section.

Chapter 6 discusses techniques for the Listening section, including how to take good notes on the lectures and the differences between the two types of lectures. It also talks about the types of questions that will be asked on the lectures and how to answer them efficiently.

Chapter 7 contains Listening section practice lectures and questions designed to be as similar to the real TOEFL lectures and questions as possible. You can check your answers and the explanations for those answers in Chapter 8.

Acing the Listening Section

Chapter 6

In This Chapter

- What listening skills the TOEFL tests
- What skills get good scores in the Listening section
- How to approach the Listening section
- The different types of Listening section questions

You probably have plenty of practice listening to people talking in English and understanding it. But that doesn't mean you'll score well on the TOEFL Listening section.

The Listening section tests very specific ways of listening to very specific kinds of lectures. And it tests your comprehension by asking multiple-choice questions about what you've heard. It's not very much like listening in a conversation, a television program or movie, or even a phone call. Keep reading to find out how to listen actively to the lectures, what you should do while you're listening, and exactly what each type of question is asking and how to answer it.

TOEFL Listening Basics

The Listening section of the TOEFL takes 60 to 90 minutes to complete and consists of two different types of lectures: conversations and academic lectures. There are two or three conversations of three to six minutes each on topics having to do with university life. Each conversation has five multiple-choice questions with four answer choices each. There are four to six academic lectures of three to six minutes each on academic topics such as history, the humanities, and science. Each academic lecture has six multiple-choice questions with four answer choices each.

The Listening section comes immediately after the Reading section. This is good because your brain has had a chance to adjust to English, especially the academic English used in the Reading passages that will be used in the academic lectures in the Listening section. You'll have also warmed up to the structure of these passages and lectures, so your ears and brain will be more ready to understand what you hear during the Listening lectures.

A conversation is more casual than an academic lecture and consists of a student talking to another person about something related to schoolwork or campus life. The structure of the academic lectures is designed to sound like a professor giving a lecture to a class, and there may be brief exchanges with students in the middle of the lecture. The lectures will follow a logical progression, the way a professor would teach a class. You may hear unfamiliar words, which are likely to be technical words or *jargon*.

Use the structural elements of the passage to help you figure out what a sentence is saying so you can understand unfamiliar words.

DEFINITION

Jargon is language that has a special meaning in a profession or academic discipline. It is either unknown or has a different meaning outside of that profession or discipline.

You are asked to answer the questions following the conversation or academic lecture based only on the information provided. This means that everything you need to answer the questions is in the conversation or lecture.

Understanding the individual words of each type of piece is only the first step to scoring well in the Listening section. Next, I talk about what skills will help you get a good score in the Listening section.

Skills That Score Points in the Listening Section

The skills rewarded with good scores in the Listening section are:

Listening carefully. You will hear six to nine total lectures, each lasting three to six minutes. While some detail questions (explained later in this chapter) will allow you to listen to a sentence again before answering the question, most will not. That means you need to focus and listen carefully to the lecture for the entire three to six minutes and try to understand as much of it as you can.

Listening in anticipation. There are a limited number of Listening question types. Once you learn these questions, you will know what information you'll need to get out of the lecture, so you can listen in anticipation of that information.

Summarizing an argument. You will likely be asked about the main idea of the lecture, so make sure you have practiced summarizing the main ideas of academic lectures before you take the TOEFL.

Writing notes. Because you only get one shot at hearing the lecture in its entirety, you should take the best notes you can. Use your knowledge of what questions will be asked about the lecture to guide the notes you take, so you'll have notes to help you answer the questions efficiently.

Listening for details in the lecture. Some of the questions will ask you about details in the lecture. You may get the chance to listen to the relevant sentence again, but you may not. So it's important to listen as carefully as you can to pick out details (and then write them in your notes).

WARNING

You cannot jump around and skip questions on the Listening section, and you only get to hear each lecture once. The Listening section requires you to be absolutely ready to both listen and then answer the questions in order. Stay focused!

The biggest challenge of the Listening section is you are only able to listen to the entire lecture one time. With practice, you can get used to listening for detail, understanding the main idea, and anticipating what questions will be asked about the lecture as you hear it.

Key Issues in the Listening Section

The following are four key issues to pay attention to in the Listening section.

Issue 1: Understand what type of question you're answering. There are five question types asked about conversations and seven types asked about academic lectures. (See the "Academic Lectures" and "Conversations" sections later in this chapter for more detail.) By the time you take the test, you should have practiced enough to know exactly how to approach each type of question—even if you can't name it. As you practice, make part of your routine identifying the type of question and how you answer it. By working consciously through the questions, you will know exactly what to do with each question on the Listening section of the real test.

Issue 2: Know which type of lecture you're hearing. The academic lectures are very different from the conversations. If you don't pay attention to the narrator's introduction to the lecture, you may not pick up on which type of lecture you're hearing until you've missed a sentence or two. Pay attention to that introduction so you're prepared for the different ways of listening to an academic lecture versus listening to a conversation.

Issue 3: Be a smart notetaker. In the Reading section, taking notes primarily consisted of drawing yourself a map of where key information was. Taking notes in the Listening section is completely different, because you can't go back to the lecture and listen again. (And a visual reference wouldn't help you much with an audio lecture anyway.) You need to listen and write down ideas and details as you hear them, including definitions of unfamiliar words that are given. This can be tricky, so you will need to practice. Remember that you'll be turning in your notes at the end of the exam, but they won't be scored with your exam.

Issue 4: Stay in the zone. If you get lost in a lecture, the Listening section can feel like a train about to run over you. The questions are asked sequentially, so you can't skip one you don't know and come back to it later. This means you have less control in this section than you do in the Reading or Writing sections, which can make you feel anxious. Be conscious about how tricky this section is logistically, stay focused, and do the best you can.

EXAM TIP

If you start to feel crowded or like you're getting off track during the Listening section, close your eyes and take four deep, slow breaths. Controlling your breath this way will help control your nerves so you can focus again.

Strategy for the Listening Section

As I just mentioned, the Listening section can be very challenging, because you only get to hear the lecture once, and you can't skip questions and come back to them later. In a way, you're really just along for the ride, and the section will go ahead with or without you. But if you can stay focused and work carefully using the following strategy, you will be able to do well in the Listening section.

What follows is a three-step process you should follow when you hit a new lecture in the Listening section of the TOEFL.

Step 1: Be an Active Listener

A lecture (either an academic lecture or a conversation) is three to six minutes long. You know what types of questions will be asked about each type of lecture, so listen carefully for different purposes. Pay special attention when you hear a word you don't know. It may be a relatively common word you're unfamiliar with, or it may be technical jargon or a term specific to the subject of the lecture. If it's jargon or technical language, the lecture will give you a definition. So pay close attention and listen for a definition.

PRACTICE TIP

As you practice the Listening section passages, note any words you do not understand. If you are having problems understanding basic, nontechnical terms, you might need to consider postponing taking the real TOEFL so you have more time to practice your listening skills.

In addition to definitions of new words, listen for the main idea or purpose of the lecture, and note any interesting details. Be ready for the questions you will be asked for each type of lecture. Pay attention to the feelings and attitudes of the speakers, and the way they relate information in the lecture, because you may see questions about attitude and structure.

Step 2: Take Good Notes

Notes are critical in the Listening section, but they are not the same kind of notes you took in the Reading section. Remember that in the Reading section you were making a map to use to go back and find details in the passage. In the Listening section, you can't go back to find details, so you'll need to take notes to help you remember what you heard. Write a word or two to describe important information in the lecture—such as details, definitions, attitudes, and structure—as you hear it. Go in order, and don't worry if you don't understand the flow or organization of the lecture as you're writing. You should understand more as you hear more of the lecture and it begins to hang together better.

At the end of the lecture, write down what the main idea was (for an academic lecture) or what the purpose was (for a conversation). This will probably be the first or second question you see once you get to the questions. If you have the main idea or purpose written down, you'll be ready to eliminate the answer choices that don't match it and answer the question easily.

Step 3: Be Alert for Common Issues

First, learn the difference between academic lectures and conversations. Academic lectures present information on one topic, while conversations involve a student talking to another person about something having to do with campus life. If you confuse which kind of lecture you're listening to, you won't be able to get the information you need to have to answer the questions.

Also, multiple speakers can be confusing to listen to. Each conversation contains two speakers, at least one of whom is a student. The academic lectures are given by a professor and may also contain one or more students. Pay attention to different tones to keep track of which speaker is which in each lecture.

Another issue is the use of rhetorical devices and idioms. The speakers in the lectures may use metaphors, irony, and idioms (see Chapter 17) to make a point. So know that the literal words you hear are sometimes not the full meaning or implication of the total phrase or sentence.

Finally, keep track of the verbal tics of the speakers. Because the speakers are using natural speech patterns, they may make pauses in speech, insert tics like "um" or "er," repeat words, or say half-sentences. Be prepared to listen through this natural speech pattern and any tics for the words, sentences, and meaning.

PRACTICE TIP

As you practice listening to conversations and academic lectures, use the preceding strategy to combat the common issues in this section. The more you practice, the easier it will be to keep track of the meaning of the lectures without having to focus on the issues so strongly.

Conversations

You will hear two or three conversations in the Listening section, and each one will be followed by five questions. Each conversation will last three to six minutes.

Your central task is to determine what the purpose of the conversation is. Why is the student talking to the other person? Is the student asking a librarian if a book is on the shelf at the library? Is the student asking another student if the dining hall is still open? The student is trying to give or receive information, and your job is to figure out what.

As you listen to the conversation, write down notes about what you hear. At the end of the conversation, think about what the purpose was and write it down. You will need it for the first question, a purpose question. There are five types of questions you will see about conversations. You may see all five after any given conversation, or you may see repeats of one or two question types and therefore not see all five types. However, be ready to answer all of them.

Purpose

A purpose question asks you what the point of the conversation is. The correct answer will cover the overall purpose of the entire conversation. The purpose will be more general than specific.

Here's how to answer a purpose question:

1. Read the question.
2. Go back to your notes and look at what you wrote down as the purpose of the conversation.
3. Eliminate the answer choices that mention details from the conversation that are not the main point, or things that were in the conversation but are misrepresented. For example, if the conversation is between two students discussing the hours the dining hall is open and they happen to mention something they ate for breakfast, one of the answer choices may mention that detail.
4. Choose the answer that best matches what you wrote in your notes.

EXAM TIP

Don't worry about identifying what type each question is. If you've practiced answering the questions, you'll know how to approach them without having to remember what they're called.

Detail

A detail question asks you about (big surprise) a detail from the conversation. It will not be something completely obscure. Instead, it will be something important to the conversation, but not the main idea. While you may or may not have written down the exact detail in your notes, you should be able to remember enough from the conversation to eliminate incorrect answer choices.

Here's how to answer a detail question:

1. Read the question.
2. Go back to your notes and see if you have anything written down about this detail.
3. Look at the answer choices and eliminate the ones that do not match. Distractors include choices that are too general, are the opposite of the correct answer, misrepresent what was said in the conversation, or were not mentioned in the conversation at all.
4. Choose the answer that best matches what you wrote in your notes.

Function

A function question for a conversation asks you what the function of saying a phrase or sentence was. You may be given the chance to listen to the relevant sentence again.

A function question asks you *why* someone said something, not *what* they said. In some cases, the speaker may have said something indirect or used an idiom, so the word-by-word meaning is not actually why the person said it. Your job is to listen to the sentence as part of the conversation, instead of just listening to the words.

Here's how to answer a function question:

1. Read the question. Listen to the sentence again, if given the option.
2. Think about the flow of the conversation. What happened before the sentence, and what happened after the sentence?
3. Determine why the speaker said the sentence.
4. Look at the answer choices and eliminate the ones that do not match the reason the speaker said the sentence.
5. Choose the answer that's left.

Opinion

An opinion question asks what the opinion or attitude is of one of the speakers in the conversation. It will ask how the speaker seems to feel about a topic, an idea, another person, or something mentioned in the conversation.

Here's how to answer an opinion question:

1. Read the question.
2. Think back to the conversation, and state in your own words what the answer to the question is.
3. Go back to the answer choices and eliminate any that do not match your answer.
4. Choose the answer that's left.

Inference

An inference question attached to a conversation usually asks you what will happen after the conversation. It is asking you about what the speakers say they plan to do, or what would be the reasonable thing for the speakers to do after the conversation. The correct answer will make sense in the context of the conversation.

Here's how to answer an inference question:

1. Read the question.
2. Think about the purpose of the conversation. Did the speaker achieve the purpose?
3. If the speaker did achieve the purpose, what should someone do next?
4. Look at the answer choices and eliminate the ones that do not match with what should happen next. Distractor answer choices will include things that were mentioned in the conversation but have already been done, are the opposite of what the speakers will do, or are misrepresentations of the speakers' intentions.
5. Choose the answer that's left.

WARNING

Don't be fooled into thinking you can't predict what the speaker will do next. The question is actually asking what one of the speakers said they'd do, so it isn't a blind prediction.

Academic Lectures

You will hear four to six academic lectures in the Listening section, and each one will be followed by six questions. The lecture will consist of a professor giving a lecture on an academic topic to students. The students may or may not interact with the professor during the lecture, so there may be multiple speakers. Each lecture will last three to six minutes.

Your central task is to determine what the main idea of the academic lecture is. Because this is a realistic academic lecture, it will not be as formal as the passages in the Reading section. The professor will use normal speech, which is sometimes more casual than written language, but at the same time will explain difficult concepts and use technical and specific words that you may not have heard before. In addition, there may be interjections or questions from students, and the professor may ask students questions about the content or other aspects of taking a college class.

As you listen to the lecture, write down notes about what you hear. Pay special attention to any words you hear that you are not familiar with. In addition, write down any details that seem significant to the overall message of the lecture. At the end of the lecture, think about what the main idea of the lecture was, and write that down. You will need it for the first question, a main idea question. There are seven types of questions you will see about academic lectures. Because there are only six questions per lecture, you will not see all of them on any one lecture. However, be ready to answer any of them.

Main Idea

A main-idea question asks you what the main idea of an academic lecture is. Only one answer choice will effectively express the main idea of the lecture.

Here's how to answer a main-idea question:

1. Read the question.
2. Go back to your notes and look at what you wrote down as the main idea of the lecture.
3. Eliminate answer choices that are too specific or misrepresent information. Distractor answer choices will mention details from the lecture that are not the main point or things that were in the lecture but are misrepresented.
4. Choose the answer that best matches what you wrote in your notes.

Detail

A detail question asks you about a detail from the academic lecture. While it is a detail, it will not be trivial. It will be important enough to the flow of the lecture that you likely noted it and wrote it down while you were listening, or can remember enough about that part of the lecture to figure out the correct answer.

Here's how to answer a detail question:

1. Read the question.
2. Go back to your notes and see if you have anything written down about this detail.
3. Look at the answer choices and eliminate the ones that do not match. Distractors include choices that are too general, are the opposite of the correct answer, misrepresent what was said in the lecture, or were not mentioned in the lecture at all.
4. Choose the answer that best matches what you wrote in your notes.

Function

A function question for an academic lecture asks you what the function is of something the professor said. You may be given the chance to listen to the relevant sentence again.

A function question asks you *why* the professor said something, not *what* he or she said. For example, the professor may have said something to support an assertion, prove a theory, or present an alternate view. Think about how the professor is making the argument and what function the sentence serves in the lecture to help the professor prove that point.

Here's how to answer a function question:

1. Read the question. Listen to the sentence again, if given the option.
2. Think about the structure of the lecture. Where does the sentence fit in?
3. What purpose does the sentence serve? Does it prove something, give an example, give an alternate view, or something else?
4. Look at the answer choices and eliminate the ones that do not match the reason the professor said the sentence.
5. Choose the answer that's left.

Opinion

An opinion question asks about the professor's opinion or attitude in the lecture. It will ask how the professor seems to feel about a topic, an idea, or something mentioned in the lecture.

Here's how to answer an opinion question:

1. Read the question.
2. Think back to the lecture and state in your own words what the answer to the question is.
3. Go back to the answer choices and eliminate any that do not match your answer.
4. Choose the answer that's left.

Inference

An inference question attached to an academic lecture is like an inference question in the Reading section. It concerns a detail from the lecture, but is not stated directly as a detail question is. Instead, you have to put details together or make a small leap to arrive at the conclusion. For example, if a speaker says, "I have class until 5 P.M.," and the question asks about a task the speaker will do after class, the answer may be "In the evening." This requires you to make the leap that the task will be done after 5 P.M., which is evening.

Inference questions are very similar to detail questions, except that the information won't be stated directly.

Here's how to answer an inference question:

1. Read the question.
2. Go back to your notes and see if you have anything written down about this detail.
3. Look at the answer choices and eliminate the ones that do not match. Distractor answers are the opposite of the correct answer, misrepresent information in the lecture, focus on details not referenced in the question, or aren't in the lecture at all.
4. Choose the answer that's left.

EXAM TIP

Detail questions and inference questions attached to academic lectures are similar enough that if you can answer one type, you can answer the other. Keep calm and power through these questions on the exam.

Organization

An organization question asks how the professor arranges the information she or he gives during the lecture. The question may ask directly how the professor organized the lecture, or it may ask how the professor made a point or proved something. The correct answer will be about the structure of the lecture, *not* the content.

Here's how to answer an organization question:

1. Read the question.
2. Think about the structure of the lecture.
3. Put the answer to the question in your own words.
4. Look at the answer choices and eliminate the ones that do not match the answer you came up with.
5. Choose the answer that's left.

Nonstandard Format

A non-standard-format question contains a table or chart with empty spaces and several sentences or phrases below the table for room for check marks. You are asked to drag and drop the sentences into the table in a way that makes sense, or check the spaces in the table that answer the question. (These questions may be worth more points than the questions with four mutually exclusive answer choices.)

Here's how to answer a non-standard-format question:

1. Read the question and the description of the table or chart and the information it contains.
2. Determine what the structure of the table or chart is and how many answer choice sentences or check marks can go in each space.
3. Go through the answer choice sentences one at a time, dragging and dropping them into the table in the proper location, or click to check the proper boxes to answer the question.

Now you should be ready to try some of the practice sections in the next chapter.

The Least You Need to Know

- The TOEFL Listening section tests your comprehension of conversations and academic lectures.
- The key to doing well in the Listening section is to stay focused and keep going even if you didn't understand everything you heard.
- When you hear a conversation, figure out what the purpose of it is and what is likely to happen after the conversation ends.
- When you hear an academic lecture, determine what the main point is.
- Study the five different types of conversation questions and the seven different types of academic-lecture Listening questions on the TOEFL so you'll know how to answer them.

Chapter 7

Listening Practice Sections

Work through these practice sections carefully, using the techniques and tips from Chapter 6. To use these practice sections, listen to the audio lectures on the website at idiotsguides.com/toefl, then answer the questions. When you finish a section, check the answers and explanations in Chapter 8 and review them carefully.

Practice Section 1

Listen to the audio track 7.1 on idiotsguides.com/toefl.

1. Why does the student visit the professor?

   (A) to ask for an extension on a paper

   (B) to ask about becoming a librarian

   (C) to ask a question about writing a paper

   (D) to ask for a recommendation

2. According to the professor, why should the student talk to a librarian?

   (A) A librarian can help the student find primary sources.

   (B) A librarian can talk to the student about becoming a librarian.

   (C) A librarian can tell the student about the differences between history and biology.

   (D) A librarian will open the library for the student on Sunday.

3. Why does the student want to start working on the paper now?

   (A) The student is getting married and needs to research the paper before her wedding.

   (B) The student needs to complete the paper before she goes to her sister's wedding.

   (C) The student knows she is slower at writing than the other students.

   (D) The student cannot decide between writing a paper on history or biology.

4. What does the professor mean when she asks, "None of the librarians could help you?"

   (A) What does a librarian do?

   (B) How many librarians helped you?

   (C) Were the librarians in the library?

   (D) Did you ask the librarians for help?

5. What will the student do when she receives the professor's email?

   (A) Go to the library's website to check the open hours on Sunday.

   (B) Write an email back asking about how to contact one of the librarians.

   (C) Forward the email to the librarians to request help finding primary sources.

   (D) Ask the professor to resend the email if she cannot figure out how to open it.

Practice Section 2

Listen to the audio track 7.2 on idiotsguides.com/toefl.

1. Why does the student visit the office?

   (A) to ask for help with paying for college

   (B) to obtain a student ID

   (C) to ask for the worker's business card

   (D) to apply for work with a professional organization

2. What is the problem with the grant?

   (A) The grant was a mistake.

   (B) The grant only works in the student's hometown.

   (C) The grant was for one year only.

   (D) The student forgot to renew the grant.

3. What will the worker do with the loan?

   (A) The worker cannot do anything with the loan.

   (B) The worker will look for alternative loans.

   (C) The worker will cancel the student's loan.

   (D) The worker will increase the amount of the loan.

4. What does the worker mean when she says "It's nothing"?

   (A) She cannot help the student.

   (B) You're welcome.

   (C) The student cannot get another loan.

   (D) The student needs to ask someone else for help.

5. What will the worker do next?

   (A) Email the student a copy of her business card.

   (B) Request a copy of the grant documentation.

   (C) Ask the student to submit a job application.

   (D) Make a note in the student's file to apply for the extra loan.

Practice Section 3

Listen to the audio track 7.3 on idiotsguides.com/toefl.

1. What is the topic of the lecture?

   (A) setting up a truck fleet for shipping products

   (B) a method of creating nuts and bolts

   (C) a horizontal manufacturing process

   (D) a manufacturing practice called vertical integration

2. According to the passage, the word *vertical* in manufacturing means

   (A) manufactured at machines stacked vertically on the factory floor

   (B) different products from the same company

   (C) from start to finish of the supply chain of a single product

   (D) all parts of a product made by the same worker

3. What does the professor think is a good reason to vertically integrate?

   (A) to save money

   (B) to make supplies you cannot purchase elsewhere

   (C) to obtain supplies quickly

   (D) to make fragile boxes

4. What did the professor mean when he says "And now I know who pays attention when I send an email!"?

   (A) The student who asked the question must have opened the email the professor sent.

   (B) The professor checks to see who pays attention by sending an email.

   (C) The professor wants to know which of the students sent an email.

   (D) The professor did not send an email to the students.

5. How does the professor demonstrate that vertical integration usually does not save money?

   (A) He cites research by economists.

   (B) He asks a rhetorical question.

   (C) He asks the students to prove it.

   (D) He uses a comparison to vertical integration in China.

6. What can you infer from the lecture?

   (A) Vertical integration saves manufacturers money.

   (B) Backward integration saves more money than forward integration.

   (C) There are reasons to vertically integrate that are not about saving money.

   (D) Products with many components are too fragile to ship easily.

Practice Section 4

Listen to the audio track 7.4 on idiotsguides.com/toefl.

1. What is the main topic of the lecture?

   (A) the early life of Julius Caesar

   (B) the rivalry between Julius Caesar and Vercingetorix

   (C) a key battle in the Gallic Wars

   (D) the Roman Civil War

2. According to the professor, Vercingetorix was

   (A) king of the Gauls

   (B) emperor of Rome

   (C) leader of the Roman army

   (D) an overthrown senator

3. Julius Caesar attacked the Gauls because

   (A) he had been challenged by Vercingetorix

   (B) it was weak because it was not unified

   (C) they would not speak Latin

   (D) they did not have a Senate

4. What does the professor mean when she says "Roman discipline had prevailed against unbridled strength, and Julius Caesar's strong leadership led the Romans to victory"?

   (A) The Romans were stronger than the Gauls were, so the Romans won.

   (B) The Romans were stronger than the Gauls were, but the Gauls won.

   (C) The Gauls were stronger than the Romans were, so the Gauls won.

   (D) The Gauls were stronger than the Romans were, but the Romans won.

5. How does the professor present Vercingetorix's plan to defend against the Romans?

   (A) in a numbered list

   (B) as an analogy

   (C) with examples of other battles using this plan

   (D) by comparing it to Julius Caesar's plan

6. What does the professor imply about Julius Caesar?
   (A) that he became king of the Gauls
   (B) that he was banned from the Senate in Rome
   (C) that he was involved in the Roman Civil War
   (D) that he was defeated by the Gauls

Chapter 8

Listening Practice Answer Keys and Explanations

Here are the answer keys and explanations for the questions you just practiced in Chapter 7.

Practice Section 1 Answer Key

1. C
2. A
3. B
4. D
5. A

Practice Section 1 Explanations

The following is a transcript of the lecture you heard.

Student: Dr. Wong, may I talk to you about the final paper?

Professor: Sure, Kelly. Come on in.

Student: Dr. Wong, I'm wondering if you could help me. I started outlining my paper last night and now I'm worried that I'm not going to be able to find enough primary sources to analyze to prove my point.

Professor: Oh. Remind me again what your topic is?

Student: I'm looking at patterns of immigration for Germans who came through Ellis Island between the Civil War and World War I.

Professor: Oh, right. None of the librarians could help you?

Student: What do you mean?

Professor: The librarians at the history library. They for sure can find all those records for you.

Student: Oh …

Professor: I'm going to make an announcement in class next week about how to get help from the librarians with primary source research. You're working on this earlier than anyone else in the class is.

Student: I have to. My sister is getting married the week before the paper is due, so I want to have it done before I go to the wedding. So I have to start now.

Professor: I wondered why you were so far ahead! Okay, then this all makes sense. Let me send you the email I use to introduce library services. It's easy to make contact with the librarians, and they can walk you through searching for census info and other records that will show immigration patterns. It's all electronic now, so it's easy to get once you know how to look for it. If you intend to go on in history, you'll need to know how to do this research anyway.

Student: I'm not sure if I'm going to go on in history. I like it, but I don't know if I want to study history or biology.

Professor: The librarians can help you and show you how to do it anyway. … I just sent you the email, so you have all the information waiting for you.

Student: Thank you! Is the library open on Sunday? I have basketball practice tomorrow but I can go Sunday.

Professor: It's open, but you should check the library website for the hours. There's a link to the website in the email I just sent you.

1. Why does the student visit the professor?

   (A) to ask for an extension on a paper

   (B) to ask about becoming a librarian

   (C) to ask a question about writing a paper

   (D) to ask for a recommendation

   The answer is C. The student comes to ask about finding primary sources. Eliminate A because the student is planning to turn the paper in early. Eliminate B because the professor suggests that the student ask a librarian for help finding primary sources, but the student does not want to become a librarian. Eliminate D because the student does not ask for a recommendation.

2. According to the professor, why should the student talk to a librarian?

   (A) A librarian can help the student find primary sources.

   (B) A librarian can talk to the students about becoming a librarian.

   (C) A librarian can tell the student about the differences between history and biology.

   (D) A librarian will open the library for the student on Sunday.

   The answer is A. The student needs help finding primary sources, and the professor tells the student to ask a librarian for help finding them. Eliminate B because becoming a librarian is not mentioned in the lecture. Eliminate C because history and biology are mentioned in the lecture, but not in the context of the librarian. Eliminate D because this is not mentioned in the lecture.

3. Why does the student want to start working on the paper now?

   (A) The student is getting married and needs to research the paper before her wedding.

   (B) The student needs to complete the paper before she goes to her sister's wedding.

   (C) The student knows she is slower at writing than the other students.

   (D) The student cannot decide between writing a paper on history or biology.

   The answer is B. The student needs to turn in the paper early, before she goes to her sister's wedding. Eliminate A because it is a misrepresentation of the lecture. Eliminate C because writing speed is not mentioned in the lecture. Eliminate D because the student knows the topic of her paper.

4. What does the professor mean when she asks, "None of the librarians could help you?"

   (A) What does a librarian do?

   (B) How many librarians helped you?

   (C) Were the librarians in the library?

   (D) Did you ask the librarians for help?

   The answer is D. The professor is trying to find out if the student asked a librarian for help finding primary sources. Eliminate A because the professor knows what librarians do. Eliminate B because the professor does not care about the number of librarians who help the student. Eliminate C because the library is not mentioned until later in the lecture.

5. What will the student do when she receives the professor's email?

   (A) Go to the library's website to check the open hours on Sunday.

   (B) Write an email back asking about how to contact one of the librarians.

   (C) Forward the email to the librarians to request help finding primary sources.

   (D) Ask the professor to resend the email if she cannot figure out how to open it.

   The answer is A. The student asks about the library's hours on Sunday and the professor tells her to click the link in the email to check the library's website. Eliminate B because the email is already about how to contact the librarians, so she does not need to request that information. Eliminate C because there is no need to forward the email to the librarians. Eliminate D because there is no indication that the student will not be able to open the email.

Practice Section 2 Answer Key

1. A
2. C
3. D
4. B
5. D

Practice Section 2 Explanations

The following is a transcript of the lecture you heard.

Staff member: Can I help you?

Student: I hope so. I need to talk to someone about my financial aid status.

Staff member: Sure. I should be able to help. Can I see your student ID, please?

Student: Here it is.

Staff member: Thanks. Let me find your file. [pause] Okay, you're all pulled up. What can I do for you?

Student: Well, I found out that a grant I got this year is only a one-year grant, so I can't get it again next year.

Staff member: Was it a federal grant?

Student: No, it was a grant I got from a professional organization in my hometown. They give it to two high school seniors every year, and last year they gave it to me. But they have to give it to someone else this year, so I can't get it, and now I don't know how I can make up the difference in tuition for next year.

Staff member: Ah. I see that grant on your record of payment for this year. I should be able to increase your loan request amount for the low-interest loan you're getting from the government to make up the difference for next year. You're maxed out on your no-interest loan, but I can increase your low-interest loan.

Student: Oh. That's great! Thank you so much.

Staff member: It's nothing. I'll have to wait until the request period in three months, though. I'll put a reminder in your file.

Student: Thank you again. This was way easier than I thought it would be.

Staff member: Well, don't forget that it's a loan, not a grant, so you will have to pay it back with interest after you graduate. But you don't have to come up with the difference now, at least.

Student: Good. I'm already working two jobs and I don't know when I could make up that money.

Staff member: I'm glad I could help you then. Let me give you my card, and if you need anything else, you can just email me and not have to come into the office.

Student: Thank you. Have a great afternoon.

1. Why does the student visit the office?

    (A) to ask for help with paying for college

    (B) to obtain a student ID

    (C) to ask for the worker's business card

    (D) to apply for work with a professional organization

    The answer is A. The student is asking for help with financial aid for college. Eliminate B because the student already has a student ID. Eliminate C because the worker gives the student a business card, but this is not the purpose of the visit. Eliminate D because the student is not applying for work.

2. What is the problem with the grant?

    (A) The grant was a mistake.

    (B) The grant only works in the student's hometown.

    (C) The grant was for one year only.

    (D) The student forgot to renew the grant.

    The answer is C. The grant is given to a different student each year, so it was for one year only. Eliminate A because the grant was not a mistake, and eliminate B because the grant was given in the student's hometown but was used at the college. Eliminate D because the student could not renew the grant.

3. What will the worker do with the loan?

    (A) The worker cannot do anything with the loan.

    (B) The worker will look for alternative loans.

    (C) The worker will cancel the student's loan.

    (D) The worker will increase the amount of the loan.

    The answer is D. The worker will request more money for one of the student's loans to offset the missing grant. Eliminate A because the worker can request more money. Eliminate B because the worker does not have to look for alternate loans but can simply increase the amount of one of the existing loans. Eliminate C because the worker will not cancel the student's loan.

4. What does the worker mean when she says, "It's nothing"?

   (A) She cannot help the student.

   (B) You're welcome.

   (C) The student cannot get another loan.

   (D) The student needs to ask someone else for help.

   The answer is B. "It's nothing" is a casual way to say "You're welcome." Eliminate A, C, and D because the worker can help the student get another loan.

5. What will the worker do next?

   (A) Email the student a copy of her business card.

   (B) Request a copy of the grant documentation.

   (C) Ask the student to submit a job application.

   (D) Make a note in the student's file to apply for the extra loan.

   The answer is D. She cannot apply for the increased loan for three more months, so she will make a note in the file to increase it in three months. Eliminate A because the student has one of her business cards already. Eliminate B because she does not need the grant documentation for anything. Eliminate C because the student is not applying for a job.

Practice Section 3 Answer Key

1. D
2. C
3. B
4. A
5. A
6. C

Practice Section 3 Explanations

The following is a transcript of the lecture you heard.

Professor: So today we're going to talk about vertical integration. Remember how we talked about how companies are trying to minimize costs for materials and other products from suppliers, while also maintaining quality? One way they try to do that is by vertically integrating. Let me explain what I mean by that. Who remembers what we were talking about with horizontal versus vertical growth?

Female student: Horizontal is different products, right?

Professor: Right. Horizontal is when a company goes into different product lines, different products, so the name alludes to how they would all be lined up in a horizontal line so you could see the different divisions and different products. So vertical is the opposite of that. It's the entire process from soup to nuts of how you make a product from the raw materials to getting it into the customer's hand. Your whole value chain, your supply chain. And most manufacturers start by buying their supplies and materials from suppliers and then paying someone else to ship their products to wherever they're sold. But some companies are doing something called vertical integration.

Male student: That was in that article you posted for us to read!

Professor: And now I know who pays attention when I send an email! Yes. The article I posted was all about vertical integration. It explains how some companies are trying to control the entire supply chain, so instead of buying supplies from someone else, they start making them themselves. So, for example, a company that makes engines will also make the parts of the engine, including the nuts and bolts and rubber tighteners and everything that goes into the engine. That's vertical integration.

Specifically, that's backward integration, because the company is integrating backward into the previous step in the process, which is making the nuts and bolts. There's also forward integration, when a company might buy a truck fleet and hire drivers to drive the finished products to stores instead of paying a shipper to do it for them.

Vertical integration used to be very popular, and many many companies did it because they thought it was saving them money, but it turns out that's not correct—it's not what the research shows. If you look at the numbers (and there are a bunch of economists who have spent a lot of time on this—really smart people), what you find out is that it's almost always cheaper to buy a part from someone else. Especially if it's a simple part, like a nut or a bolt. Think about it—if you're an engine factory and you have people trained to put these complicated engines together, and you have to pay them that rate to do something complicated, and then you have to start up an entirely new operation to make something simple, and you have to hire different people and pay them a different amount per hour, you're causing a lot of work and expense. And in the meantime, if it's really just a bolt, you can probably buy that bolt from some guy who turns them out in his garage with three workers helping him, or from a factory in China. And it's probably cheaper to pay a trucking company to ship your products for you, too.

The only exception is if you can't find anyone to give you the quality you need—because either your supply is too specialized so no one knows how to do it, or they won't set up their factory to make it for you, or the products they're making are too low quality for you to use. If you can't find what you need to buy that you're happy with, then it makes tons of sense to vertically integrate to get the part you need or the service you need. An example of this would be that you make a product that's very fragile, and you can't find good boxes to ship it in that are the right size and shape and material to keep your product safe. It makes sense for you to manufacture those boxes so you can ship your product to customers.

So that's vertical integration.

1. What is the topic of the lecture?

   (A) setting up a truck fleet for shipping products

   (B) a method of creating nuts and bolts

   (C) a horizontal manufacturing process

   (D) a manufacturing practice called vertical integration

   The answer is D. The passage is about vertical integration, a practice in manufacturing that involves controlling the entire supply chain. Eliminate A because the truck fleet was only a small part of the lecture. Eliminate B because nuts and bolts are only a small part of the lecture. Eliminate C because the lecture is not about horizontal integration.

2. According to the passage, the word *vertical* in manufacturing means

   (A) manufactured at machines stacked vertically on the factory floor

   (B) different products from the same company

   (C) from start to finish of the supply chain of a single product

   (D) all parts of a product made by the same worker

   The answer is C. *Vertical* means having to do with the entire manufacturing process of a single product, from beginning to end. Eliminate A because there is nothing in the passage about stacking machines. Eliminate B because it describes *horizontal,* not *vertical.* Eliminate D because *vertical* does not mean the same worker must make all parts.

3. What does the professor think is a good reason to vertically integrate?

   (A) to save money

   (B) to make supplies you cannot purchase elsewhere

   (C) to obtain supplies quickly

   (D) to make fragile boxes

   The answer is B. The professor states that a good reason to vertically integrate is to make supplies you cannot find elsewhere or cannot find of the quality you need. Eliminate A because the professor states that vertical integration does not save money. Eliminate C because there is no information in the passage about obtaining supplies quickly. Eliminate D because this is a misrepresentation of the part of the lecture about boxes.

4. What did the professor mean when she says, "And now I know who pays attention when I send an email!"?

   (A) The student who asked the question must have opened the email the professor sent.

   (B) The professor checks to see who pays attention by sending an email.

   (C) The professor wants to know which of the students sent an email.

   (D) The professor did not send an email to the students.

   The answer is A. The professor is saying that by referencing an article the professor sent by email, he knows that the student must have opened the email. Eliminate B because it is not specifically about the student. Eliminate C because the students did not send an email—the professor did. Eliminate D because the professor did send an email to the students.

5. How does the professor demonstrate that vertical integration usually does not save money?

   (A) He cites research by economists.

   (B) He asks a rhetorical question.

   (C) He asks the students to prove it.

   (D) He uses a comparison to vertical integration in China.

   The answer is A. The professor states that economists have done research showing that it is cheaper to buy parts from suppliers than to make them. Eliminate B and C because he doesn't ask a rhetorical question or ask his students to prove anything. Eliminate D because this is a misrepresentation of his mention of China.

6. What can you infer from the lecture?

   (A) Vertical integration saves manufacturers money.

   (B) Backward integration saves more money than forward integration.

   (C) There are reasons to vertically integrate that are not about saving money.

   (D) Products with many components are too fragile to ship easily.

   The answer is C. The lecture gives a need for quality and specific features that can't be found elsewhere as a reason to vertically integrate. Eliminate A because the lecture states that this is not true. Eliminate B because there is no information about this in the lecture. Eliminate D because this is a misrepresentation of the lecture.

Practice Section 4 Answer Key

1. C
2. A
3. B
4. D
5. A
6. C

Practice Section 4 Explanations

The following is a transcript of the lecture you heard.

Professor: I trust you all had a good weekend and read the sections I assigned for today. I'm going to be talking about the Gallic Wars this week and I want to make sure we're all on the same page. Okay? Okay.

When we left off, Julius Caesar had just been elected. When he was elected to the office of Consul in Rome, he saw that Gaul could easily be conquered because it was weak from internal fighting and tribal disputes. In short, it wasn't unified, so it was a prime target for takeover by Rome. Julius Caesar attacked, and started the Gallic Wars, and ended up doing battle with Vercingetorix of the Alemanni, who was proclaimed king of the Gauls at Gergovia in 52 B.C.E. Vercingetorix made as many alliances as he could, so the Gallic Wars were a lot like the Peloponnesian War, with the Gauls winning some here and the Romans winning some there. Eventually, Vercingetorix and 70,000 Gallic warriors were besieged in the hilltop fortress of Alesia. Is everyone still with me?

Female student: I think so. But in the textbook it talks about the "Dun of Alesia." When did that happen?

Professor: Ah, good detail! *Dun* is the Gallic word for "fortress," so the Dun of Alesia is the hilltop fortress of Alesia I just mentioned. Is that clear?

Female student: Um, yeah.

Professor: Eventually, Caesar had 23,000 legionaries, and the food situation in Alesia was deteriorating, so much so that the women and children had to camp between the two armies to save food for essential military personnel. It was bad, and they needed help. Gallic soldiers on horseback went scouting and foraging. Meanwhile, the Romans were constructing walls and ditches, stone and wooden ramparts, and towers and turrets. One famous part of this battle is the way Caesar employed Roman siege engineering to full effect. He really used construction techniques in ways no one had seen before.

Fortunately for the Gauls, Vercingetorix had a plan. The backup plan employed by Vercingetorix was a phased plan, like most military operations:

1. The Gallic Cavalry escaped, prompting Caesar to build ramparts and ditches, which there are pictures of in the textbook, if you want to get an idea of the layout.
2. The Gauls in Alesia would hold out for as long as they could, waiting for a large master plan that would be shown in later stages.
3. The cavalry would recruit other Gauls to come help.
4. The Gauls in Alesia would make Fascines and rams for their breaking-out operation.
5. The garrison of Alesia would coordinate with a massive relief army, and the relievers smashed the wall.

Vercingetorix's plan was solid but didn't end in success for the Gauls. The Romans somehow held the Gauls at bay despite being outnumbered 5 to 1, and the Gauls in Alesia were soon forced to surrender. Roman discipline had prevailed against unbridled strength, and Julius Caesar's strong leadership led the Romans to victory.

Later, Julius Caesar wrote up all his successes and failures in the *Commentarii de Bello Gallico*, or *Commentary of the Gallic Wars*, so we have a record of everything that happened, at least from his point of view. Interestingly, part of the reason the Roman Civil War started in 49 B.C.E. was the Roman Senate's refusal to give Caesar a triumph for his many victories in Gaul. So, indirectly, the Gallic Wars led to the Roman Senate's overthrow. On Wednesday, I'm going to go more in depth about some other battles of the Gallic Wars and we'll talk about the quiz from last week.

1. What is the main topic of the lecture?

   (A) the early life of Julius Caesar

   (B) the rivalry between Julius Caesar and Vercingetorix

   (C) a key battle in the Gallic Wars

   (D) the Roman Civil War

   The answer is C. The lecture is about the battle of the fortress of Alesia in the Gallic Wars. Eliminate A because the lecture does not contain information about Julius Caesar's early life. Eliminate B because any rivalry between Caesar and Vercingetorix is not explained in the lecture. Eliminate D because this is only mentioned at the very end of the lecture.

2. According to the professor, Vercingetorix was

    (A) king of the Gauls

    (B) emperor of Rome

    (C) leader of the Roman army

    (D) an overthrown senator

    The answer is A. Vercingetorix was king of the Gauls and led the Gallic army. Eliminate B, C, and D because he was not Roman.

3. Julius Caesar attacked the Gauls because

    (A) he had been challenged by Vercingetorix

    (B) it was weak because it was not unified

    (C) they would not speak Latin

    (D) they did not have a Senate

    The answer is B. The Gauls were not organized or united, so they were weak and an easy target. Eliminate A and C because there is nothing about either of these in the lecture. Eliminate D because the Senate mentioned in the lecture is the Roman Senate.

4. What does the professor mean when she says, "Roman discipline had prevailed against unbridled strength, and Julius Caesar's strong leadership led the Romans to victory"?

    (A) The Romans were stronger than the Gauls were, so the Romans won.

    (B) The Romans were stronger than the Gauls were, but the Gauls won.

    (C) The Gauls were stronger than the Romans were, so the Gauls won.

    (D) The Gauls were stronger than the Romans were, but the Romans won.

    The answer is D. The Gauls were stronger, but the Romans were more organized and had better discipline, so they won. Eliminate A and B because they are opposite of what the passage indicates. Eliminate C because it correctly assesses who was stronger, but not the outcome.

5. How does the professor present Vercingetorix's plan to defend against the Romans?

    (A) in a numbered list

    (B) as an analogy

    (C) with examples of other battles using this plan

    (D) by comparing it to Julius Caesar's plan

    The answer is A. The professor lists five numbered stages of the plan. Eliminate B and D because there is no analogy or comparison in the way the professor presents the plan. Eliminate C because she does not give examples.

6. What does the professor imply about Julius Caesar?

   (A) that he became king of the Gauls

   (B) that he was banned from the Senate in Rome

   (C) that he was involved in the Roman Civil War

   (D) that he was defeated by the Gauls

   The answer is C. The passage states that lack of recognition for Julius Caesar was a contributing factor of the Roman Civil War. Eliminate A and D because he was neither king of nor defeated by the Gauls. Eliminate B because there is no evidence that he was banned from the Senate.

Part 4

TOEFL Speaking

This part covers the TOEFL Speaking section. This section may be the most feared section on the TOEFL, as it requires reading, listening carefully, and speaking into a recording device with only one chance to record.

Chapter 9 explores the different elements of Speaking section questions, including prompts, passages, and lectures. It also details the best techniques you can use to prepare for and speak your responses to the questions.

Chapter 10 consists of Speaking section prompts, passages, and lectures you'd encounter on the real exam. You can assess the strength of your responses with the scoring guide in Chapter 11.

Acing the Speaking Section

Chapter

9

In This Chapter

- What speaking skills the TOEFL tests
- What skills get good scores in the Speaking section
- How to approach the Speaking section
- The different types of Speaking section questions

You may feel completely comfortable carrying on a conversation about current events in English, but that doesn't mean you'll automatically do well on the TOEFL Speaking section. The Speaking questions are very formulaic, and the raters who listen to your responses and score them are looking for specific formats and answers.

The Speaking section tests very specific ways of answering very specific types and formats of the written or spoken passages (or prompts). This section does not resemble carrying on a conversation in English at all. You are asked to write and then deliver a speech in a very short amount of time. That may sound daunting, but with enough practice, you can conquer this section efficiently.

TOEFL Speaking Basics

The Speaking section of the TOEFL consists of six questions over a total of 20 minutes. Each has a prompt and then the question. For each question, you will be given time to read or listen to the passage, 15 to 30 seconds to prepare your response, and 45 to 60 seconds to speak your response.

The prompts might not resemble many situations you have been in before or will be in in the future. There are two very specific types of tasks you will be asked to do:

Independent tasks are prompts that ask you for your own story, argument, or position on a topic. There are two types of independent questions: description and opinion.

Integrated tasks are prompts (which are written, recorded, or a combination of the two) that ask you to summarize and sometimes interpret information or the opinions of others. There are four types of integrated questions: summarize opinion, summarize reading and lecture, summarize problem, and summarize lecture.

PRACTICE TIP

You *must* understand which type of question you're answering. If you're given an independent task and you don't give new information, or you're given an integrated task and you only give your own opinion without summarizing the prompts, you will not score well on the questions. So make sure you're clear on all six question types and what your job is in each one. (I explain them in depth at the end of this chapter.)

The great thing about the TOEFL Speaking section is that it comes right after a mandatory 10-minute break, during which you may use the restroom, do jumping jacks to use up energy, get a drink, or whatever else you need. This means that, if nothing else, you shouldn't be physically uncomfortable during this section. There's a lot to be said for being able to sit still during a test section.

The not-so-great thing about the Speaking section is that it can be easy to get freaked out about having to a) speak in English, b) speak on a topic you've just been given, and c) have your speech graded and scored by unknown mysterious graders at a later date.

Unless you're a prodigy who learned English by reading books and watching movies, you've practiced speaking English. But in all those situations in which you've spoken English, you've been speaking to or with other human beings. Most likely, you were speaking in the same room with them and got plenty of feedback—verbal and nonverbal—on what you were saying and how you were saying it. You probably spent time speaking with other people who either helped you along if you didn't know a word or phrase or verb tense, or corrected you kindly if you spoke incorrectly. Even if you were speaking without being able to see the other person—on the phone or by computer connection—your speaking partner probably helped you along, or at least let you know when they didn't understand you.

But on the TOEFL, there's no immediate feedback on how you're doing, and that can make the Speaking section scary. You get no help as you go along, and if you get too nervous you can freeze up and forget words you know. That's why I'm listing my two biggest tips for the Speaking section:

First, remember that you're being scored compared to other non-native English speakers taking the TOEFL, not against the general population of native English speakers. When you're speaking in real life, you're often speaking with native English speakers. Not so on the TOEFL. Everyone who takes this test learned English and is going through the same test-taking experience you are. So you don't have to be perfect; you just have to speak as well as you personally can.

Second, you can practice the Speaking tasks enough to get past the fear of freezing up. The more you practice speaking on random topics and passages you've just been given, the more likely you'll be able to sail through this section. So practice—a lot.

PRACTICE TIP

Have you ever heard of aversion therapy? It means exposing yourself to something scary until it no longer scares you. That's what you should do in the Speaking section—practice so many questions that you no longer feel any fear about speaking into the microphone when you get to the actual exam.

Everyone who takes the TOEFL worries the most about the Speaking section. *Everyone.* And there's no reason to think you'll do worse on this section than any of the other people taking it will, relative to your actual speaking skills. So take a deep breath, and let's start preparing for the Speaking section.

As much as I've discussed the aspects of this section that require, you know, actually speaking, it's vital to remember that you can't get anywhere without completely answering the questions the test asks. And the prompts and tasks you're being asked to do are not fundamentally different from any of the other parts of the TOEFL (or from any other standardized test involving reading and responding to reading). Next, I talk about what skills will help you get a good score in the Speaking section.

Skills That Score Points in the Speaking Section

The skills rewarded with good scores in the Speaking section are as follows:

Organization. Be sure your answer makes sense logically, whether by telling a story chronologically, making an argument and supporting it, or summarizing arguments in an order that makes sense. Don't jump around, and don't use nonsequiturs. You want the graders to listen to your answer and believe it flows logically.

Understanding dialogue. Listen carefully and actively. Pay attention at the beginning, especially so you know who is speaking and what role the speaker has.

Understanding written text. Written text is often easier to understand than spoken dialogue is, so stay focused when you are given a written prompt.

Sticking to an argument. You would be shocked at the number of people who take the vague topic of the question and prompt and go off on a tangent. Don't be one of them. Understand the question and prompt, and stick to that topic. If you're making an argument, stick to one position. It is better to use less of your allotted speaking time than it is to ramble or go off-topic.

Supporting an argument. In addition to making arguments and sticking to them, you need to support what you argue with reasoning and facts.

Summarizing an argument. In integrated tasks, you will be asked to summarize arguments made by writers or speakers. Be sure to pay attention so you can effectively sum up the different positions presented in a task's prompt.

Writing notes. You have very little time to take notes on the reading or dialogue—only as long as it takes to listen to or read the prompts. Use this time wisely to write down words or phrases that will remind you of what you need to say in your response. You'll turn in the notes at the end of the exam, but they won't be used as part of your grade.

Speaking from notes. You will only have a few brief seconds to write notes to prompt you for your spoken response, so you must be ready to speak from sparse notes and not a full script that includes each word you intend to say.

Speaking fluently. It's the Speaking section, so of course it's important that you be able to speak in English in a way that is understandable and demonstrates fluency in the language.

WARNING

The six questions in the Speaking section are always the same six types of questions. Do *not* lose focus on which type of question you're answering and accidentally give your opinion on a question asking for a summary, or vice versa.

All are skills you can practice, so if you're not sure you're good at one of these yet, keep working on it.

Key Issues in the Speaking Section

The following are eight key issues to pay attention to in the Speaking section.

Issue 1: Understand what type of question you're answering. There are six question types. (See the "Question Types" section later in this chapter for more detail.) By the time you take the test, you should have practiced enough to know exactly how to approach each type of question—even if you can't name it. As you practice, make identifying the type of question and how you answer it part of your routine. Don't just blindly take each practice question as it comes. By working consciously through the questions, you will know exactly what to do with each question on the Speaking section of the real test.

Issue 2: Organization is everything. Understanding how the base passages are organized and organizing your response in a way that makes sense to the grader are equally important. If you don't understand how the passage you're reading or listening to is organized, you will have a difficult time formulating a good response to it. As you practice, pay particular attention to how passages tend to be organized, and be very deliberate about how you arrange your response.

Later in this chapter, I discuss each type of Speaking task and how you should organize each one. Learn these and use them while you practice, and you'll save time and energy when you get to the tasks on the real exam.

Issue 3: You don't have time to write down every word. Please don't try to write down every word! The only time you have to take notes is the time you spend listening to or reading the passages, and if you try to write down every word, you'll miss important parts of the passages.

By the same token, there is no way for you to write down every word you need to speak during your response. Just by the numbers, if you have 15 to 30 seconds to prepare, there's no way you can write down every word you'll say in 45 to 60 seconds. You'll have to write down notes that give you an outline of what you'll speak, but not a script. It may be easier, in fact, to draw a picture of what you want to say if you're a visual learner. As you practice, you'll learn what to write or draw that helps you remember and give the best response.

Issue 4: Practice summarizing what you're going to say and saying it. If you have a lot of practice speaking from an outline or a few notes, you will already be able to do this well. But most people need to practice speaking from notes instead of a script and making it sound natural and fluent. It can be challenging to take a word or phrase and turn it into a sentence or two explaining your point. You can—and should—practice reading a story, summarizing it in a few notes, and using your notes as a prompt to retell the story. This is exactly what you'll be doing in the integrated tasks.

EXAM TIP

Some students who have taken the TOEFL report that it is easier to summarize and speak during the exam when they think of themselves as actors speaking in character. Think of yourself as an actor playing a student taking a test, and you may speak more smoothly.

Issue 5: Thoughts count more than pronunciation ... Without a good foundation, you can't build a house that will last. And without good organization and a well-supported argument, you can't respond well to a question in the Speaking section of the TOEFL. It's absolutely vital to practice responding to the six different types of questions consciously, paying attention to all the actions you take. If you can construct six well-understood, well-planned responses, your pronunciation will be far less important to your score.

Issue 6: … But pay attention to your pronunciation. The graders have to be able to understand your response to score it highly. There's no expectation that you won't have an accent (you probably wouldn't be taking the TOEFL if you had no accent whatsoever), but if they can't understand what you're saying, there's no way for them to give you a good score.

If you're concerned about your accent and pronunciation, find a native speaker friend and ask that friend to listen to you speak without any visual clues (for example, by closing their eyes or by talking on the phone) and give their honest appraisal of how difficult you are to understand.

Issue 7: There's no need for fancy words. You may have heard the saying that you shouldn't use a ten-dollar word (a fancy, longer vocabulary word) when a one-dollar word (a simple and direct word) will suffice. That is absolutely true on the TOEFL. The graders will be more impressed if you communicate your ideas clearly and directly than if you throw in big words in an effort to sound more advanced. Especially under the pressure of the test, you could misuse a longer word and end up hurting your own argument, so it's best to stick to the words you know, even if you think they sound too basic. If you're communicating your ideas effectively and fluently, you'll score well.

Issue 8: Speak correctly, but use idioms if they fit. The TOEFL is not the time to use informal speech. We all know that one form of fluency is being able to speak casually and use slang, but this will not help your score on the Speaking section. Speak as clearly and simply as possible without using slang and overly casual language. On the other hand, feel free to use *idioms* that are appropriate to the topic you're speaking about, as long as they are not too informal. Use of idioms can display your fluency.

DEFINITION

An **idiom**, also known as a figure of speech, is an expression that has a different meaning than the literal meaning of the individual words. An example of an idiom is "it's raining cats and dogs" to mean "it's raining very hard." You can find examples and explanations of idioms in Chapter 17.

Strategy for the Speaking Section

As I mentioned at the beginning of the chapter, the Speaking section is not just about your ability to pronounce words or put sentences together. The Speaking section tests your ability to read and listen in English, but it also tests your ability to make an argument, analyze an argument, express an opinion, and support your opinion. In fact, in the Speaking section, it is more important to make a good argument than it is to have perfect diction, fluency, and pronunciation. That's why this strategy is focused more on the content of the questions and how to answer the questions than it is on speaking skills per se.

What follows is a standard operating procedure for each of the six questions in the Speaking section.

Step 1: Determine the Main Idea

You will be asked to read or listen to a passage or dialogue, or read one passage and listen to another. These are the *base passages* (or *base dialogues*). No matter what type of question you are asked about the base passage, you will need to know what the main idea of the passage is.

Some of the questions will be very straightforward and ask you to discuss the main idea of the base passage, while others will ask you to discuss the main idea of the base passage in relation to your own opinion or to discuss different points of view of two speakers. But in both cases, the questions will require that you understand the main idea of the base passage in order to formulate an adequate response.

So you'll need to read and listen carefully to determine what the main idea is. Depending on the structure of the base passage, the main idea will be in different places. For a passage giving information on a topic, the main idea is most likely to be in the first paragraph of the base passage, and reiterated again at the end of the passage. If the base passage is a story or anecdote, the main idea is likely to be toward the end of the passage. If the passage is spoken, listen to the inflection of the speaker's voice to get clues about the main idea.

Write down what the main idea is on your note paper so you can stay focused on it as you prepare for the spoken response.

EXAM TIP

Don't let fear of speaking into a recording device distract you from the main purpose of this section—understanding what you read and hear, and making a good argument about it. If you can focus on the content of the question, your speech will flow naturally.

Step 2: Organize Your Ideas

Once you've read or listened to the base passages, you will be given a question and 15 to 30 seconds in which to prepare your answer. Use your time wisely by organizing your ideas before you do anything else.

Identify which type of question you're being asked and what your job is in your spoken response, based on the explanation of question types at the end of this chapter. The questions are always presented in the same order, so you should be able to identify the question type as soon as you turn to it, based on which number it is in the section. Once you know which question type you're dealing with, you'll know what kind of response is expected and how to organize your ideas in order to speak effectively.

In general, you'll want to use a top-down strategy, in which you state your opinion or main idea first and then provide supporting details or a descriptive strategy that mention opinions, facts, or processes from the passage. Quickly write notes on your note paper with the main points of your response, leaving room for supporting details.

Step 3: Add Support

Fill in the space left in your notes for details, based on the type of question you're answering. If the response is describing the passage, fill in supporting facts. If the response asks for your own opinion or a story, fill in details from your own experience. Be sure you have one supporting detail for each main point or description you have in your notes.

If the question asks for a story or opinion based on something that happened to you, you do not have to tell the truth! You may not have had the experience asked for in the question, or may not be able to think of anything that fits. Don't worry; you can make up details and no one will care. If the question is based on details from the passage, however, you need to use facts or details that can be found in the passage.

Step 4: Create a Conclusion

The best way to end your spoken response is with a strong, definite statement. The worst way to end your spoken response is by trailing off vaguely as if you don't know what to say. If you plan out the last statement you're going to say, you can end strongly. The simplest way to end strongly is to restate your main point as the last sentence.

In real life, you would not end a conversation by restating what you'd said at the beginning. But in real life you also wouldn't be given a time limit on speaking, along with 15 to 30 seconds to prepare to speak on a topic you have little interest in. So don't worry about sounding forced or trite; the graders don't care about that. All they care about is your ability to construct and express an argument in spoken English that makes sense and indicates you understand the base passage.

So look back to the beginning of your notes for the first thing you're going to say, and restate it to finish up. Don't worry about being clever—just be definite.

PRACTICE TIP

Download an app to your phone or computer that lets you record sound on it. This will allow you to practice recording and listening to your responses in order to make changes and improvements.

Now that you know how to do all four steps, practice them until you can do them all in the 15 to 30 seconds allotted before you must begin speaking your response. While 15 to 30 seconds sounds like a ridiculously small amount of time to prep to speak on a topic you've just seen, if you can determine the main idea while you're reading or listening, you will have enough time to do the other three steps.

Question Types

Let's talk about the six different questions you'll be asked on the Speaking section, and what format you should use to answer each one.

Now that you've prepped the passage, you're ready to roll with the actual questions. The following are the different types of questions you can be asked in the Speaking section, and how to answer each one.

Description

The first independent question is a description question. Description questions ask you to describe something you like—whether it's something you like to do, someplace you'd like to go, or something else stating your preference—and support your position with details and examples. You will have 15 seconds to prepare and 45 seconds to speak.

Here's how to answer a description question:

1. State what you would like, prefer, admire, or enjoy.
2. Give a reason, and provide a specific detail for that reason.

3. Give a second reason, and provide a specific detail for that reason.
4. Give a third reason, and provide a specific detail for that reason.
5. State your conclusion.

Here's an example of how that might look in the notes you write during your preparation time:

Hero = father.

Smartest man.

Hardest worker. Worked two jobs = college.

Bravest. Saved neighbor from burning house.

That's why.

These notes follow the question type format and will give you enough information to be able to speak for 45 seconds on why you admire your father.

Opinion

The second independent question is an opinion question. Opinion questions give you two options and ask you which you prefer. Your job in the response is to tell which option you prefer and why. You will have 15 seconds to prepare and 45 seconds to speak.

Here's how to answer an opinion question:

1. State which option you prefer.
2. Give a reason, and provide a specific detail for that reason.
3. Give a second reason, and provide a specific detail for that reason.
4. Give a third reason, and provide a specific detail for that reason.
5. State your conclusion.

Here's an example of how that might look in the notes you write during your preparation time:

Hands-on > theory.

No substitute for experience. Theory isn't truth.

Learn more quickly by doing. Repetition = learning curve.

Develop reflexes. Experience makes muscle memory.

That's why experience > theory.

These notes follow the question type format and will give you enough information to be able to speak for 45 seconds on whether you prefer hands-on experience or theoretical study.

WARNING

Students sometimes get anxious or tripped up because they don't have a strong opinion or preference for one of the independent questions. Don't worry about the accuracy of your response—just pick a side and make an argument in favor of it. The grader will never know (or care) if it's your real opinion.

Summarize Opinion

The first integrated question is a summarize-opinion question. Summarize-opinion questions ask you to read an announcement about something related to a university campus, then listen to two speakers discussing the announcement. The question will ask you to summarize the opinion of one of the speakers. You will have 30 seconds to prepare and 60 seconds to speak.

Here's how to answer a summarize-opinion question:

1. State what the speaker's opinion is.
2. Give a reason, and provide a specific detail for that reason.
3. Give a second reason, and provide a specific detail for that reason.
4. State your conclusion.

Here's an example of how that might look in the notes you write during your preparation time:

Schedule change is bad.

Riders will miss bus. Be late for class.

New schedule makes class schedule impossible.

That's why.

These notes follow the question type format and will give you enough information to be able to speak for 60 seconds on how the woman in the conversation feels about the announcement of a campus bus schedule change.

Summarize Reading and Lecture

The second integrated question is a summarize–reading and lecture question. Summarize–reading and lecture questions ask you to read a short passage and then listen to a professor giving a lecture about the topic of the passage. The question will ask you to summarize something the professor said related to the reading. You have 30 seconds to prepare and 60 seconds to speak.

Here's how to answer a summarize–reading and lecture question:

1. State how the lecture relates to the reading.
2. Give a detail from the reading, and explain how the lecture relates to that detail.
3. Give another detail from the reading, and explain how the lecture relates to that detail.
4. State your conclusion.

Here's an example of how that might look in the notes you write during your preparation time:

Plastics help textile production

Weaving = natural materials. Knitting = plastics.

Plastics work in any climate.

That's how.

PRACTICE TIP

As you practice for the Speaking section, time yourself during the preparation section for each question type so you can judge exactly how much detail you can (and need to!) write in the time allowed. If you practice enough, you'll develop a feel for how much you can write down in your prep time.

These notes follow the question type format and will give you enough information to be able to speak for 60 seconds on what the professor says about the reading on how plastics have changed the process of textile production.

Summarize Problem

The third integrated question is a summarize-problem question. Summarize-problem questions ask you to listen to a conversation between two people about a topic related to campus life. The question will ask you to summarize the problem described in the conversation. You will have 20 seconds to prepare and 60 seconds to speak.

Here's how to answer a summarize-problem question:

1. State the problem in the conversation.
2. Summarize the solutions offered in the conversation.
3. Give your opinion about which solution is best.
4. Give a reason for preferring that solution, and provide a specific detail about that reason.
5. Give another reason for preferring that solution, and provide a specific detail about that reason.
6. State your conclusion.

Here's an example of how that might look in the notes you write during your preparation time:

Man can't take two classes he needs

Could take one class now and other next semester, or both during summer school.

Take one now, other next semester.

No guarantee both offered in summer school.

First class still useful if he changes major.

That's why he should take one now and one later.

These notes follow the question type format and will give you enough information to be able to speak for 60 seconds on the man's problem of fitting two conflicting classes into his schedule.

Summarize Lecture

The fourth integrated question is a summarize-lecture question. Summarize-lecture questions ask you to listen to a professor giving a lecture about an academic topic. The question will ask you to summarize the information in the lecture. You will have 20 seconds to prepare and 60 seconds to speak.

Here's how to answer a summarize-lecture question:

1. State the main idea of the lecture.
2. Give a point from the lecture, and provide a specific detail about that point.
3. Give another point from the lecture, and provide a specific detail about that point.
4. Give a third point from the lecture, and provide a specific detail about that point.
5. State your conclusion.

Here's an example of how that might look in the notes you write during your preparation time:

Fish becoming extinct or evolving.

Pollution killing some species.

As pollution spreads species disappear.

Some fish change to adapt.

That's how we know fish are going extinct or evolving.

These notes follow the question type format and will give you enough information to be able to speak for 60 seconds on a professor's lecture about fish and pollution.

Now you should be ready to try some of the practice sections in the next chapter.

The Least You Need to Know

- Everyone is scared of the TOEFL Speaking section. Just remember that you're being scored compared to other non-native English speakers taking the TOEFL, not the general population of native English speakers.
- Practice writing notes to help you speak, but don't expect to take overly detailed notes in the short time provided.
- Study the six different types of Speaking questions on the TOEFL so you'll know how to answer them.

Speaking Practice Sections

Chapter 10

Work through these practice sections carefully, using the techniques and tips from Chapter 9. As you work through them, be sure to time yourself based on the time estimates provided so you replicate the experience of the real exam. You can time yourself with a stopwatch, an alarm clock, the timer on a microwave, or the alarm on your phone. Use these sections for the prompts and passages, and listen to the audio lectures on the website at idiotsguides.com/toefl. Make sure you have paper and a pencil to take notes.

To practice your speaking, use a tape recorder or download a free app for your phone or computer to speak into and then play back to listen to yourself. If you download the app, do so before you sit down to practice these sections, so you have time to figure out how to record and play back with the app.

These practice sections are designed to get you used to responding to the prompt and speaking your response. Practice Section 1 contains only written prompts. Practice Sections 2 and 3 contain combined reading and listening prompts. Practice Section 4 contains only listening prompts.

When you finish a section, check the explanations in Chapter 11 and review them carefully.

Practice Section 1

Read the prompt and give yourself 15 seconds to prep and write notes. Then take 45 seconds to record your response.

1. Discuss a book or movie that has informed your view on life. Please include specific examples and details in your explanation.

Read the prompt and give yourself 15 seconds to prep and write notes. Then take 45 seconds to record your response.

2. Some students live in university dormitories, while others live in private apartments. Which housing situation do you think is better for students, and why?

Practice Section 2

In this question, you will read a short passage about a situation occurring on a university campus, and then listen to a conversation about the passage. You will then answer a question using information from both the reading passage and the conversation. After you hear the question, you will have 30 seconds to prepare your response and 60 seconds to speak.

State College computing center is planning to change the hours of some of its services. Read the notice that is posted on the door of the computing center. You will have 45 seconds to read the notice. Begin reading now.

> **Notice**
>
> To all university computing center users: beginning next semester, no student will be allowed to print out papers after midnight on Friday, Saturday, or Sunday nights. The computing center will still be open for those who need to use the computers, but the printing rooms will be closed and locked until the center reopens at 8 A.M. Saturday, Sunday, and Monday mornings. Thank you for your understanding.

Listen to audio track 10.1 on idiotsguides.com/toefl.

Now get ready to answer the question. Give yourself 30 seconds to create notes for your response. Then take 60 seconds to speak your response.

1. The woman expresses her opinion of the notice by the computing center. State her opinion and explain the reasons she gives for having that opinion.

Practice Section 3

In this question, you will read a short passage on an academic subject and then listen to a talk on the same topic. You will then answer a question using information from both the reading passage and the talk. After you hear the question, you will have 30 seconds to prepare your response and 60 seconds to speak.

Read the passage about mammal milk production. You will have 45 seconds to read the notice. Begin reading now.

> Mammals are animals that produce milk for their young to drink. The hormones that trigger the birth process also trigger the mother mammal's system to begin producing milk. The first milk that comes from the mother's udder is called colostrum, and it contains special fats and enzymes that coat the newborn's stomach and prepare it for the fully developed milk that comes after the colostrum.
>
> Once the colostrum is out of the mother's system, she begins producing milk. The milk is a special combination of the exact nutrients, proteins, sugars, and fats that the young of her species needs to develop and grow. Horse milk is not like sheep milk and is not like cow milk, as each is specially evolved to be the perfect food for the newborns of its species.

Listen to audio track 10.2 on idiotsguides.com/toefl.

Now get ready to answer the question. Give yourself 30 seconds to create notes for your response. Then take 60 seconds to speak your response.

1. The professor describes the relationship of sheep and cows and milk production. Explain how they are different from and similar to each other.

Practice Section 4

In this question, you will hear a conversation. Then you will be asked to talk about the conversation and give your opinion about the subject of the conversation. You will be given 20 seconds to prepare. Then you will be given 60 seconds to speak.

Listen to the audio track 10.3 on idiotsguides.com/toefl.

Give yourself 20 seconds to create notes for your response. Then take 60 seconds to speak your response.

1. The students discuss which of the exams the woman should study for first. Describe the two exams. Then explain which exam you feel she should study for first, and why.

In this question, you will listen to part of a lecture. Then you will be asked to summarize information from the lecture. You will be given 20 seconds to prepare. Then you will be given 60 seconds to speak.

Listen to audio track 10.4 on idiotsguides.com/toefl.

Give yourself 20 seconds to create notes for your response. Then take 60 seconds to speak your response.

2. Using data and examples from the lecture, explain how tanks were developed during World War I.

Chapter 11

Speaking Practice Explanations

There is obviously no one correct answer for spoken response, so there is no answer key for the Speaking questions you used for practice in Chapter 10. Instead, in this chapter you'll find the transcript of the lectures for each practice question along with the reading passage. In addition, I've provided a discussion of what an excellent response would cover, so you can assess whether your own response contained the correct number of elements and addressed the topic adequately.

Practice Section 1 Explanations

Read the prompt and give yourself 15 seconds to prep and write notes. Then take 45 seconds to record your response.

1. Discuss a book or movie that has informed your view on life. Please include specific examples and details in your explanation.

   An excellent response will mention one specific book or movie and give at least two examples from the book or movie that have changed your view on life, and explain how these examples changed your view.

Read the prompt and give yourself 15 seconds to prep and write notes. Then take 45 seconds to record your response.

2. Some students live in university dormitories, while others live in private apartments. Which housing situation do you think is better for students, and why?

   An excellent response will pick one side of the question and will not argue both sides. It will use at least two strong reasons for the opinion expressed in the response and will support those reasons with facts or examples.

Practice Section 2 Explanations

In this question, you will read a short passage about a situation occurring on a university campus, and then listen to a conversation about the passage. You will then answer a question using information from both the reading passage and the conversation. After you hear the question, you will have 30 seconds to prepare your response and 60 seconds to speak.

State College computing center is planning to change the hours of some of its services. Read the notice that is posted on the door of the computing center. You will have 45 seconds to read the notice. Begin reading now.

Notice

To all university computing center users: beginning next semester, no student will be allowed to print out papers after midnight on Friday, Saturday, or Sunday nights. The computing center will still be open for those who need to use the computers, but the printing rooms will be closed and locked until the center reopens at 8 A.M. Saturday, Sunday, and Monday mornings. Thank you for your understanding.

The following is a transcript of the conversation you heard.

Woman: Did you see the notice on the door of the computing center?

Man: No. What did it say?

Woman: It says that they are going to be locking the printer rooms at midnight on Fridays, Saturdays, and Sundays. How am I going to print out my papers now?

Man: You can print them out before midnight, right? I don't see why this is a big deal.

Woman: On Fridays and Saturdays I work at my campus job until 10 P.M. So it's 10:30 before I can get to the computing center to write a paper. I don't think I'm going to be able to finish before midnight. And even if I don't have to turn anything in over the weekend, what about being closed Sunday nights? I have a paper due every Monday morning at 8 A.M. If I don't finish before midnight, then I can't print it out, because the computing center doesn't open again the next morning in time.

Now get ready to answer the question. Give yourself 30 seconds to create notes for your response. Then take 60 seconds to speak your response.

1. The woman expresses her opinion of the notice by the computing center. State her opinion and explain the reasons she gives for having that opinion.

   An excellent response will state that the woman is not happy that the printing rooms will be closed at midnight on Fridays, Saturdays, and Sundays because she is concerned that she will not have enough time to finish and print a paper between 10:30 P.M. and midnight on Fridays or Saturdays. In addition, she cannot print her paper due Monday morning if she is not finished in time to print before midnight on Sunday nights because the computing center doesn't open on Monday until the same time her paper is due.

Practice Section 3 Explanations

In this question, you will read a short passage on an academic subject and then listen to a talk on the same topic. You will then answer a question using information from both the reading passage and the talk. After you hear the question, you will have 30 seconds to prepare your response and 60 seconds to speak.

Read the passage about mammal milk production. You will have 45 seconds to read the notice. Begin reading now.

> Mammals are animals that produce milk for their young to drink. The hormones that trigger the birth process also trigger the mother mammal's system to begin producing milk. The first milk that comes from the mother's udder is called colostrum, and it contains special fats and enzymes that coat the newborn's stomach and prepare it for the fully developed milk that comes after the colostrum.
>
> Once the colostrum is out of the mother's system, she begins producing milk. The milk is a special combination of the exact nutrients, proteins, sugars, and fats that the young of her species needs to develop and grow. Horse milk is not like sheep milk and is not like cow milk, as each is specially evolved to be the perfect food for the newborns of its species.

The following is a transcript of the lecture you heard.

> Professor: In the last class, I know we finished up with the ways that mammals produce milk, and how the hormones that make the female animal go into labor also stimulate her to start producing milk. So today we're going to talk a little more specifically about how that works, and how they produce the milk, and how they hold it, and how animals are different from each other.
>
> So if we talk about cows, regular cows, and sheep, they are very different in the ways they produce milk. Cows produce milk and it gets stored in the udders and milk glands, and there are reserves up above the udders. They produce and produce and produce, and then they're filled up and stop producing milk, and it hurts and they need the calf to feed, or to be milked. So they're milked and all the milk is taken so they're emptied out completely, and once they're empty they start making milk again, and make milk until they're filled all the way up, and then they get milked, and the cycle continues.
>
> In contrast, sheep are what we call "constant producers." They're just making a little bit of milk all the time. And it's rare that they fill all the way up before one of their lambs feed, but even while the lamb is feeding they're producing more milk. So that means that the fat and sugar balance and everything is different from cow milk to sheep milk because of the way they make milk differently.

Now get ready to answer the question. Give yourself 30 seconds to create notes for your response. Then take 60 seconds to speak your response.

1. The professor describes the relationship of sheep and cows and milk production. Explain how they are different from and similar to each other.

   An excellent answer will cover the way milk production is triggered in both sheep and cows by the hormones that trigger labor, and that both animals produce colostrum. It will also cover the difference that cows produce until they are full and then stop, and only begin producing again after they are emptied, while sheep produce constantly, even while they are being emptied.

Practice Section 4 Explanations

In this question, you will hear a conversation. Then you will be asked to talk about the conversation and give your opinion about the subject of the conversation. You will be given 20 seconds to prepare. Then you will be given 60 seconds to speak.

The following is a transcript of the conversation you heard.

Man: Hey Kelly, what's up?

Woman: I'm just really stressed out, Eric. I have two exams tomorrow and I don't know how I'm going to study for both of them tonight.

Man: Why not? You've got plenty of time.

Woman: I know, but when I'm studying for Chemistry I start worrying about Spanish, and when I'm studying for Spanish I start worrying about Chemistry.

Man: You just have to pick one and do that and not think about the other, and then do the same thing. Which one are you going to pick to go first?

Woman: Well, I feel like Spanish is going to be easier. It's all grammar, so the more exercises I do in the back of the book the more I know, and I can probably get through all the ones I need to do in an hour. But then I think that I should start with Chemistry because it's going to take me longer to study for that. All that memorization of all the different kinds of bonds. I'm afraid that if I don't do that first I'll run out of time.

Man: That's a tough decision. I don't know which one I would do first.

Give yourself 20 seconds to create notes for your response. Then take 60 seconds to speak your response.

1. The students discuss which of the exams the woman should study for first. Describe the two exams. Then explain which exam you feel she should study for first, and why.

   An excellent response will describe the Spanish and Chemistry exams, and will then pick one for the woman to study for and will give at least one reason she should study for that exam first.

In this question, you will listen to part of a lecture. Then you will be asked to summarize information from the lecture. You will be given 20 seconds to prepare. Then you will be given 60 seconds to speak.

The following is a transcript of the lecture you heard.

Professor: As World War I dragged on, it settled into trench warfare in late 1914. With each side literally entrenched, it was nearly impossible for either side to get the upper hand. The defenders were virtually invulnerable, the attackers were disadvantaged, and the two sides, the Allies and the Central Powers, were evenly matched. Therefore, a new invention was needed to shift the battle—the armored, armed car. Artillery was very strong; so were machine guns; and the massive steel foundries promised that enough steel was available to make hundreds of thousands of armored cars. The official name for the armored car was "Armored Fighting Vehicle" (in German, *Panzerkampfwagen*), but the codename "tank" stuck.

The first tanks were Rolls-Royces and Model Ts covered in boiler plating and equipped with machine guns, artillery guns, and treads to help them cover unstable or uneven terrain. Tanks were first deployed in 1916 at the Battle of the Somme, with the British using early tanks to gain some ground on the Germans. The German troops they assaulted were horrified to see an armored vehicle impervious to their rifles—and, for the most part, their grenades—but most of the tanks had been lost to artillery or mechanical failure within the hour. Still, the world had been changed forever, and military battles would never be the same again.

Give yourself 20 seconds to create notes for your response. Then take 60 seconds to speak your response.

2. Using data and examples from the lecture, explain how tanks were developed during World War I.

   An excellent answer will explain that World War I was deadlocked because of trench warfare, so the British began building armed, armored cars, and that these tanks scared the Germans when they began using them in battle, even though many of the tanks did not survive the battle.

TOEFL Writing

Part

5

This part explores the TOEFL Writing section and the specific types of writing that achieve a high score in this section of the test.

Chapter 12 looks at the differences between the writing you use every day and the writing that the raters are looking for on the TOEFL, and helps you design a plan to be able to write quick and efficient responses to the prompts in the Writing section.

Chapter 13 contains Writing section prompts designed to give you the experience you need to begin writing immediately during the real exam. You can check your responses against the scoring guide in Chapter 14.

Chapter 12

Acing the Writing Section

In This Chapter

- What writing skills the TOEFL tests
- What skills get good scores in the Writing section
- How to approach the Writing section
- Writing the integrated writing task essay
- Writing the independent writing task essay

You may be able to write a letter, an email, or even an academic paper in English, but that doesn't mean you have practiced the writing style rewarded with a good score on the TOEFL Writing section. This chapter will teach you how to write essays that score well.

The TOEFL Writing section asks you to write essays in a very specific format. Writing fluently in that format is a skill that can be learned, so read this chapter carefully and then practice using the Writing prompts in the practice sections.

TOEFL Writing Basics

The Writing section of the TOEFL consists of two writing prompts. One prompt, called the *integrated writing task*, involves reading a short passage, listening to a brief audio lecture, and writing a response. You are given 20 minutes to write a 150- to 225-word essay.

The second writing prompt is called the *independent writing task*. You have 30 minutes to write a response to a question which conveys your opinion on it. Essays should be 300 words or more.

The Writing section is the last section of the TOEFL, which has both disadvantages and advantages. The disadvantage is you will be tired by the end of the exam, and it may be tempting not to do your best on this section. The advantages, however, are stronger. You will have been practicing reading, listening, and writing in English in this setting already, so your brain will be in an English writing mode. You will also be in an academic paper mindset after reading and listening to so many of them in the previous sections of the TOEFL, so your mind will gravitate to this style as you write your own essays.

The true challenge of the Writing section is keeping your energy up. Yes, it comes at the end of the exam, but it is just as important as any of the other sections. If you learn the strategies for planning and writing a good essay, you will be fast and fluid enough not to waste time in this section and will be focused throughout.

DEFINITION

Integrated means "dealing with two or more equal parts." That's what you're doing in the integrated writing task—looking at the relationship between the lecture and the passage.

It is key to note that in the integrated writing task you will be asked to write a response to both written and audio text. You do not need to bring in outside information to write your response—everything you need to know factually to formulate an excellent response is in the materials you have read and listened to. In the independent writing task, however, you will need to bring in your own reasoning and data.

Remember that the writing style you use in the TOEFL Writing section is not the same style you use to write an email, or even some school papers. The TOEFL rewards certain skills with a good score. Next, I talk about what skills will help you get a good score in the Writing section.

PRACTICE TIP

Go to the TOEFL website at ets.org/toefl and download the free practice questions, including the prompts for the TOEFL Writing section. On the homepage, click **Prepare for the Test.** On the left side of the page, click **Sample Questions**, and you will be taken to the download page. You can use these to practice brainstorming ideas and writing an outline.

Skills That Score Points in the Writing Section

The skills rewarded with good scores in the Writing section are as follows:

Reading efficiently. The passage you are given to read is not long, but you need to read it in three minutes in order to have enough time to listen to the audio response and write your essay based on what you read and heard. So it's important for you to get as much information out of the passage as quickly and directly as you can. Stay focused, and read for meaning.

Listening carefully. You will already know the topic of what you are listening to from having read the passage. This will help you understand more of what the speaker is saying, but you still need to listen carefully to the full audio section to understand it.

Writing good notes. You do not need to take extensive notes on the passage you read, because it is not that long. But take as many quick notes as you can on the audio portion so you can use them to help you formulate your response. For the independent writing task, you can probably write your notes in the form of an outline to combine two steps.

Organizing an outline. As soon as you read the question telling you what to write on, make an outline to figure out how you will organize your essay. The faster you can do this, the sooner you can begin the actual writing, and the more time you'll have to write a thoughtful response that covers the topic with fluency.

Writing efficiently. You only have 20 minutes to write 150 to 225 words that make sense and make your point. You do not have access to a dictionary, so you should use simple words that you are already familiar with. This will help you write with intention and focus.

Editing quickly. If you practice within the time limits enough, you will be able to leave yourself a minute at the end of the section to go through your essay and edit it for typos, misspellings, poor grammar, and other fluency issues. Fluency can be the difference in a good score and an almost-good score, so editing matters.

If you can develop these skills, you will be rewarded with a good score on the Writing section. The essays that score the highest on this section are written with focus and control. Fluency is important, but sticking to the topic and making your point are the backbone of your essays.

Key Issues in the Writing Section

The following are four key issues to pay attention to in the Reading section.

Issue 1: Understand what type of essay you're writing. Your job in the essay for the integrated writing task is to explain the relationship between the ideas in the passage and the ideas in the lecture, based on what the question asks you. It is not to give your own opinion on the topic.

In contrast, the independent writing task is only asking for your opinion. Your opinion must be backed up with supporting details or facts, but your opinion is your own. To make your point, you need to be able to think of examples and reasoning that will support your opinion.

Issue 2: Organization is everything. You can have the best thoughts in the world, but if you don't organize your essays, the raters will not be able to understand what you are trying to say. Stick with a logical essay structure that builds your point and uses strong transition words, and you will score well on the Writing section.

Issue 3: Keep the raters in mind. The raters are actual human people who are paid to read and score your essays. They have very little time to read your essay and decide which score to give it. So you should make it as easy as possible for them to give you a high score after reading your essay quickly. Use a definite structure, transition words, strong support for your argument, and a definite closing.

Issue 4: Watch your time. Twenty minutes is not a long time to write an essay responding to two different pieces of information. Thirty minutes is a better time frame for writing an opinion essay, but it can still be tight. Keep your eye on the clock so you don't run out of time and end up with a half-finished essay.

EXAM TIP

If you've practiced writing the two kinds of essays, you should be able to write them within the time limit. If you start to get nervous on the exam about the time you have left, stop, take a deep breath, and think about how you've already practiced this in the allotted time. You can do this!

Strategy for the Writing Section

The Writing section asks you to produce very specific types of essays written in a standard, consistent format. So if you practice writing several essays of each style, you will become faster and more skilled at writing essays that will score well in this format. As with everything else, the more you practice, the easier it will be to do on the real exam.

If, as you are practicing, you discover you are having significant difficulty writing essays that express your ideas, you may need to take a break from preparing for the TOEFL and do some more practice with writing in English in general. If you can't write the TOEFL essays, you will struggle in an academic program in English. Give yourself time to prepare adequately so you can do well on the TOEFL and in your program.

There are four steps to writing, and practicing for writing, high-scoring essays in the Writing section. These steps work for both the integrated writing task and the independent writing task.

Step 1: Write to the Correct Task

The two Writing section tasks are asking you to do two different things. The integrated writing task asks you to take two pieces of communication—a written passage and a listening section—and compare the information in both. The question after the listening portion will tell you exactly how you should compare this information. It is vital to read the passage efficiently and also listen very carefully to the lecture, while taking good notes, so you can understand the way the information in the two pieces is different and similar. Comparing and contrasting the passage and lecture is key to writing a good integrated writing task essay.

The independent writing task is based solely on a topic and question. There is no other text or information given to you. This means the essay you write is solely your own opinion, and you need to come up with, out of your own mind, reasoning, ideas, and facts to support your opinion and to convince a rater of your point of view.

Be sure you are clear on which one of these tasks you are writing. If you give your own opinion in the integrated writing task, you will not answer the question correctly and you will earn a lower score on that essay. So know exactly what you're answering.

Step 2: Preplan Your Response

You can plan, right now, most of what you're going to write in your TOEFL Writing section essays. That's because much of what you're writing consists of standard structures and forms. The actual topics will only be given to you when you begin the section, but you can create and work with the structures you're going to use right now.

Create one essay structure for the integrated writing task that gives you a framework for discussing the relationships between two sets of ideas. Create a different essay structure for the independent writing task that gives you a framework for giving your own opinion and providing supporting facts. Practice these forms, and you will be set when you get to the Writing section of the exam.

Step 3: Read and Listen

If you've been reading this book in order, you've already worked on your reading and listening skills for the types of passages and lectures found in the TOEFL. If you are skipping around in this book, go back and practice those skills in the Reading and Listening section chapters.

The difference between a reading passage in the Reading section and one in the Writing section is that the Reading passages are so long you need to make a map of them to tell you what information is where in them. The passages in the Writing section are short enough that you probably do not need to take notes, which means you need even more focus while you read a passage in the Writing section. Read carefully, quickly, and with intention to understand the overall message.

Listening in both the Listening section and Writing section are similar because both require that you listen carefully to a lecture on the same topic that you already have some information about. In the Listening section, you may have heard another lecture about the topic; in the Writing section, you are listening to a lecture on the same topic as the passage you just read. This means you do not need to spend the first few minutes of the lecture figuring out what the topic of the lecture is about, but can pay attention to the actual content and details from the first sentence.

You do need to take notes while you listen. You will be asked about similarities and differences between the written passage and the audio lecture. As you listen, you can note any words or phrases you hear that you notice are similar or different from what you read in the passage. Then when it is time to write your essay, you will have that information there and will not have to risk having forgotten what you heard.

PRACTICE TIP

Your task while reading and listening is to figure out what the main ideas of both the passage and the lecture are. As soon as you figure out what the main ideas are, you'll know if the essay is about comparing similarities or contrasting differences.

Step 4: Put It Together

As you write the essays in the TOEFL Writing section, you will need to combine the structures you've created with the content you've read and listened to. The best way to do this is to practice. The more you practice the steps and combining the structure with the content, the better you will become at writing essays that are organized and fluent. These kinds of essays are easy for the raters to read, and to give good scores to.

Integrated Writing Task

The integrated writing task is the first task in the Writing section. You will be given a written passage to read in three minutes. The passage will be short enough to read in the allotted three minutes, but you will have to stay focused and read without becoming distracted and without struggling over words in order to finish.

Once you have read the passage, you will put on headphones and be given a lecture to listen to. This audio lecture will be on the same topic as the passage you just read, and may or may not directly reference the passage. The lecture will last for several minutes, during which time you will not be able to see the reading passage. You will, however, be able to take notes while you listen. Take notes on anything that stands out to you as being similar or different from the written passage.

The lecture will either support or challenge or cast doubt on what you read in the passage. In other words, the lecture either goes with the passage or goes against the passage. Determine as quickly as you can whether it agrees or disagrees with the passage. Then you will be able to listen for supporting details to use in your response.

After the lecture is over, the reading passage will be visible on the computer screen again. You will see directions to write the response in 20 minutes, along with a question prompt. The question prompts look like this:

> "Summarize the points made in the lecture you just heard, explaining how they are similar to the points made in the reading passage."
>
> "Summarize the points made in the lecture, being sure to explain how they challenge the arguments made in the passage."

The clock will begin counting down from 20 minutes. You should make a brief outline based on one of the following forms.

For an essay in which the lecture supports the passage, your outline should look like this:

> Lecture supports passage
>
> [1 way it supports]
>
> [2 way it supports]
>
> [3 way it supports]

You will have heard the three ways the lecture supports the passage when you listened to it, and you may have even written down those ways in your notes. Put them in the outline.

For an essay in which the lecture goes against what the passage said, your outline should look like this:

> Lecture contradicts passage
>
> [1 contradiction]
>
> [2 contradiction]
>
> [3 contradiction]

You will have heard the three ways the lecture contradicts the passage when you listened to it, and you may have even written down those ways in your notes. Put them in the outline.

EXAM TIP

Write an essay that gets the job done simply and clearly. If you have time left, go back in and make things sound more elegant, but don't spend time initially on nuance.

With your outline in front of you to consult, you will start writing. But you won't just start from scratch. Instead, you'll use a template. You need one template for a supporting essay and one for a contradicting essay.

This template is a frame for an essay in which the lecture agrees with the passage:

> The lecture states that **[fill in specific information here]**. This confirms the information in the passage, which discussed **[fill in specific information]**. **[More details about the specific information.]**

> First, the lecture said that **[fill in specific information]**. This was very similar to the information in the passage, which stated **[fill in specific information]. [More details about the specific information.]**
>
> Second, the passage stated **[fill in specific information]**. This was supported when the lecture confirmed that **[fill in specific information]. [More details about the specific information.]**
>
> Third, the passage and lecture agreed on **[fill in specific information]. [More details about the specific information.]**

Use this template when the lecture contradicts the passage:

> While the passage stated that **[fill in specific information]**, the lecture did not have the same point of view. The lecture stated that **[fill in specific information]**. There are several details on which the lecture contradicted the passage.
>
> First, while the passage stated that **[fill in specific information]**, the lecture says that **[fill in specific information]**.
>
> Second, the lecture says that **[fill in specific information]**. This contradicts the claim of the passage, that **[fill in specific information]**.
>
> Third, while the passage stated **[fill in specific information]**, the lecture says that **[fill in specific information]**.

Write your own templates, using words that you know and use with confidence. You can see that the templates are simple and do not use fancy words, but they give a definite structure. This way the rater knows exactly where the argument is going and can see the details and the direction of the essay. An essay that is easy to read and understand and makes a clear point is an essay the rater can give a good score to.

You will not gain more points by writing a long, rambling introduction and conclusion. The raters know that you only have 20 minutes in which to write this essay. They are also given such a short time to read and grade the essays that they need to focus on your organization and your reasoning and evidence. Anything designed just to add length will not help your score.

As you type your essay, combine the template words with the specific information you wrote down in your notes and outline. By merging the two, you will create an organized essay with a strong frame that is supported with details and observations from the passage and lecture.

Use your templates to practice writing integrated writing task essays. The first time you use them, they may seem strange and unnatural. As you practice more, however, they will become more natural to use. By the time you get to the real TOEFL exam, you will be able to use your templates quickly and efficiently.

Integrated Writing Scoring Rubric

The *rubric* for the integrated writing task focuses on organization, details, and fluency.

DEFINITION

A **rubric** is a standard of performance that tells you what qualities are necessary to achieve a certain level of performance.

The highest score you can receive on the integrated writing task is 5. The lowest score you can receive is 0. Let's talk about what qualities an essay must have to earn each possible score on the TOEFL.

To earn a score of 5, an essay must take the important information from the lecture and relate it to corresponding important information from the passage. Very minor word choice or grammar errors do not affect the flow of the essay.

To earn a score of 4, an essay must make a good connection between information from the lecture and information from the passage, although some connections may not be drawn out completely and there may be some vagueness in the argument. Minor word choice and grammar errors are present, but do not seriously impact readability of the essay.

To earn a score of 3, an essay connects the ideas in the lecture with the ideas in the passage but is either vague, leaves out an important point from both the lecture and the passage, confuses ideas from the lecture and passage, or has so many grammar and word choice errors that it affects understandability.

To earn a score of 2, an essay must confuse the differences between the lecture and the passage, leave out several important points from the lecture and passage, and contain grammar and word choice errors significant enough to make understanding the essay difficult.

To earn a score of 1, an essay must be generally poor, with little relevance to the topic; undeveloped ideas; no support or reasoning for the ideas stated; and significant word choice, grammar, and usage errors.

To earn a score of 0, an essay must be copied directly from the passage, written on a different topic or in a way that's extremely difficult to understand, written in a language other than English, consist of random characters, or left blank.

Note that fluency and use of words and grammar is only part of the criteria for each score. So if you learn to write a very tight essay with strong organization that connects ideas from the lecture and the passage and brings out the relationship between them, you will score well. If you create and use a template with strong organization and connections, you have already achieved many of the tasks necessary to score well. In addition, spending one minute at the end of the section to catch and correct fluency errors and typos can pay off with a higher score.

WARNING

It can be tempting to simply restate the points you hear in the lecture or read in the passage. But remember that the raters are looking for the relationship between the ideas in the lecture and passage. Be sure to discuss those relationships.

Independent Writing Task

The independent writing task is the second task in the Writing section. You will be given a question as a prompt, and then given 30 minutes to write an essay giving your opinion on the question. Question prompts for the independent writing task look like this:

> Do you agree or disagree with the following opinion?
>
> Children should only be required to attend school until they can read and do basic math. More than this amount of formal education should be optional, as most people do not need more than basic literacy and math skills to function well in society.

Unlike the integrated writing task, the independent writing task doesn't require you to spend time reading or listening to any information about the topic. Instead, you read the question and immediately begin formulating your response. If you find this difficult, you can use the Listening section as practice to warm up your brainstorming powers before you get to the Writing section. It will also help you practice formulating responses to question prompts.

The open-question format gives you great freedom, because you are able to write your own opinion on the topic and support it with whatever examples you have—reasoning, commonly known facts (from history, science, and literature), details and anecdotes from your own life, and other data. Your job is to create a persuasive case that will convince the raters that your opinion is correct because you give strong evidence to support your points.

There are three components of a successful independent writing task essay. The first is the ideas themselves. When you decide which side you will argue on the essay, pick the side you can think of the strongest supporting points for. This may not be the side you actually believe, but if you can come up with strong reasoning and support, your essay will be better.

The second component of a successful essay is your fluency. The next few chapters address topics including vocabulary, word choice, and grammar. The more you practice these—and the more time you spend immersed in listening, reading, speaking, and writing English in all formats—the better you will do.

The third component of a successful essay is organization. As soon as you read the question and the clock starts ticking down from 30 minutes, you should be putting your pencil to the note paper to brainstorm your points and write down an outline. In general, your outline should look like this:

> Supporting [one point of view]
>
> [Reason 1]
>
> [Reason 2]
>
> [Reason 3]
>
> [Point of view] is clearly correct.

Pretty simple and direct. If you follow this outline, you will stay on topic when you write the essay.

Like you did in the independent writing task, you should create your own template using the kinds of words and style you write and feel comfortable with. The basic structure of your template should look like this:

> Some people feel that **[state position opposite to the one you're going to take].** It is evident, however, that **[your position]** is a better course of action. I will explain why in this essay.
>
> While you could argue that **[reason supporting opposite view],** in fact, the opposite is true. **[Reasoning and facts supporting your claim.]**
>
> In addition, **[another fact supporting your point that connects to the claim in the second paragraph].** This means that **[add more support for your reasoning].**
>
> Moreover, **[an argument the other side could use]** might actually cause **[something that supports your case].** That proves that **[the other position]** is not well thought out and will not be true in the long run.
>
> In conclusion, the evidence shows that **[your point of view]** is correct. While others may make a strong case for **[opposite point of view],** when the evidence is examined, the case becomes clear.

This template is clear, logical, and organized. It uses transition words and provides a frame to allow you to build an argument logically. Remember that you will not get a higher score by padding your essay with rambling, rhetorical questions or fancy words used incorrectly. Create a template using simple, clear words you can remember and use when you practice and when you are in the real TOEFL exam.

EXAM TIP

If you're concerned that you'll forget the elements of your template, write them down quickly on your note paper as soon as you begin the Writing section, before you make your outline.

The more you practice using your template, the more comfortable you will become with it. The more comfortable you are with the template, the more time you can spend on the real exam checking your word choices, grammar, and other fluency issues and coming up with airtight reasoning to support your argument.

Independent Writing Scoring Rubric

The highest score you can receive on the independent writing task is 5. The lowest score you can receive is 0. Let's talk about what qualities an essay must have to earn each possible score on the TOEFL.

To earn a score of 5, an essay must address the topic directly. It integrates information from both the passage and the lecture, and uses strong organization and a logical progression of ideas. It makes sense throughout and does not jump from point to point, but rather uses appropriate transitions. The language used is fluent and displays understanding of English words and sentence structure. A few minor grammar or word errors are acceptable.

To earn a score of 4, an essay must address the topic directly, although it may not have a strong focus. The essay is organized and structured well, but some points may be supported better than others. It makes sense throughout, but it may not be fluid in transitions and may jump around. The language use is fluent overall but has some errors in word choice and grammar.

To earn a score of 3, an essay must address the topic and have some developed explanations and details. It is organized, but the ideas may not connect well and the transitions are not strong. The language use is good but there are errors in word choice, grammar, and conventions.

To earn a score of 2, an essay must be related to the topic but with a limited response that is not developed in ideas or support. It is not organized and does not communicate a coherent idea, and does not support the ideas with reasoning or details. Word choice is inadequate, and there are significant errors.

To earn a score of 1, an essay must be generally poor, with little relevance to the topic; undeveloped ideas; no support or reasoning for the ideas stated; and significant word choice, grammar, and usage errors.

To earn a score of 0, an essay must be copied directly from the question, written on a different topic, written in a language other than English, consist of random characters, or left blank.

Note that fluency and use of words and grammar is only part of the criteria for each score. So if you learn to write a very tight essay with strong organization, good connection of ideas, and strong support in terms of reasoning and details from the passage and lecture, you can score higher than you would just on the basis of writing fluently. If you create and use a template with definite organization and connections, you have already achieved many of the tasks necessary to score well. In addition, spending one minute at the end of the section to catch and correct fluency errors and typos can pay off with a higher score.

Now you should be ready to try some of the practice sections in the next chapter.

The Least You Need to Know

- The TOEFL tests a very specific way of writing, which you can learn to do.
- The integrated writing task wants you to write about relationships between the ideas in the lecture and the passage.
- The independent writing task wants you to write your opinion on a question and support it with strong reasoning.
- Create templates for the two Writing tasks to make writing the essays easier and give them strong organization.

Chapter 13

Writing Practice Sections

Work through these practice sections carefully, using the techniques and tips from Chapter 12. As you work through the practice sections, be sure to time yourself based on the estimates provided so you replicate the experience of the real exam. Use these sections for the prompts and passages, but type your responses into a computer so you get the experience of typing an essay instead of handwriting it.

Do the integrated writing task first. Give yourself three minutes to read the passage. Next, listen to the audio lectures on the website at idiotsguides.com/toefl. Finally, look at the question, and take 20 minutes to type the essay into a document on a computer.

Do the independent writing task second. Read the question prompt, then take 30 minutes to write your outline and type your essay into a document on a computer.

When you finish a section, check the explanations in Chapter 14 and review them carefully.

Practice Section 1

Integrated writing task:

Reading:

In order to keep our bones healthy, human beings need a daily intake of calcium and magnesium. Calcium is absorbed by the bones and strengthens them, and magnesium aids in the absorption of the calcium. The single best source for calcium is cow's milk and other cow dairy products, which have high levels of calcium that can be easily absorbed into the bones. The level of magnesium in cow's milk is high enough to aid effective absorption of the calcium.

Evidence that cow's milk products are the best sources of calcium is that cultures that drink cow's milk and eat cow dairy products have taller people than cultures that do not consume cow dairy. The bones of the people in cultures without cow dairy do not have the constant sources of calcium necessary to aid in bone growth, so the people in these cultures have remained shorter in stature than those in cow dairy-consuming cultures.

Further evidence that cow's milk is the best source of calcium for the human body is that cultures that have ample cow's milk to feed children tend to have lower infant mortality rates than cultures that cannot afford adequate cow's milk. Without cow dairy to strengthen infants' bones, the rate of death from malnutrition is greater.

Lecture: Listen to audio track 13.1 on idiotsguides.com/toefl.

1. Summarize the points made in the lecture, being sure to explain how they cast doubt on specific points made in the reading passage.

Independent writing task:

2. Do you agree or disagree with the following statement? Use specific details and examples to support your answer.

   Students should choose a university major that prepares them for high-paying careers.

Practice Section 2

Integrated writing task:

Reading:

A pandemic is an episode of one infectious disease that spreads throughout vast geographic areas and populations. Recent pandemics have included H1N1, or swine flu, in 2009. H1N1 was a respiratory virus that manifested itself as flu symptoms, followed three to six days later by breathing difficulty. The disease quickly spread throughout the world. In the spring, the government of Mexico shut down all business operations. Four hundred schools in 18 states were closed in the United States in May. Airline operations and hotels were affected in Asia.

Some epidemiologists dispute the idea that H1N1 was a true pandemic, because very few people were actually killed by the disease. While it is true that it spread over a wide area, it did not cause deaths or largely compromise public health. The disruptions in business and government operations were largely preemptive, not resulting from the actual effects of the disease. In effect, these experts say, the claim that H1N1 was a pandemic is a worldwide episode of "crying wolf," or calling an alarm when there is no true emergency. They ask that the term pandemic be reserved for spreads of disease that infect larger percentages of the world population.

Lecture: Listen to audio track 13.2 on idiotsguides.com/toefl.

1. Summarize the points in the lecture, being sure to explain how they challenge specific arguments made in the reading passage.

Independent writing task:

2. Do you agree or disagree with the following statement? Use specific details and examples to support your answer.

   It is better to study subjects that have practical applications than subjects that are theoretical.

Practice Section 3

Integrated writing task:

Reading:

Perhaps the most famous poetic form, the sonnet originated in Europe in the thirteenth century and became popular with aspiring poets in many languages because of its combination of structure and flexibility. While early poets, writing in various languages, embraced the sonnet, it remains a popular form for poets today. The original Italian sonnet has been transformed in the 800 years since its creation into multiple variations that achieve different moods.

A sonnet contains a set number of lines—usually 14 but sometimes 12—and a specific structure that includes a strict pattern of rhymes of the last sound of each line. The most common rhyme pattern is *a-b-a-b*, *c-d-c-d*, *e-f-e-f*, *g-g*, which is the rhyme pattern of the English sonnet, also known as the Shakespearean sonnet (because it was the form used by Shakespeare to write his famous sonnets). In addition to the well-known rhyme scheme, Shakespearean sonnets are also recognized for using iambic pentameter, a form of internal rhythm. In iambic pentameter, two syllables—one unstressed and one stressed—are paired. This pattern of unstressed followed by stressed is repeated five times within each line.

Lecture: Listen to audio track 13.3 on idiotsguides.com/toefl.

1. Summarize the points made in the lecture, being sure to specifically explain how they highlight certain points also made in the reading passage.

Independent writing task:

2. Do you agree or disagree with the following statement? Use specific details and examples to support your answer.

   Playing a team sport teaches valuable lessons that cannot be learned in another way.

Practice Section 4

Integrated writing task:

Reading:

Long considered a prime source of nutrition of humans, chicken eggs are almost entirely edible. There are five parts of a chicken egg: the hard shell, the outer membrane, the inner membrane, the white (albumen), and the yolk. The shell, while not harmful, is generally not eaten by humans, nor is the outer membrane, which is attached to the shell. The inner membrane, albumen, and yolk are routinely eaten by humans in many cultures across the earth.

The yolk is designed to nourish a growing chicken embryo, and is high in minerals, cholesterol, fat, and vitamins. If the egg is fertilized, the yolk will give the embryo everything it needs to develop and grow before it is ready to hatch. If the egg is not fertilized, it can be consumed by humans, either raw or in cooked form. When eaten by humans, the yolk is considered delicious and highly nutritious but too full of cholesterol and other fat to be consumed regularly. Some medical and nutrition experts recommend consuming no more than three egg yolks a week for a healthy diet. The albumen has little vitamin or mineral content, but is one of the purest forms of protein available to humans for consumption. It is low in fat, has no cholesterol, and is considered safe to be consumed on a daily basis for a healthy, low-fat diet.

Lecture: Listen to audio track 13.4 on idiotsguides.com/toefl.

1. Summarize the points made in the lecture, being sure to explain how they cast doubt on specific points made in the reading passage.

Independent writing task:

2. Do you agree or disagree with the following statement? Use specific details and examples to support your answer.

   Reading books is more worthwhile than exploring the internet.

Writing Practice Explanations

Chapter
14

There is obviously no one correct answer for an essay question, so there is no answer key for the Writing questions you used for practice in Chapter 13. Instead, in this chapter you'll find the transcript of the lectures for each integrated writing task along with the reading passage. In addition, I've provided a benchmark essay for each question that would receive a 5, so you can assess whether your own essay contained the correct number of elements and addressed the topic adequately.

Compare your essay with the sample essay here and go paragraph by paragraph to make sure you've covered the important points. Also compare your structure and transition words to the sample essay here to make sure the template you're using is creating a strong-enough structure. If you are concerned about your fluency and use of word choice, idioms, and grammar, ask a friend who is a native speaker to read your essay and tell you if you have made any errors you didn't catch on your own.

Practice Section 1 Explanations

Integrated writing task:

Reading:

In order to keep our bones healthy, human beings need a daily intake of calcium and magnesium. Calcium is absorbed by the bones and strengthens them, and magnesium aids in the absorption of the calcium. The single best source for calcium is cow's milk and other cow dairy products, which have high levels of calcium that can be easily absorbed into the bones. The level of magnesium in cow's milk is high enough to aid effective absorption of the calcium.

Evidence that cow's milk products are the best sources of calcium is that cultures that drink cow's milk and eat cow dairy products have taller people than cultures that do not consume cow dairy. The bones of the people in cultures without cow dairy do not have the constant sources of calcium necessary to aid in bone growth, so the people in these cultures have remained shorter in stature than those in cow dairy–consuming cultures.

Further evidence that cow's milk is the best source of calcium for the human body is that cultures that have ample cow's milk to feed children tend to have lower infant mortality rates than cultures that cannot afford adequate cow's milk. Without cow dairy to strengthen infants' bones, the rate of death from malnutrition is greater.

Lecture:

For years, doctors and nutritionists considered cow's milk and dairy to be the best source of calcium for humans and the primary way to keep human bones strong. New evidence and reasoning, however, calls that theory into question and suggests that consumption of cow's milk may actually prevent absorption of calcium into the bones.

Cow's milk is high in protein, and too much protein can leech calcium from bones. Because of the balance of protein and calcium in cow's milk, the net amount absorbed may be negligible. Nonprotein sources of calcium, such as broccoli and oranges, do not have this problem, and may therefore contain more calcium that can actually be absorbed by the human body.

The claim that cultures that consume more cow's milk grow taller because of better calcium absorption misunderstands the function of calcium in the bones. Calcium makes bones stronger, but does not make them longer. If anything, the fat content in cow's milk and the resulting extra calories in the average diet is most likely responsible for the increased height of people in cultures that drink cow's milk.

By the same token, infant mortality is not related to calcium absorption. However, cultures with enough wealth to afford cow's milk for all babies are more likely to have better nutrition and health practices overall, which would account for better infant mortality rates.

1. Summarize the points made in the lecture, being sure to explain how they cast doubt on specific points made in the reading passage.

   Sample essay that would score a 5:

   The lecturer talks about the claims that cow's milk is the best source of calcium for humans to ingest. She says that the passage is incorrect, that cow's milk is not the best source of calcium for humans, and gives several reasons why this is true.

   First, she says that because there is so much protein in cow's milk, it prevents the bones from absorbing all the calcium in the milk. The passage says that because there is so much calcium in milk, it is the best source for humans to strengthen their bones. The lecture contradicts this with the information that the high level of protein means that all that calcium can't be absorbed.

   Second, she says that the claim in the passage that increased calcium in bones makes humans grow taller is false. She states that calcium doesn't make bones grow longer, but that there is another reason drinking more milk could make people taller: the higher fat and calories.

   Last, she says that when the passage states that feeding infants leads to lower infant mortality rates, it is bad logic. Instead, the lecturer says that milk has nothing to do with infant mortality, but that people who can afford more milk for their baby have more money and better health overall, so the mortality rate is lower.

Independent writing task:

2. Do you agree or disagree with the following statement? Use specific details and examples to support your answer.

   Students should choose a university major that prepares them for high-paying careers.

   Sample essay that would score a 5:

   While some people may feel that students should choose a university major that prepares them for high-paying careers, I do not agree. I feel that students should choose a university major that they really enjoy instead.

   For one thing, it's good to enjoy what you do. We have the rest of our lives to work at jobs doing things because we have to do them. University is our last chance to work hard at something because we enjoy it. If students pick something only because it will lead to a job later, they miss out on their last chance to work because of passion, not duty.

   For another thing, if a student chooses a major just because it will lead to a high-paying career, the student will not truly enjoy the classes and will not work hard at them. If the student doesn't work hard, his or her grades will be poor, and he or she will not be able to get a good job that pays well out of university. And the first job sets up the rest of a person's career. So the whole point of choosing a major just to make a lot of money will be lost.

Finally, it is a person's duty to maximize their own potential. Part of potential is exercising your mind and stretching into thoughts and ideas and feelings that are not just practical and focused. If all students choose majors that are purely practical, what will happen to all the other departments, like art and music and literature? If no one studies them, those majors may just fade away, and then the human race will be less educated and less thoughtful. We will lose our true potential. We owe it to future generations to keep studying the majors that bring beauty into our lives, not just the majors that lead to high-paying careers.

Practice Section 2 Explanations

Integrated writing task:

Reading:

A pandemic is an episode of one infectious disease that spreads throughout vast geographic areas and populations. Recent pandemics have included H1N1, or swine flu, in 2009. H1N1 was a respiratory virus that manifested itself as flu symptoms, followed three to six days later by breathing difficulty. The disease quickly spread throughout the world. In the spring, the government of Mexico shut down all business operations. Four hundred schools in 18 states were closed in the United States in May. Airline operations and hotels were affected in Asia.

Some epidemiologists dispute the idea that H1N1 was a true pandemic, because very few people were actually killed by the disease. While it is true that it spread over a wide area, it did not cause deaths or largely compromise public health. The disruptions in business and government operations were largely preemptive, not resulting from the actual effects of the disease. In effect, these experts say, the claim that H1N1 was a pandemic is a worldwide episode of "crying wolf," or calling an alarm when there is no true emergency. They ask that the term pandemic be reserved for spreads of disease that infect larger percentages of the world population.

Lecture:

Today we're going to talk about H1N1, also called the swine flu. H1N1 was a disease that was initially observed in Mexico. It spread very quickly because people who had it didn't realize they were infected until it had already infected someone else. H1N1 started out like a normal flu, with ordinary symptoms—chills, ache, fever, dizziness. After a few days, however, the victim started having problems breathing and intense respiratory distress.

H1N1 was not a lethal disease. In fact, only a few hundred people worldwide were killed by the virus. However, doctors and public health officials were baffled because of the way the disease spread. Transmission was no more likely to occur from a victim to the people the victim lived closely with, although these people were in close contact and were likely to be sharing utensils and dishes. In contrast, casual contact or proximity was just as likely to spread the disease from victim to victim.

Because of this unusual transmission pattern, public health officials classify H1N1 as a pandemic. They claim that because we were unable to stop the spread of the virus, that classifies it as a pandemic, regardless of the number of deaths the disease caused. They feel that the idea that a pandemic results in massive loss of life is a misunderstanding of the definition of the word *pandemic*.

1. Summarize the points in the lecture, being sure to explain how they challenge specific arguments made in the reading passage.

   Sample essay that would score a 5:

   In the lecture, the professor talks about a disease called H1N1 that spread throughout the world. The professor disputes the claim in the reading passage that H1N1 should not be classified as a pandemic.

   The professor initially explains H1N1 and talks about how it was like a regular flu, but then turned into breathing problems, which was not like a regular flu. It was severe, but did not cause most of its victims to die. The reason the passage says H1N1 is not a pandemic is that it did not cause widespread deaths.

   The lecture then talks about how strange it was that people who lived in the same house with someone who got H1N1 did not always catch the virus from the victim. People who had casual contact with the victim could catch the virus just as easily as someone who was sharing the same house. That made the virus very strange, and that is why the professor says it should be called a pandemic. She says the definition of a pandemic is a disease that can't be stopped from infecting people. In contrast to the passage, she says that the number of deaths from the disease doesn't have anything to do with calling it a pandemic.

Independent writing task:

2. Do you agree or disagree with the following statement? Use specific details and examples to support your answer.

   It is better to study subjects that have practical applications than subjects that are theoretical.

   Sample essay that would earn a 5:

   The idea that it is better to study subjects that have practical applications than subjects that are theoretical is correct. Studying theoretical subjects is ultimately not worth the time it requires to study them, while studying practical subjects always pays off.

   To begin, theoretical subjects may be interesting, but there is no way to know if they are actually true or not. Imagine spending years studying something, only to realize that there is no way to know if what you studied was real or just an idea that cannot possibly happen. If everything you studied is false, or even unprovable, you have wasted your entire life on a fiction.

   In contrast, practical applications relate directly to life, so you know that they are true and worth studying. The only reason not to study a practical application is if you are not interested in the subject. For instance, someone who does not own a car probably should not study auto mechanics. But even if you are not interested in a subject with a practical application, you know it has been proven to be true, and that more discoveries will be made that will also be proven to be true, because they can be tested.

Furthermore, studying practical applications means that you will always have skills that will allow you to have a job and make money. Theoretical subjects can be fun and can expand your mind, but you can't buy food and pay your rent with an expanded mind. You have to be able to survive in the world by working, and practical subjects are the subjects that prepare you to do paid work, especially highly paid work. Practical subjects are the only subjects it makes sense to study seriously, although theoretical subjects are okay to study occasionally, just for fun.

Practice Section 3 Explanations

Integrated writing task:

Reading:

Perhaps the most famous poetic form, the sonnet originated in Europe in the thirteenth century and became popular with aspiring poets in many languages because of its combination of structure and flexibility. While early poets, writing in various languages, embraced the sonnet, it remains a popular form for poets today. The original Italian sonnet has been transformed in the 800 years since its creation into multiple variations that achieve different moods.

A sonnet contains a set number of lines—usually 14 but sometimes 12—and a specific structure that includes a strict pattern of rhymes of the last sound of each line. The most common rhyme pattern is *a-b-a-b*, *c-d-c-d*, *e-f-e-f*, *g-g*, which is the rhyme pattern of the English sonnet, also known as the Shakespearean sonnet (because it was the form used by Shakespeare to write his famous sonnets). In addition to the well-known rhyme scheme, Shakespearean sonnets are also recognized for using iambic pentameter, a form of internal rhythm. In iambic pentameter, two syllables—one unstressed and one stressed—are paired. This pattern of unstressed followed by stressed is repeated five times within each line.

Lecture:

William Shakespeare's Sonnet 18 is often known by its famous first line, "Shall I compare thee to a summer's day?" The poem is often considered one of the most beautiful and romantic poems written in the English language. It is written in the form of an Italian or Petrarchan sonnet, which describes one loved and longed for, often an unrequited or unattainable love. Shakespeare uses language to effectively convey strong and tender emotion through the form of the sounds he chooses to put together.

Shakespeare's secret weapon in constructing Sonnet 18 is iambic pentameter, a way of writing poetry that gives each line 10 syllables. These 10 syllables are paired into five pairs in which the first syllable is unstressed and the second is stressed, like this: *la-DA la-DA la-DA la-DA la-DA*. Something about this pattern creates energy but soothes the listener at the same time. When repeated over the 14 lines of a traditional sonnet, with the classic *a-b-a-b*, *c-d-c-d*, *e-f-e-f*, *g-g* rhyming scheme, the sonnet sounds lilting and gentle, filled with movement, and complete.

Modern poets have followed Shakespeare's example of using classic forms and careful choice of language to create a specific emotional effect for the reader or listener of the poem, but few have approached the emotional resonance—reflected by the lasting popularity—of Shakespeare's 154 sonnets, and especially Sonnet 18.

1. Summarize the points made in the lecture, being sure to specifically explain how they highlight certain points also made in the reading passage.

   Sample essay that would score a 5:

   The lecture talks about William Shakespeare's Sonnet 18 which is also called "Shall I Compare Thee to a Summer's Day." This poem is an example of the sonnet, which is explained in the reading passage and described technically. The lecture describes how Shakespeare took the technical form of the sonnet and used it to get a specific emotional effect.

   Shakespeare wrote Sonnet 18 as a love sonnet, which was the traditional form of an Italian sonnet. In this type of sonnet, the person the poet writes about may not love the poet as much as the poet loves the object of the poem.

   The lecture shows how Shakespeare used the traditional *a-b-a-b, c-d-c-d, e-f-e-f, g-g* rhyme scheme to create a complete structure. It also discusses the way Shakespeare used iambic pentameter, which means that he put 10 syllables in each line of the poem. The 10 syllables were in five pairs, with the first syllable in each pair unstressed and the second syllable stressed, so the whole line had motion and created a romantic effect. The passage describes the rhyme scheme and iambic pentameter, but the lecture shows how they were used in Sonnet 18.

Independent writing task:

2. Do you agree or disagree with the following statement? Use specific details and examples to support your answer.

   Playing a team sport teaches valuable lessons that cannot be learned in another way.

   I agree with the statement that playing a team sport teaches valuable lessons that cannot be learned in another way. While many of the elements of team sports can be learned in other ways, the total experience of playing team sports cannot be replicated by any other activity.

   The main benefits of playing a team sport are learning perseverance, athletic skills, to work as part of a team, and to be there for teammates even when you don't want to be. It is true that there are other activities that can teach one or even two of these lessons, but no other activities teach all four.

   There are activities that are similar to team sports—playing music with a group or doing theater productions, for instance—that teach some of the aspects of cooperation, with everyone doing a different part to create a whole that is better than all the individual parts. But these do not teach athletic skills or the same kind of physical perseverance that team sports do.

   Even individual sports, such as running and swimming, in which a player is doing athletic activity on the same team as others, are not true "team sports" because the individual athletes do not depend on each other for their performance. If you have a good race, you still come in first place even if your teammates do not race well that day.

In contrast, a team sport like soccer, basketball, or football teaches you to each play your own part so others can play theirs, or no one does well. No matter how well a forward plays soccer in a match, if the rest of the team does not play well, the forward doesn't win all alone. Everyone must work together to learn perseverance and athletic skills, and then play their individual roles together so they do not let the team down, even when they do not feel like playing.

Practice Section 4 Explanations

Integrated writing task:

Reading:

Long considered a prime source of nutrition of humans, chicken eggs are almost entirely edible. There are five parts of a chicken egg: the hard shell, the outer membrane, the inner membrane, the white (albumen), and the yolk. The shell, while not harmful, is generally not eaten by humans, nor is the outer membrane, which is attached to the shell. The inner membrane, albumen, and yolk are routinely eaten by humans in many cultures across the earth.

The yolk is designed to nourish a growing chicken embryo, and is high in minerals, cholesterol, fat, and vitamins. If the egg is fertilized, the yolk will give the embryo everything it needs to develop and grow before it is ready to hatch. If the egg is not fertilized, it can be consumed by humans, either raw or in cooked form. When eaten by humans, the yolk is considered delicious and highly nutritious but too full of cholesterol and other fat to be consumed regularly. Some medical and nutrition experts recommend consuming no more than three egg yolks a week for a healthy diet. The albumen has little vitamin or mineral content, but is one of the purest forms of protein available to humans for consumption. It is low in fat, has no cholesterol, and is considered safe to be consumed on a daily basis for a healthy, low-fat diet.

Lecture:

For a long time, scientists and nutritionists thought that consuming chicken egg yolks, even in moderation, was unhealthy for humans. They based this theory on the fact that egg yolks contain high amounts of cholesterol and other fats, and that cholesterol is known to cause heart problems in humans along with other health problems.

In recent years, however, it has been discovered that the potential danger of consuming chicken egg yolks has been grossly exaggerated. While the yolks do contain high levels of cholesterol, more of that has been discovered to be high-density lipoprotein, or "good" cholesterol, than low-density lipoprotein, or "bad" cholesterol. In addition, there are substances in the yolk that were previously unidentified that may help the body process the fats and cholesterols in the yolks to protect the human body from negative effects. Interestingly, the substances in the yolk may make it easier for the human body to process and use all the protein in the albumen, or egg white, of an egg. So people who have been consuming egg whites and discarding the yolks for health reasons may have inadvertently been hindering their bodies accessing the full nutrition of the whites. The current recommendation is for humans to eat both the yolk and the albumen, and not to restrict consumption of chicken eggs to only three times per week.

1. Summarize the points made in the lecture, being sure to explain how they cast doubt on specific points made in the reading passage.

   Sample essay that would score a 5:

   The lecture discusses how nutritious chicken eggs are for humans to eat. It explains why some claims in the reading passage that eggs are not healthy for humans are false.

   The lecture talks about the claim in the passage that egg yolks are unhealthy because they contain too much cholesterol and fat for humans to eat regularly. The passage says that the levels of these make them too unhealthy for humans. The lecture, however, says that scientists now know that the cholesterol is the good kind of cholesterol, not the bad kind of cholesterol, so yolks are much healthier than previously thought.

   In addition, the lecture says that scientists now know that there is another substance in yolks that helps the body process the cholesterol and fats in the yolk. Also, this substance helps the body process all the protein in the egg whites, so when people eat just the whites and not the yolks to try to be healthy, they might not get all the benefits of the whites. The lecture ends by disputing the reading passage that humans should limit their egg consumption to three eggs a week.

Independent writing task:

2. Do you agree or disagree with the following statement? Use specific details and examples to support your answer.

   Reading books is more worthwhile than exploring the internet.

   The statement that reading books is more worthwhile than exploring the internet makes no sense. Exploring the internet includes all the benefits of reading books but many more that books can't give you. It makes far more sense to explore the internet.

   While reading books is a wonderful activity, you can read books on the internet. There are all kinds of books on the internet, both for free and that you can pay for, written as regular text on web pages, or readable through e-readers that you can download onto your computer. Almost any book that you can read in paperback or hardback form you can read on the internet. Moreover, there are many books that have only been published on the internet, so you can't even read them in paperback or hardback form. This means that the internet is even better than reading books.

   In addition, the educational things you can do on the internet are so much richer than reading a book can be. When you read a book, you are transported to the world that the author creates, but on the internet you can communicate with real human beings from all over the world. Together you can share your worlds with each other, and create a story with all of you in it, making something bigger than a book could be because it involves real people in real places, and makes the world smaller.

Overall, the idea that books are better than the internet sounds like it comes from someone who has not spent time doing anything productive on the internet. While it is true that there are many ways to waste time on the internet, like watching videos of kittens, there are many more valuable and productive things to do on the internet. Videos are only a tiny part of what can be done on the internet, and anyone with the initiative to look for more educational activities can easily find them.

Vocabulary and Fluency for All Sections of the TOEFL

Part 6

This part explores a variety of topics related to reading, writing, listening, and speaking English. Learning these concepts will help you not only practice for and take the TOEFL exam, but also prepare you to communicate with others in English in your daily life and in an academic setting.

Chapter 15 explores vocabulary and how to build it. The chapter begins with a discussion of Latin and Greek roots of words (with tables of common roots) and finishes with a list of the top words to learn for the TOEFL.

Chapter 16 contains a grammar review of the parts of speech and looks at common usage problems. Chapter 17 explores idiomatic expressions, both as parts of prepositional phrases and as standalone expressions.

Chapter 18 explores issues in fluency, including structure, organization, transition words, and deciphering words in context.

Vocabulary You Need to Know

Chapter 15

In This Chapter

- Why vocabulary is important on the TOEFL
- Learning Latin and Greek roots
- 250 words to learn for the TOEFL

The more words you know in English, the better you'll do on the TOEFL. It's a simple equation, but it holds true, because the whole point of the TOEFL is words in combination—in the passages you read and listen to, in the questions you're asked, and in the essay answers you write. If you don't understand the words you read or hear, you can't answer the questions. If you don't understand the words in the questions, you can't answer the questions. And if you don't know the words to write what you think, you can't answer the questions.

Now that I've convinced you to learn more words, it's time to talk about how. The more you read and listen to English, the more words you'll encounter in context. So read and listen to English texts as much as possible. It will also help you to learn vocabulary by studying it outright. In this chapter, I give you tables of root words to help you decipher words you haven't seen before. I also list 250 words you should know for the TOEFL.

Using Roots to Learn Vocabulary

English is full of words from other languages, and because of this has an enormous vocabulary compared to many other languages. One open-source dictionary project has counted 55,000 English words in its lexicon, and more are being added to the dictionary all the time.

This makes it extremely difficult to learn all the words in the English language, or even many of them. One way to be able to decipher words you have not seen before is to learn common roots of words. If you memorize some of the roots, then you will be able to use your knowledge of the roots to figure out what the words mean, even when you haven't encountered those exact words before.

The two languages that have contributed the most commonly used roots to English are ancient Greek and Latin. Following are two tables of common roots, one from Latin and one from ancient Greek. These tables list the roots used most frequently in English, and are by no means complete. If you memorize the information in these tables, you'll increase your chances of being able to decipher more words on the TOEFL.

PRACTICE TIP

If you want to increase your chances of knowing even more words, do an internet search for Latin roots or Greek roots and you'll find lists of hundreds of roots.

Latin Roots

Latin Root	English Meaning
act	do
agri	field
amo	love
ann	year
aud	hear
bene, beni	good
cap	head
centr	center
cide	kill
clud, clus	close
cor, corp	body
dic, dict	say
doc	teach
fac, fact	do, make
fer	carry
form	shape
ject	throw
man	hand
miss, mit	send
mob, mot	move
multi	many, much
ped	foot
port	carry
sist, stat	stand
spec	look

Greek Roots

Greek Root	English Meaning
anthr	man
ast	star
auto	self
biblio	book
bio	life
chron	time
cosm	universe
cycl	circle
dem	people
gen	birth
geo	earth
graph	writing
hydr	water
iatr	medical care
mania	madness
meter	measure
micro	small
neo	new
ology	study of
opt	eye
phone	sound
psych	mind, soul
scope	see
tele	far
therm	heat

Vocabulary Words to Know for the TOEFL

Following are five lists of 50 vocabulary words you should know before you take the TOEFL. They're separated into lists of 50 words to make them easier for you to keep track of. To use these lists most effectively, write down each word on an index card. Then, look up each word in a dictionary or on Visual Thesaurus (visualthesaurus.com) to find the definition and synonyms and antonyms of the word, and write those down on the other side of the card. Now you have flash cards and can drill yourself on these words whenever you have a few extra minutes to kill.

List 1

abet
abridge
academic
accede
accord
adverse
aesthetic
affable
allay
allude
allure
ally
amenable
amiable
analogy
anonymous
anthology
antithesis
apathy
apology
appraise
apprise
articulate
ascetic
askance
atheist
attribute
aura
auspicious
authentic
authenticate
authority
autocrat
avarice
averse
awry
banal
bane
banter
bated
belie
belief
benefit
benevolent
bereave
bias
bibliography
bizarre
bland
blandishment

List 2

blemish
blight
blithe
bombast
boor
bore
cabal
callous
candid
capricious
captious
caricature
captivate
castigate
catholic
character
chauvinist
chronic
circumference
circumspect
circumvent
civic
civil
claim
coalesce
coercion
cogent
collide
collude
commode
commute
compendium
compensate
complacent
concede
condone
confederate
consensus
consternation
consummate
copious
cosmopolitan
countenance
craven
credible
credulous
crucial
culpable
cursory

List 3

curt
cynic
dearth
deism
delete
delineate
deluge
demagogue
denounce
deplete
depraved
deprecate
depreciate
devoid
devout
didactic
different
diffident
dilemma
discreet
discrete
dissent
diverge
diverse
divulge
dogma
edict
edify
egregious
elicit
ensue
epigram
epitaph
epithet
equitable
exceptionable
exceptional
exodus
exotic
exploit
export
extinct
façade
facetious
feign
fervid
fiction
flagrant
flaunt
fragrant

List 4

forensic
frustration
garish
garnish
genesis
glib
glide
hail
hale
harbinger
heinous
hiatus
historic
histrionic
hovel
hover
hyperbole
hypothesis
illicit
illumine
imminent
immune
impeach
impeccable
implicit
import
impugn
incumbent
ingenious
ingenuous
inhibit
insidious
ire
jargon
ken
labyrinth
latent
lethal
literacy
literary
lucent
malicious
malignant
maudlin
meddle
mettle
mimic
misnomer
mundane
myriad

List 5

nettle
noisome
notorious
novice
oblivious
obsessive
obviate
onus
panacea
paradox
parody
pedantic
peruse
plagiarism
prelude
profession
professor
proximity
radical
refute
reign
rein
research
respite
revile
rue
salacious
sacrosanct
sanguine
scourge
sinister
soporific
sovereign
standpoint
stoic
supine
tangible
taunt
taut
temporal
temporary
tenuous
transgression
transitory
vaunt
version
vicious
viscous
waive
zealous

Now that you've worked through this chapter, don't stop learning new vocabulary. Read as many different types of writing in English as you can, and pay attention to any words you don't know. Keep a list of the words you read and don't know so you can look them up later. There's no way (and no need) to learn every word in the English language, but you'll improve your score on the TOEFL by knowing more words.

The Least You Need to Know

- The more English words you can understand and use, the better you'll do on the TOEFL.
- Learning Latin and Greek roots can help you guess at meanings of words you haven't seen before.
- Learning the 250 words on the lists in this chapter will give you a boost in your vocabulary.

Chapter

16

Grammar Review

In This Chapter

- What nouns are and how to use them
- How pronouns are different from nouns
- What verbs are and why tense is important
- When to use adjectives and adverbs
- Why prepositions are where it's at

This chapter is entitled "Grammar Review," but it could also be titled "Parts of Speech," because it's going to give you a quick and solid review of the parts of speech in English that you need to be able to use on the TOEFL. If you studied English in school, you probably learned about all of these parts of speech when you first started learning English. If you learned by speaking with native speakers and reading, these names might be new to you. Whatever the case, the concepts are simple, and you should learn or relearn them quickly.

Decades ago, kids in elementary school in the United States used to spend time circling words and writing notes next to them in their books to learn which parts of speech were which. That's not done in U.S. schools anymore, but it's still important to know which words fill which function in a sentence. I'm not going to make you do any circling or special notation, but I will talk about the different parts of speech so you understand how words go together.

Nouns

Nouns are words that are a person, place, thing, or idea. A sentence must contain a noun. Some examples of nouns are:

feelings

Abraham Lincoln

car

parking lot

kittens

Oklahoma

Nouns can be singular or plural and counted or uncounted. I've provided some examples to show you the difference between the types.

Singular	Plural
puppy	puppies
car	cars
idea	ideas

Counted	Noncounted
dogs	freedom
houses	ice cream
dollar bills	money

A singular noun that refers to a group of things is called a *collective noun. Team*, *herd*, and *squadron* are all collective nouns.

PRACTICE TIP

A noun that does not refer to a specific thing is called a common noun. Examples of common nouns are *teacher, school,* and *apple.*

Noun Forms

Nouns can be subjects or objects. A subject is a noun that performs an action in a sentence. An object is a noun that has an action performed on it in a sentence. For example:

Bob played the violin.

Bob is the subject and *violin* is the object. Both *Bob* and *violin* are nouns. Here's another example:

The monkeys stole coconuts from the cart.

The nouns in this sentence are *monkeys*, *coconuts*, and *cart. Monkeys* is the subject, because they do the stealing. *Coconuts* is the object, because the coconuts are stolen by the monkeys. *Cart* is the object of the phrase *of the cart.*

Proper Nouns

Proper nouns are nouns that refer to specific people, places, things, or ideas. Proper nouns are usually capitalized:

Adam Smith

Spokane

Count Dracula

Kleenex

Rosicrucianism

PRACTICE TIP

An abstract noun is a noun that expresses an idea that's not tangible, like "love" or "truth."

Pronouns

Pronouns are words that take the place of one or more nouns. They are used in place of the original noun to avoid repetition and awkward speech. Examples of pronouns are the following:

me

my

she

her

he

his

it

its

they

their

them

these

those

that

which

who

whom

what

whose

Look at how pronouns can take the place of nouns. Instead of saying:

I love my new teacher because my new teacher has a good sense of humor.

You can say:

I love my new teacher because she has a good sense of humor.

In that sentence, the pronoun *she* takes the place of *teacher* so you don't have to repeat the noun.

Pronouns must agree with the number of nouns they replace. If a pronoun replaces a singular noun, it must be a singular pronoun—for example, *the man* becomes *him*. If a noun replaces a plural noun, it must be a plural pronoun—for example, *the men* becomes *them*.

Pronouns must also agree with the gender of the noun they replace. A masculine noun becomes a masculine pronoun—for example, *the man* becomes *him*. A feminine noun becomes a feminine pronoun—for example, *the girl* becomes *her*.

When you write, be sure it is obvious which noun a pronoun refers to, or replace confusing pronouns with the nouns they refer to. The following sentence contains confusing pronouns:

> My dad asked my brother to take the dog for a walk, but he wouldn't go.

It is not clear whether the word *he* refers to "my dad," "my brother," or "the dog." Instead, say:

> My dad asked my brother to take the dog for a walk, but the dog wouldn't go.

Possessive pronouns show who or what owns something else. Possessive pronouns do not take apostrophes:

> The chair is hers.
>
> The dogs knew that all the bones in the garage were theirs.

Verbs

Verbs are words that express actions or conditions. A sentence must contain a verb. Examples of verbs include:

> walk
>
> have eaten
>
> catapulted
>
> will be
>
> had read
>
> would have pretended

As you can see, some verbs are single words, while other verbs use what are called *helping verbs* to change the time condition, or tense, of the verb. You should understand verb tenses and verb conjugations (also called *subject-verb agreement*).

Verb Tenses

Verb tenses let you express when in time an action or condition took place. The simplest tense is present tense, which tells what is happening right now:

I walk down the street.

She eats a hamburger.

Kelly and Yumiko have the flu.

Another simple tense is past tense, which tells what happened once in the past and is finished:

Roberto ate an apple.

We were late to the meeting.

The Supreme Court ruled on the case.

The other tenses all take helper verbs. Present continuing tense is made of a helper (the present tense of the verb "to be") plus the *-ing* form of the verb:

She is walking to the store.

We are waiting for the news.

Alexander and DeJuan are collecting papers.

Past perfect tense is created by using a helper (a form of the verb "to have") and the past participle of the verb. Use "had" and the participle to express something that happened once before something else happened:

We had eaten before we went to the party.

He had seen the movie before.

The DJ had played that song three times already.

PRACTICE TIP

If you're concerned about your skill with verb tenses, take 10 minutes a few times a day to find reading material on the internet and practice determining which tense each verb is. After a few days of consistent practice, you'll be much better at understanding which tense indicates which time frame of action.

Use "have" or "has" and the participle to express something that happened in the past and is continuing (see the "Verb Conjugations" section for more on subject-verb agreement):

I have gone to Mexico.

The girls have driven 500 miles today.

My boss has designed a new office space for the company.

Future tenses use the helper "will" plus the infinitive of the verb (minus "to") to show that something will happen:

I will go to Boston for Christmas.

The dogs will sleep all afternoon.

The cells will divide every eight hours.

Use "will" plus the past tense helper "have" to make a more complex future tense in which you are in the future looking back at something that happened after the present time:

The airplane will have been in the air for four hours already.

I will have written two papers by this time next week.

My mother will have traveled all weekend by the time she arrives here.

Listening or reading to understand which tenses are being used in a lecture or passage can help you work out a time line of events to gain more understanding of the passage. Using correct tenses to express time when you are speaking and writing on the TOEFL allows the raters to understand what you are saying or writing and grade you higher than if you use imprecise tenses or mix tenses inappropriately in your response.

Verb Conjugations

Verb conjugations, also known as subject-verb agreement, means that you use the correct form of the verb to match the subject of the sentence. Here's a traditional conjugation chart:

Singular	Plural
I am	we are
you are	you are
he/she/it is	they are

Most verbs don't have as many forms, depending on the subject of the sentence, but the verbs do change based on whether the subject is singular or plural:

Singular	Plural
I walk	we walk
you walk	you walk
he/she/it walks	they walk

So the trick is just to make sure they match, even if there are words in between the subject and the verb:

The lady eats.

The lady eats a burger.

The lady with the hat eats a burger.

The lady with the blue hat and green gloves eats a juicy cheeseburger.

The lady by the door with the blue hat and green gloves eats a juicy cheeseburger.

EXAM TIP

If you're taking the TOEFL and you get confused about subject-verb agreement, stop for a second and strip the sentence down to its basic subject and verb, ignoring all the other words surrounding them. When they're isolated, you should be able to make them agree.

Adjectives

Adjectives are words that modify or describe another word in the sentence. Adjectives are used to add more detail to writing and almost always go before the word they modify:

the black cat

stinky cheese

the delightful song

a rushing river

While adjectives are a way to add detail to your writing, they can also be seen as a lazy prop. If you choose more descriptive nouns and verbs, you won't have to rely on adjectives to get your meaning across. On the TOEFL, you will get a higher score on the Writing and Speaking responses by using better verbs and nouns rather than more adjectives.

Make sure you understand adjectives of comparison. The comparative form is used when you are describing one of two things. The superlative form is used when you are describing one of three things. Here are some examples:

Adjective	Comparative	Superlative
good	better	best
bad	worse	worst
big	bigger	biggest
slow	slower	slowest

Adverbs

Adverbs are words that describe verbs, adjectives, and other adverbs. They answer the questions *how*, *when*, *where*, and *why*.

He drove the car slowly through the woods.

He threw the barely eaten croissant into the garbage.

I never ride a bike.

You can often recognize adverbs because most of them end in *-ly*. Adverbs that do *not* end in *-ly* are called *flat adverbs*.

Adverbs can go in multiple locations in a sentence, so they cannot be identified solely by where they appear. Changing the location of an adverb can change the meaning of a sentence, but the meaning could also stay the same.

Here's a case where changing the location changes the meaning:

I almost read the entire book. (I didn't read the book.)

I read almost the entire book. (I read most of the book but not the entire thing.)

And here's an instance where placement of the adverb doesn't affect the meaning:

She removed the necklace from the box carefully.

She removed the necklace carefully from the box.

Prepositions

Prepositions are words that connect nouns and pronouns to the rest of a sentence. They show movement or action, as well as place and time. Here is a list of some common prepositions:

to

from

on

upon

about

under

behind

toward

past

beside

before

after

during

at

by

WARNING

Prepositions can be the toughest parts of speech to understand for people learning another language. In the next chapter, I talk about idiomatic prepositions and include a list of commonly misused idiomatic prepositions in English.

A phrase containing a preposition and a noun is called a *prepositional phrase:*

to the store

at home

beside the stove

Prepositions show how concepts are related. Prepositional phrases can add detail and information to a sentence without sounding overly complicated.

This grammar review has explained some of the rules and conventions to follow in English. Once you know the rules, the best way to improve your English is to continue to use it by reading, listening, speaking, and writing English as often as you can.

The Least You Need to Know

- Words can be sorted into parts of speech, each of which serves a different function in a sentence.
- Nouns are people, places, things, and ideas. Pronouns are shorthand for the nouns they refer to.
- Verbs show action or condition, and need to be in the correct tense and conjugation.
- Adjectives and adverbs describe other words in sentences.
- Prepositions are words that connect nouns to other parts of a sentence.

Idiomatic Expressions

Chapter
17

In This Chapter

- What an idiomatic expression is
- Common prepositional idioms
- Other idiomatic expressions

An idiomatic expression, or idiom (*ID-ee-um*), is any phrase that means something different than the meaning of the individual words. An example of an idiom is the phrase "ace in the hole." Reading that phrase, it seems to mean something about having an ace (presumably a playing card) in a hole. However, the real meaning of the phrase is "an advantage that is kept hidden until the person holding it has the right opportunity to use it."

As you can see, idioms can be very difficult, if not impossible, to understand if you did not grow up speaking the language. You know and use the idioms in your native language without realizing it. When it comes to English, some estimates say there are as many as 25,000 idioms in the language! Obviously, I am not going to cover all those idioms in this chapter, but I hope to give you enough of a start that you can understand some common idiomatic ways of expressing thoughts in English, along with the knowledge that if the literal words of something you read or hear don't make sense in context, you might be reading or hearing an idiom.

Prepositional Phrase Idioms

If you recall from the previous chapter, prepositions are those little words that connect ideas, express relationships, and give a sense of movement or direction. Prepositions are small, but if used incorrectly, you sound nonfluent, and you can also give a meaning you didn't intend to give.

The bad thing about idiomatic prepositions is that they sometimes won't make sense to you if a different preposition is used in the equivalent phrase in your native language. Have you ever had the experience of directly translating a prepositional phrase from your language to English and having a native English speaker correct your preposition? It doesn't make sense to your ear, but "that's just the way we say it in English."

WARNING

When I say "that's just the way we say it in English," I mean American English. Canadian English, British English, Australian English, New Zealander English, South African English, and other forms of English all have their own idiomatic expressions. Sometimes two native speakers don't know what the other is saying because idioms can be regional—even prepositional idioms.

The good news is that idiomatic prepositions make up a very small percentage of English idioms, which means that you could learn all of them and use them with fluency—eventually. You do not have to know every single prepositional idiom before taking the TOEFL. But you should know some common ones.

Here is a list of common prepositional idioms in which the preposition comes at the end of the phrase. When there are two acceptable prepositions that lend different meanings to the phrase, the difference in meaning is in parentheses:

accountable for (responsible for)

accountable to (responsible to someone)

according to

adapt from (change something already in existence)

adapt to (become accustomed to)

agree on/upon (make a decision)

agree to (decide on a course of action)

agree with (have the same opinion)

annoyed at/with (irked at a person)

annoyed by (irritated by something)

apart from

assist at (help at an event)

assist with (help someone)

because of

choose between (choice of two things)

choose from (make a choice from an array)

contend for (compete for something)

contend with (struggle with something)

depart for (leave for a destination)

depart from (leave from a destination)

due to

favor for/to (do a good deed for someone)

favor from (receive a good deed from someone)

from now on

grateful for (thankful for something good)

grateful to (thankful to a person)

impatient for (wishing an event would happen soon)

impatient with (wishing a person would hurry up)

in addition to

in case of

in common with

in favor of

in front of

instead of

lack of

part from (leave a person)

part with (give up a possession)

profit from

rather than

regardless of

suspicious of

time for (to have time in which to do something)

time to (the hour at which to do something)

with regard for

with regard to

Here's a list of idiomatic prepositions in which the preposition is at the beginning of the phrase:

by accident

on behalf of

on business

by chance

in conclusion

under control

without fail

at first

in the future

by heart

for instance

at last

at the latest

at least

by no means

by mistake

at the moment

for now

at once

on purpose

in private

at a profit

at any rate

at risk

in secret

by the time

on time

by the way

PRACTICE TIP

Make flashcards of these common idiomatic prepositional phrases. Write the phrase on one side and a sample sentence on the other. You can even draw a picture on the card to help you remember the meaning.

As you read and listen to English, you will notice more idioms involving prepositions. Write them down and learn them. Pay attention to prepositional idioms in your own language and compare them to equivalent prepositional phrases in English. Can you see any patterns?

Common Idiomatic Expressions

Following is a table of 100 common idioms in American English.

10-4	I hear and acknowledge what you said
24/7	constantly
a dime a dozen	common and therefore cheap
a penny for your thoughts	a way of asking what someone's thinking
about to	be on the point of doing something
add insult to injury	make a bad situation worse
after all	at the end of a situation
all of a sudden	suddenly
an arm and a leg	very expensive
as if	resembling
as long as	if
at face value	literally
back and forth	going from one side of something to another
better off	improved
break a leg	wishing good luck
break up	separate
by the way	giving extra information
come on	go faster
come up	happen without warning
come up with	find something
cut corners	skimp on quality
deal with	take on or fix a situation
draw the line	stop at a certain action
easier said than done	not as easy as it sounds
end up	an unexpected ending
figure out	solve something
fill in	put information into a form
find out	learn something
first of all	the first item on a list
for sure	definitely
get back to	return contact with someone

continues

continued

get into	become interested in
go ahead	start something
go on	continue
hang out	spend time with
have to do with	be connected to something else
hit the books	study
hold on	wait
hurry up	go faster
in case	if
in effect	practically
in fact	what actually happens
in hot water	in trouble
in other words	the same thing explained a different way
in terms of	with regard to
in the nick of time	just before time expired
in time	with enough time
kill two birds with one stone	get two results with effort for only one of them
kind of	somewhat
lend a hand	help
look up	search for information in a reference source
make sense	be logical
make sure	check to see if something is true
matter of fact	very practical in tone
miss the boat	lose the chance to do something because of inaction
money talks	money has influence
more or less	somewhat
my bad	an apology for making an error
of course	certainly
on the ball	prepared
on the fence	not making a decision
on the other hand	an opposing idea from the first one proposed
on the point of	almost beginning to
on time	at the correct time

once in a blue moon	not very often
open to	willing to learn or hear something
pick up	obtain
piece of cake	easy
point out	draw attention to
poker face	not giving away one's feelings with one's expression
put out (verb)	create something
put out (condition)	annoyed or angry at something
right away	immediately
run into	encounter something
see eye to eye	have the same opinion
show up	arrive
sick and tired of	to be annoyed or angry at something repeated
so far	up to this point
sort of	almost
take care	a salutation wishing someone well
take care of	to be in charge of or look after something
take it easy	relax
take over	take control of
take place	happen
the last straw	the final thing that pushes someone or something to the limit
the best of both worlds situation	something that has good characteristics from both sides of a
the grass is always greener on the other side	things look better for other people than for you
time-out	let's take a break
turn in	give something to someone else
turn out	show up
turn up	appear unexpectedly
two cents' worth	your opinion, to give your opinion or ideas
under the weather	sick
up to	to this point
used to	be accustomed to
what goes around comes around	your actions and attitude will be returned to you

continues

continued

what goes up must come down	there's a consequence for every action
with a pinch of salt	do not take literally
word of mouth	information told from one person to another
work out	how something ends up happening; also, to exercise

EXAM TIP

If you hear or read a phrase on the exam that truly does not make sense to you in context, it's probably an idiom. Try not to focus on the individual words, but instead see if you can pick up the meaning of the entire phrase from the framework of the rest of the sentence or passage.

Once you have learned the idioms I've shared with you, the internet is full of lists of common—and not-so-common—idioms in American English that you can challenge yourself to learn. The more idioms you know and can use correctly, the more fluent you will be.

The Least You Need to Know

- Idioms are expressions that don't make sense if you read the words literally.
- Prepositional idioms (idiomatic prepositions) are phrases that always use the same preposition.
- You can't learn the many English idioms, but you should learn as many as you can to help you on the TOEFL.

Chapter 18

Fluency

In This Chapter

- Using structure and solid organization for your Speaking and Writing responses
- Using transition words effectively
- What if you really don't know the word?
- Reading and listening effectively
- Writing and speaking without hesitating

In general, it's easy to get so focused on the topics you can study technically and memorize that you don't allow yourself to pay attention to the flow issues that help you become truly fluent. In this chapter, I'll cover all those issues that aren't specifically about grammar or vocabulary but can still trip you up in reading, listening, speaking, and writing in English. This chapter will help you not only with the TOEFL exam, but also with the admissions essays you'll write to get into your academic program of choice and everything you'll read and write while you're in that program.

First, I touch on structural and organization issues. I wrote about using templates to organize your responses in Chapters 9 and 12. Here I get into the general ideas of organization and typical structure in written English. The rest of the chapter will cover transition words, context, and fluency.

Structure and Organization

In some cultures and languages, beautiful writing is prized. In the United States, clear writing is the goal—which is not to say that people don't enjoy poetry or well-written fiction. But for academic writing, business writing, and even everyday person-to-person communication (letters, emails, texts, memos, reports), people prefer clarity. And clarity means structure.

The classic structure taught in school in the United States for an essay or speech is the five-paragraph essay. The format of the five-paragraph essay is as follows:

> Paragraph 1: State the issue and tell which side you will argue.
>
> Paragraph 2: Give a reason for your point of view and support it with data, facts, examples, or reasoning.
>
> Paragraph 3: Give a second reason for your point of view and support it with data, facts, examples, or reasoning.

Paragraph 4: Give a third reason for your point of view and support it with data, facts, examples, or reasoning.

Paragraph 5: Restate the issue and state how you proved your side.

Students learn this structure in elementary school and continue using it through middle school, high school, and all forms of higher education. Professionals write reports and memos based on the five-paragraph essay concept (with more or fewer reasoning paragraphs between the introduction and conclusion paragraphs, of course). People in the United States are used to it and expect it.

This means that you will do better on a test of English if you follow this structure, too. Go back and look at the templates for the Speaking and Writing sections in Chapters 9 and 12: they're set up as five-paragraph essays. That's because it seems to be the most standard way of setting up an essay in English. The raters are familiar with this structure.

Because the raters know this structure, they will be able to read more quickly and will have an easier time understanding your point. Remember the rubric for grading Writing essays? You get points for organization and structure. Using the five-paragraph essay by default in the Writing section makes it more likely the raters will give you a higher score.

You should also organize your responses on the Speaking section in a format close to the five-paragraph essay structure. You may not need to give three separate examples or reasons in response to some of the questions. However, doing an introduction in which you state the question and your position, add reasons for your position, and conclude with a restatement of your point is a good format that will allow the raters to better understand your argument and give it a higher score than they would a response that was not as well-organized.

EXAM TIP

If you run out of time or genuinely don't know what to say or write, start by stating the topic, come up with three points that relate somehow to the topic, and finish by restating the topic. At least your organization will be strong.

Transition Words

One of the ways you can tell what a passage or lecture is saying is by noticing the transition words that take you from one idea to another. Transition words tell you if the author or speaker is continuing with the same idea or switching to a different or even opposite idea. Transition words also tell you where one paragraph or idea ends and another begins. In other words, transition words and phrases are the signposts in an essay or spoken response that tell the reader and listener where they are in the piece and where the piece is going.

By the same token, you can use transition words in your own writing and spoken responses to increase your chances of the raters giving you better scores. A rater can recognize the structure and organization of your essay or spoken response by noting the transition words you use. Even if you are not sure of your answer and aren't confident you're using the right words or pronouncing some words correctly, if you use appropriate transition words, you will score better than you would if you didn't use any.

Some transition words are:

additionally
also
and
as a result
but
finally
first
for example
for instance
furthermore
however
in addition
in conclusion
in contrast
in fact
in summary
lastly
likewise
more importantly
moreover
on the other hand
second
similarly
therefore

PRACTICE TIP

Some transition words are going to feel more normal for you to use than others. Use different transition words while you practice to figure out which ones feel most natural to you so you can use them on the exam.

Transition words make the structure of a piece blatantly obvious. This is excellent when you're reading or listening and trying to understand what's being communicated. It's even more excellent when you're responding either in the Writing or Speaking section and you want the raters to give you a high score on your response. As you work on your writing and speaking, practice using different transition words with a template based on the five-paragraph essay until you find ones that feel natural to you to use.

Deciphering Words in Context

Even if you have a large vocabulary and have worked on learning Latin and Greek roots and lists of words (see Chapter 15), you still may encounter unfamiliar words on the TOEFL. Let's not forget there are thousands of commonly catalogued words in English, so it's possible that you'll hit some words on the exam you simply haven't seen before or have seen but don't know the exact meaning of.

You can help yourself understand a passage or lecture better if you practice figuring out words in the context of the sentence or paragraph they're in. You'll have to adjust your strategy depending on whether you're reading or listening, because they have different ways of delivering information and require different ways of managing time.

Your strategy will be relatively simple for reading passages, because you'll have a bit of time to spend figuring out the meaning of words you don't know while you're reading. Read through the passage and make a mental note of any words you don't know. Did you understand the point of the sentence without understanding that word? Sometimes you get the meaning of the sentence and realize it didn't even matter that you didn't know one specific word.

If you did not understand the meaning of the sentence without knowing that word, you'll have to do a little sleuthing. Pretend the word is a blank and use your reading skills to look at the rest of the sentence and figure out what kind of word should go into the blank. Do you know what part of speech it should be—noun, verb, adjective? Once you know which part of speech it is, work backward by figuring out what you already know about the spot containing the word you don't know. Is it part of a list of similar things? Are you told anything else about it in that sentence, the previous sentence, or the following sentence? Whatever you can use to help you is fair game.

And you don't need to figure out the exact meaning, either. It's okay just to know if the unfamiliar word is positive or negative, for example (if that makes sense in context). Just getting a vague idea of the meaning can help you to understand enough of the sentence to understand the paragraph and be able to formulate a response (or answer the multiple-choice questions, if it's the Reading section).

You'll have to use a different strategy when listening to a lecture, because you don't have any time to go back and look at the word or the sentence around the word. For a lecture, you have to figure it out as you hear the words, which doesn't give you much flexibility. You'll have to pick up as much of the sentence as possible and ignore the word you don't know.

That's right—ignore it. You don't have time to go back and use the "pretend it's a blank" technique you can use for a reading passage. And you can't even spend time wondering about it because then you'll miss the next sentence in the lecture. Essentially, you're sacrificing one word for the whole lecture.

WARNING

It is unlikely that one word will make or break your comprehension of an entire passage or lecture. So don't get so bogged down in figuring out the meaning of an unknown word that you run out of time or stop paying attention to the rest of the passage or lecture.

So listen carefully, but if you don't understand a word, don't think about it too much. You might get the meaning of the sentence anyway, and even if you don't, you can probably get the message of the paragraph. If you're in the Listening section, you may get the chance to listen to that sentence again to attempt to decipher the word. If not, it is likely that you will still be able to formulate a good response to the lecture or answer the multiple-choice questions.

Fluency for Reading and Listening

Fluency is an interesting word that means different things to different people. People usually think of it in terms of how well they can speak and, occasionally, write. But it also applies to reading and listening, too. It's one thing to be able to read simple texts, and to read slowly; it's another to be able to read more complicated pieces with technical or specific language, and to do so in a time limit.

It's also different to listen to conversations on specific topics or lectures on academic subjects without being able to watch the speaker. Most people practice listening to a different language by watching television or videos or talking in person to native speakers. Having to listen for understanding without being able to see the speaker's lips and body language is difficult and represents a higher level of listening skills.

I wish there was a magic bullet that would increase your reading and listening fluency. The solution is simply to read and listen with intention (you can find tips on how to do this in Chapters 3 and 6).

For reading practice, find academic passages of six to eight paragraphs on the internet or in textbooks and give yourself 10 minutes to read them. Write a quick summary of what you read. Then go back and reread to see how closely your summary matches and to take a closer look at the sections you didn't fully understand the first time. Repeat this process with at least one passage every night until you can understand the entire passage the first time through.

For listening practice, find videos of people giving academic lectures with subtitles, or use a television with a rewind feature and *captioning*. Turn away from the video or television and listen to part of the lecture. Write down a quick summary of what you heard. Then rewind and watch with the captions on and determine how closely your summary matches and try to understand any parts you didn't get the first time. Do one listening passage every night until you can understand everything the first time through.

DEFINITION

Captions are the words that run across the bottom of the television or movie screen and tell you what the announcer and characters are saying. Watching videos or television with the captions on will help your comprehension.

Fluency for Writing and Speaking

Fluency for writing and speaking involves using the correct grammar, choosing appropriate words and spelling them correctly, using correct capitalization and punctuation, and having proper pronunciation. If you are going to take the TOEFL, you must be able to use proper grammar and make appropriate word choices. If you are not confident in your ability to do these things, consider delaying taking the TOEFL until you have studied enough to feel ready.

Once you know you have near-perfect grammar, word choice, and spelling, you will need to work on capitalization and punctuation (for writing), following conventions, and pronunciation (for speaking). Once again, the best way to improve is to study and practice. There are punctuation and capitalization guides available on the internet. Consider purchasing a subscription to the online dictionary Visual Thesaurus (visualthesaurus.com), which has correct pronunciations for 55,000 words in American English for you to listen to.

Once you have your resources in place for studying fluency, practice timing yourself writing essays (remember: five-paragraph essays) on academic topics. Ask a native speaker friend to read your essays and help you identify mistakes you made, so you can learn as you go. The more you write and the more instruction you receive, the better you'll become at writing for the TOEFL.

Also, practice speaking on academic topics in 45- or 60-second time periods. Record your speech using an app on your phone or computer, then send the file to a native speaker friend to critique. As with writing, the more you practice and the more instruction you receive, the better you'll be.

The Least You Need to Know

- Having a definite structure to your words can help you get a better score on the Writing and Speaking sections of the TOEFL.
- Transition words are signposts that increase your chances of getting better scores from the raters.
- If you don't recognize a word in a passage or lecture, you may be able to figure it out in context. If you still can't figure it out—and it's not critical to getting the main idea of the passage or lecture—feel free to move on.
- You can improve your reading and listening skills by practicing the types of passages and lectures you'll encounter on the TOEFL.
- You can improve your fluency in speaking and writing by practicing the types of responses you'll give on the TOEFL and asking a native speaker to point out your mistakes.

Full-Length Practice Tests

Part

7

This part gives you the chance to practice what you've learned in this book, with two full-length tests. Chapters 19 and 21 contain full-length TOEFL exams, with Reading, Listening, Speaking, and Writing sections. Chapters 20 and 22 contain the answer keys and explanations for each exam.

Chapter 19

Practice Test 1

Now that you have studied and worked through the practice sections for all four sections of the TOEFL, it's time to take a full-length practice test. Set aside four hours in a quiet place near a computer, with a clean surface to work on. You should circle your answers to the multiple-choice questions in the Reading and Listening sections in the book. For the Speaking section, speak your response into your phone or a computer with voice-recoding software. For the Writing section, type your responses into a blank document on your computer. Make sure you have several pieces of blank paper to use for note-taking.

Be sure to give yourself a 10-minute break after the Listening section and before the Speaking section. Stay focused and keep going.

Good luck!

Reading Section

Give yourself 60 minutes to complete this section. Circle your answers to the questions in the book. You may take notes on your blank paper.

Passage 1

Types of Muscle in the Human Body

The human body contains muscle, a soft tissue made of protein filaments. The filaments move and flex in different ways to make the muscles contract and expand, supporting the body and producing motion. There are two primary types of muscle—skeletal ("voluntary") muscle and smooth ("involuntary") muscle. While the differences between skeletal muscle and smooth muscle are taught in elementary schools around the world, few of us were taught the differences between the two types of skeletal muscles: slow-twitch muscles and fast-twitch muscles. Slow-twitch and fast-twitch muscles are named for the relative speeds at which they twitch, or contract. The two types of muscle have different structures, compositions, actions, and functions and work together to keep our bodies in motion.

Slow-twitch muscles, officially called Type I muscles, are the muscles that provide endurance. They conduct oxygen and contain blood capillaries that give them a red color, so they are sometimes referred to as "red muscles." Slow-twitch muscles do not contract with significant force, but this is offset by the fact that they can contract for longer periods of time. Slow-twitch muscles process fats and carbohydrates to use as fuel for aerobic activity, carrying oxygen for endurance activities, such as long-distance running and cycling.

Fast-twitch muscles, officially called Type II muscles, are the muscles that provide strength and speed. There are two subtypes of fast-twitch muscles. Type IIa muscles are called intermediate fast-twitch muscles, and perform both aerobic and anaerobic functions equally. Type IIb muscles are what are traditionally thought of as fast-twitch muscles.

Fast-twitch muscles do not conduct oxygen, and are not red in color but white. They perform anaerobic activity, not aerobic, but contract quickly and forcefully. Fast-twitch muscles are the muscles that build bulk through weightlifting and other use because of the strength of contraction, and are useful in activities requiring speed and force, such as sprinting.

In general, the muscle fibers in our skeletal muscles are divided evenly between slow-twitch and fast-twitch muscles, but each individual's specific mix of types of muscles is determined genetically. This means that we may be predisposed to be better at some athletic activities than others. It may be true that we are "born runners," or weightlifters, or swimmers because of our skeletal and muscle structures.

However, humans have the ability to change our bodies and prevail over genetics by altering which form of muscle is prominent in our bodies. The more we work one of the two types, the more predominant that type will become. This can be seen in professional and elite athletes, who have muscle structures that reflect the different demands of their particular sports. For example, sprinters' bodies and long-distance runners' bodies reflect the fact that sprinters use fast-twitch muscles more predominately and long-distance runners use slow-twitch muscles more predominately. This change does not happen overnight, however, and is the result of years of specific and intentional training.

This is not to say that elite athletes only focus on one type of muscle and ignore the other type. Even endurance athletes need well-developed fast-twitch muscles, and sprint and weight athletes need well-developed slow-twitch muscles. Many athletes focus on working both types of muscles specifically, through different forms of athletic training, to maintain balance and support for their sports. They also support the development of balanced muscle types through diet, as the two types of muscle are fueled by different nutrients.

Researchers have gone from the basic discovery that muscle is comprised of bundled protein fibers and expanded on that knowledge to understand exactly how the different types of muscles function. This has allowed sports medicine and athletic performance researchers to create programs to train athletes to achieve better performance with fewer injuries. These athletic gains based on understanding slow-twitch and fast-twitch muscles and how they function are being used in medicine to heal patients more quickly and with less lasting trauma.

1. What is the main idea of the passage?

   (A) The two main types of muscle are skeletal and smooth.

   (B) Skeletal and smooth muscles are known as Type I and Type II muscles, respectively.

   (C) The two types of skeletal muscles, slow-twitch and fast-twitch, have different functions and uses.

   (D) Slow-twitch and fast-twitch muscles can be trained with different exercises.

2. The word *anaerobic* in the passage is closest in meaning to

   (A) cardio

   (B) using oxygen

   (C) not using oxygen

   (D) fast

3. The word *twitch* in the passage is closest in meaning to

   (A) shake

   (B) freeze

   (C) run

   (D) fiber

4. The phrase *two types* in the passage refers to

   (A) smooth and skeletal

   (B) voluntary and involuntary

   (C) Type IIa and Type IIb

   (D) slow-twitch and fast-twitch

5. In the second paragraph, why does the author include the information about the length of contractions?

   (A) to explain how slow-twitch muscles provide endurance

   (B) to give evidence that slow-twitch muscles are red

   (C) to show why capillaries carry oxygen

   (D) to describe why strength training is necessary

6. Which of the following can be inferred from the fourth paragraph about the color of fast-twitch muscles?

   (A) The color of fast-twitch muscles is determined by the strength of their contractions.

   (B) The color of fast-twitch muscles varies from person to person.

   (C) The color of fast-twitch muscles is red.

   (D) The color of fast-twitch muscles is determined by them not carrying oxygen.

7. According to the passage, sprinters use more fast-twitch muscles than slow-twitch muscles because

   (A) sprinting involves endurance more than speed and strength

   (B) sprinting involves speed and strength more than endurance

   (C) sprinters are born with more fast-twitch muscles

   (D) sprinters use more oxygen than long-distance runners

8. The author implies in the eighth paragraph that understanding the differences between fast-twitch and slow-twitch muscles can

   (A) help athletes prevent injury and heal faster

   (B) cause genetic changes in athletes

   (C) inspire more athletes to become sprinters

   (D) increase the oxygen processed by the two types of muscles

9. According to the passage, all of the following are true about fast-twitch and slow-twitch muscles EXCEPT

   (A) Each person has a mix of slow-twitch and fast-twitch muscles.

   (B) A person can change the mix of fast-twitch and slow-twitch muscles in the body.

   (C) Athletes can train both fast-twitch and slow-twitch muscles.

   (D) Working one type of muscle strengthens that type of muscle.

10. Sum up the passage by choosing three of the six sentences below and putting them in the correct order following the introductory sentence. The incorrect sentences will express information that was not in the passage or were minor ideas in the passage. This question is worth 2 points.

    There are two types of skeletal muscle in the human body: fast-twitch muscle and slow-twitch muscle.

    *

    *

    *

    1. Fast-twitch muscle is responsible for endurance, while slow-twitch muscle is responsible for speed and strength.
    2. Fast-twitch muscle is responsible for speed and strength, while slow-twitch muscle is responsible for endurance.
    3. Long-distance runners must train for more hours a day than sprinters, because the slow-twitch muscles take longer to become fully developed than fast-twitch muscles.
    4. Fast-twitch muscles and slow-twitch muscles can be identified by the color they are.
    5. By understanding the differences between the two types of muscle, athletes, trainers, and doctors can help athletes perform better and can heal patients with muscle injuries.
    6. Humans all have both types of muscle, but athletes strengthen the type of muscle they use more in training and performance.

This is not to say that elite athletes only focus on one type of muscle and ignore the other type. Even endurance athletes need well-developed fast-twitch muscles, and sprint and weight athletes need well-developed slow-twitch muscles. Many athletes focus on working both types of muscles specifically, through different forms of athletic training, to maintain balance and support for their sports. They also support the development of balanced muscle types through diet, as the two types of muscle are fueled by different nutrients.

11. Which of the following choices best expresses the essential meaning of the highlighted sentence in the passage? Incorrect choices will change the meaning or leave out important details.

    (A) The type of muscle athletes work with primarily will be the type of muscle they work on almost exclusively, although some athletes may choose to balance their muscles by working the other type occasionally.

    (B) The type of muscle an athlete works primarily will determine how much success that athlete has in a chosen sport.

    (C) Athletes who use one type of muscle primarily do not need to focus on the other type of muscle, although they will be better balanced if they do.

    (D) Athletes who use one type of muscle primarily still need to work on the other type of muscle for balance and to stay in condition for their chosen sport.

12. The passage implies that
    (A) athletes have more muscles than nonathletes
    (B) there is a connection between athletic performance and medicine
    (C) athletes cannot train for their sports if they do not understand the differences between fast-twitch and slow-twitch muscles
    (D) the genetic preset a person has of the mix of fast-twitch muscles and slow-twitch muscles can be changed with enough work

Passage 2

Carthage: From Founding to Conquest

The works of Carthaginian traders and merchants are truly astonishing. They are credited with the invention of clear glass and the bireme—or two-decked—galley, among many other noteworthy achievements. The modern-day city of Barcelona is named after the famous Barca family of Carthage. However, Carthage is far less well known by modern scholars than it should be, considering the contributions made to the world by this great civilization and by its fascinating military history.

Legend has it that the first Queen of Carthage, Dido, fled Phoenicia after her brother killed her husband. She landed in North Africa and asked the locals for a piece of land that could be "bounded by a bull's hide." The locals agreed, thinking that the land that could be encircled by the skin of a cow was not considerable. Dido, however, ripped the bull's hide into thin strips and enclosed a vast space. The locals, having agreed to give her land that could be enclosed by a bull's hide, were forced to comply and give her a large amount of land, which she took. On that land she built Carthage. Dido eventually committed suicide, but the city she began flourished.

As Carthage grew up, it obtained an empire, mostly by sea trade on the Mediterranean. The Carthaginians were in control of Spain and the lucrative silver mines there, and so they expanded into southern Gaul. The Romans were intimidated by the Carthaginian expansion. Sea warfare was not Rome's strength, so its navy was undeveloped. The Carthaginians, however, had hundreds of trade fleets that could easily be equipped with rams and ballistae, making it easy for them to make an oversized fleet in a week's notice. The Romans were afraid of a massive Carthaginian assault that could land half a mile from Rome and the Senate houses at any time. They decided to use land fighting to cripple the Carthaginians, because land was where the farms and cities were. The Romans had the best army, and Carthage had the best navy. The battle shaped up to pit a massive naval power against a massive land power.

Thus began the Punic Wars. The Carthaginians were defeated in the First Punic War, and they had to cede to Rome their territory in Sicily and Gaul. In the Second Punic War, the Carthaginians were blessed with a fabulous general in Hannibal Barca, who was a legendary military genius. He took elephants, a massive force of ancient armies, Carthaginian African soldiers from Libya and Poeni, and Iberian infantry, among other things. He marched over the Alps, crushing the Romans at Lake Trasimene and the river Trebia. His greatest achievement, however, was the destruction of the Roman army at Cannae.

Outnumbered, Hannibal engineered a plan to ambush the Romans, in which he killed 40,000 Romans for the loss of only 5,000 Carthaginians. He deployed his infantry in a crescent formation, horns to the rear, and the Romans advanced right into it. The crescent reversed itself, horns to the enemy, so to the Romans it looked like the Carthaginian front line was crumbling. This encouraged them, and they had their entire army attack the Carthaginian "front line." At that time, Hannibal gave the signal. Thousands of fresh Carthaginian forces swooped in from behind hills and surrounded the Romans on three sides. Then Hannibal gave another signal. The Spanish cavalry swung around and surrounded the Romans again. Roman morale was dashed. They fought to the last man, with no Roman survivors. All that remained of an entire generation of Roman young men was a heap of corpses.

Despite the efforts of Hannibal, however, the Romans eventually prevailed and confiscated Carthaginian holdings in Spain. In the Third Punic War, the inevitable end came for Carthage. In 168 B.C.E., Carthage was captured by Scipio Aemilianus. He ordered the inhabitants of the city enslaved or put to the sword, and the entire city taken apart brick by brick until Carthage was just a heap of rubble. Then he ordered that salt be sprinkled on the site where the city once stood, so not even weeds would grow in memory of Carthage.

13. What is the main idea of the passage?

    (A) to describe the rise and fall of Carthage

    (B) to explain who Dido was

    (C) to detail Hannibal's contribution to military strategy

    (D) to question the importance of Carthage in history

14. The word *locals* in the passage is closest in meaning to

    (A) generals

    (B) residents

    (C) cities

    (D) houses

15. The word *fleet* in the passage is closest in meaning to

    (A) swift and easy

    (B) lightweight vessel

    (C) group of ships

    (D) army battalion

16. The word *crescent* in the passage is closest in meaning to

    (A) half-moon shape

    (B) cylindrical shape

    (C) oval shape

    (D) cross shape

17. In the fifth paragraph, the word *them* refers to
    (A) horns
    (B) crescents
    (C) Carthaginians
    (D) Romans
18. In the fourth paragraph, the author mentions elephants and African soldiers in order to
    (A) give examples of Hannibal's military genius
    (B) question the authenticity of Hannibal's methods
    (C) deny claims that the Roman army was superior
    (D) maintain an antimilitary stance
19. It can be inferred from the passage that
    (A) Carthage would have survived if Hannibal had not been its military leader
    (B) naval power is less important than army power
    (C) Carthage was not as great as Rome
    (D) a larger army can be defeated by a smaller army if the larger army is trapped
20. Which of the following can be inferred from the passage about Rome's military power?
    (A) Rome's larger army did not defeat Carthage in every battle.
    (B) Rome's larger army provided a rapid defeat of Carthage.
    (C) Rome's military power was earned through battling Carthage.
    (D) Rome's military power was no match for Hannibal's strategy.
21. The passage states that Carthage obtained most of its territory
    (A) by defeating Rome at sea
    (B) by trading along the Mediterranean
    (C) by battling African soldiers
    (D) by marking out an area with cow hide
22. The author of the passage mentions the order that salt be sprinkled on the grounds of Carthage in order to
    (A) build a case against Rome's military superiority
    (B) explain why Hannibal used the crescent formation
    (C) describe the environmental conditions at Carthage
    (D) indicate how final Carthage's defeat was

Outnumbered, Hannibal engineered a plan to ambush the Romans, in which he killed 40,000 Romans for the loss of only 5,000 Carthaginians. He deployed his infantry in a crescent formation, horns to the rear, and the Romans advanced right into it. The crescent reversed itself, horns to the enemy, so to the Romans it looked like the Carthaginian front line was crumbling. This encouraged them, and they had their entire army attack the Carthaginian "front line." At that time, Hannibal gave the signal. Thousands of fresh Carthaginian forces swooped in from behind hills and surrounded the Romans on three sides. Then Hannibal gave another signal. The Spanish cavalry swung around and surrounded the Romans again. Roman morale was dashed. They fought to the last man, with no Roman survivors. All that remained of an entire generation of Roman young men was a heap of corpses.

23. Which of the following choices best expresses the essential meaning of the highlighted sentence in the passage? Incorrect choices will change the meaning or leave out important details.
    (A) Hannibal gave two signals to tell two different armies to advance, trapping the Roman army in the middle and killing all the Roman soldiers.
    (B) Hannibal gave two different signals to two different armies to advance, trapping the Roman army in the middle, and the Roman army surrendered.
    (C) First Hannibal gave a signal to the Carthaginian army, then to the Spanish army. After the signals, the Roman army admitted defeat.
    (D) First Hannibal gave a signal to the Spanish army, then to the Carthaginian army. After the signals, the Roman army was defeated.

24. According to the passage, which of the following was responsible for the Carthaginian win at Cannae?
    (A) the Spanish cavalry
    (B) Scipio Aemilianus
    (C) Hannibal's strategy
    (D) sea trade on the Mediterranean

Passage 3

The United States Senate Hierarchy

The Senate is part of the bicameral legislature of the United States, called the United States Congress. The United States Congress is made up of two houses: the House of Representatives (the lower house) and the Senate (the upper house). Members of the House of Representatives are elected by voters in the states they represent, and the number of representatives a state sends to the House is determined by the total population of that state. The Senate is comprised of two senators from each state, no matter what the population of the state is, elected by the voters of that state. Senators serve six-year terms, with the two senators from each state serving staggered terms so they are never both up for reelection at the same time. Senators may be reelected an unlimited number of times. There are no term limits in the United States Congress. The lack of term limits has created hierarchies in the Senate.

The official hierarchy in the Senate consists of the majority and the minority, which refer to the number of senators each of the two parties (Democrats and Republicans) has in the Senate. The party with the most members is called the majority party, and the party with the second largest number of members is called the minority party. Members of another party are not considered in the majority and minority calculation unless they officially caucus with one of the two major parties.

The majority party always has more power than the minority party, simply because in a straight vote the majority party will have more votes than the minority party. This does not mean that on any individual bill the majority party will win, because senators can always vote across party lines. But the majority party tends to be a voting bloc, as does the minority party, so the majority party controls most of the legislation passed in a session.

The leader of the majority party within the Senate is called the Senate majority leader, and the leader of the minority party within the Senate is called the Senate minority leader. Together they are called floor leaders. The Democrats began the practice of electing a floor leader in 1920 when they were the minority party, and the Republicans soon followed suit. Thus, electing floor leaders is a tradition in the Senate but not written into the Senate rules. The floor leaders speak as the official representatives of their party within the Senate and externally. The Senate majority leader serves as the voice of the Senate and may serve as the voice of the entire Congress, depending on the makeup of the House of Representatives. The Senate majority leader also schedules debates and votes, thereby controlling the schedule of the Senate. The Senate majority leader does not preside over the Senate, however—that task is reserved for the vice president, although few vice presidents have presided over actual debates in the last 60 years. The Senate may elect a president pro tempore to act in the vice president's place to preside over debates.

The two senators for each state also have an official hierarchy. The senator who has been in office for longer is called the senior senator, while the senator who has been in office for less time is called the junior senator. As these honorifics have no relationship to the ages of the senators, it is possible for a junior senator to be older than a senior senator. These titles are merely a tradition, however, and do not serve a practical purpose. The only privilege the senior senator has over the junior senator is in the choosing of physical offices.

The hierarchical traditions of the United States Senate are an interesting mix of the formal system under the monarchy of England and the democratic ideals of the Roman Senate. The official hierarchy does not adequately express the unofficial but traditional hierarchy of status and power within the Senate, which is a holdover from the English monarchy. Even 240 years after the creation of the United States Senate, the English roots of our nation remain represented by the traditions of our elected bodies.

25. The main idea of the passage is

    (A) to discuss the Senate majority leader

    (B) to explain the U.S. bicameral legislature

    (C) to determine which party has the majority in the U.S. Senate

    (D) to describe the hierarchy of the U.S. Senate

26. The word *majority* in the passage is closest in meaning to

    (A) larger

    (B) smaller

    (C) older

    (D) newer

27. The word *bloc* in the passage is closest in meaning to

    (A) government

    (B) prevent

    (C) unit

    (D) achievement

28. The word *voice* in the passage is closest in meaning to

    (A) spokesperson

    (B) singer

    (C) secretary

    (D) president

29. The phrase *these honorifics* in the passage refers to

    (A) Senate majority leader and Senate minority leader

    (B) senator and representative

    (C) senior senator and junior senator

    (D) president pro tempore and vice president

30. The author mentions the titles "junior senator" and "senior senator" in the paragraph in order to

    (A) list the two most important positions in the Senate

    (B) give an example of hierarchies that have little practical effect

    (C) explain the process of becoming president pro tempore of the Senate

    (D) reject the assertion that the Senate majority leader has the most power in the Senate

31. Which of the following can be inferred from the passage about the Senate minority leader?

    (A) The Senate minority leader is a senior senator.

    (B) The Senate minority leader gets paid less than the Senate majority leader.

    (C) The Senate minority leader only speaks once the Senate majority leader has spoken.

    (D) The Senate minority leader has less power to influence votes than the Senate majority leader.

32. You can infer from the passage that

    (A) larger states have more senators than smaller states

    (B) states all have the same number of senators, no matter the size or population

    (C) population size determines the number of senators a state has, not physical size

    (D) states with senior senators have more senators than states with only junior senators

33. All of the following can be inferred from the passage EXCEPT

    (A) The Senate majority leader and Senate minority leader are chosen by their respective parties.

    (B) A voting bloc means that all members of the bloc vote the same way on an issue.

    (C) The junior senator gets to choose an office before the senior senator.

    (D) The Senate majority leader does not run voting procedures in the Senate.

34. According to the third paragraph, the majority party has more power because

    (A) it has the title "majority party"

    (B) it has a bigger budget than the minority party

    (C) it has a stronger leader than the minority party

    (D) it has more votes than the minority party

The leader of the majority party within the Senate is called the Senate majority leader, and the leader of the minority party within the Senate is called the Senate minority leader. Together they are called floor leaders. The Democrats began the practice of electing a floor leader in 1920 when they were the minority party, and the Republicans soon followed suit. Thus, electing floor leaders is a tradition in the Senate but not written into the Senate rules. The floor leaders speak as the official representatives of their party within the Senate and externally.

35. Which of the following choices best expresses the essential meaning of the highlighted sentence in the passage? Incorrect choices will change the meaning or leave out important details.

    (A) The floor leaders, also called the Senate majority leader and the Senate minority leader, are the leaders of their respective parties in the Senate.

    (B) The Senate majority leader is one of the floor leaders who leads his or her respective party in the Senate.

    (C) The Senate majority leader and Senate minority leader are elected by their parties by tradition but not by a rule.

    (D) The Senate floor leaders are elected through a process dating back to 1920.

36. Look at the four bullets in the passage and indicate where the sentence below should be inserted.

    The senior senator has no official power over the junior senator, and the junior senator does not need to defer to the senior senator.

    (A) The senior senator has no official power over the junior senator, and the junior senator does not need to defer to the senior senator. •The two senators for each state also have an official hierarchy. •The senator who has been in office for longer is called the senior senator, while the senator who has been in office for less time is called the junior senator. •As these honorifics have no relationship to the ages of the senators, it is possible for a junior senator to be older than a senior senator. These titles are merely a tradition, however, and do not serve a practical purpose. •The only privilege the senior senator has over the junior senator is in the choosing of physical offices.

    (B) •The two senators for each state also have an official hierarchy. The senior senator has no official power over the junior senator, and the junior senator does not need to defer to the senior senator. •The senator who has been in office for longer is called the senior senator, while the senator who has been in office for less time is called the junior senator. •As these honorifics have no relationship to the ages of the senators, it is possible for a junior senator to be older than a senior senator. These titles are merely a tradition, however, and do not serve a practical purpose. •The only privilege the senior senator has over the junior senator is in the choosing of physical offices.

    (C) •The two senators for each state also have an official hierarchy. •The senator who has been in office for longer is called the senior senator, while the senator who has been in office for less time is called the junior senator. The senior senator has no official power over the junior senator, and the junior senator does not need to defer to the senior senator. •As these honorifics have no relationship to the ages of the senators, it is possible for a junior senator to be older than a senior senator. These titles are merely a tradition, however, and do not serve a practical purpose. •The only privilege the senior senator has over the junior senator is in the choosing of physical offices.

    (D) •The two senators for each state also have an official hierarchy. •The senator who has been in office for longer is called the senior senator, while the senator who has been in office for less time is called the junior senator. •As these honorifics have no relationship to the ages of the senators, it is possible for a junior senator to be older than a senior senator. These titles are merely a tradition, however, and do not serve a practical purpose. The senior senator has no official power over the junior senator, and the junior senator does not need to defer to the senior senator. •The only privilege the senior senator has over the junior senator is in the choosing of physical offices.

Listening Section

Give yourself 60 minutes to complete this section.

Lecture 1

Listen to audio track 19.1 on idiotsguides.com/toefl.

1. Why does the student visit the library?

   (A) to check out a book

   (B) to ask for help with research

   (C) to pick up material for a class

   (D) to use the internet

2. Why could the librarian not give the student the course pack?

   (A) The librarian could not find the student's account in the system.

   (B) The student needed to print the course pack on a computer.

   (C) The internet was down.

   (D) The student had not paid for the course pack yet.

3. How can the student pay for the course pack?

   (A) by giving the librarian cash

   (B) by giving the librarian a credit card

   (C) by using a credit card on the internet

   (D) by giving cash to the professor

Listen to audio track 19.2 on idiotsguides.com/toefl.

4. What did the librarian mean?

   (A) Everything at her desk is free.

   (B) She can't process a credit card at that desk.

   (C) The course pack is too expensive.

   (D) The student does not need to pay for the course pack.

5. What will the student do now?

   (A) Use a credit card to order the course pack on a computer in the library.

   (B) Give the librarian his credit card to pay for the course pack.

   (C) Email his professor to ask about buying the course pack.

   (D) Make copies of important readings for a political theories class.

Lecture 2

Listen to audio track 19.3 on idiotsguides.com/toefl.

6. Why does the student visit Health Services?

   (A) The student is feeling sick.

   (B) The student needs to buy insurance.

   (C) The student needs to pay the doctor.

   (D) The student needs to enroll as a full-time student.

7. How much does the student have to pay for the visit to Health Services?

   (A) nothing, as she is a full-time student

   (B) nothing, because she will be billed later

   (C) twenty dollars, and insurance will cover the rest

   (D) a fee determined by a sliding scale

8. According to the health worker, why will the prescription be filled at the pharmacy on West University?

   (A) The pharmacy is in the Social Work building.

   (B) The pharmacy may not have the prescription the student needs.

   (C) The pharmacy is part of the university health system.

   (D) The pharmacy is close to the student's room.

Listen to audio track 19.4 on idiotsguides.com/toefl.

9. What did the health worker mean?

   (A) The student needs to wait in a crowded waiting room with no room to sit down.

   (B) The student should wait, but may not get to see a nurse practitioner.

   (C) She could get the student a short appointment in 30 minutes.

   (D) She could get the student an appointment that lasts 30 minutes in three hours.

10. What will the student do in half an hour?

    (A) go to the pharmacy

    (B) be examined by the nurse practitioner

    (C) pay an office visit fee

    (D) go to class

Lecture 3

Listen to audio track 19.5 on idiotsguides.com/toefl.

11. What is the topic of the lecture?

    (A) martial arts

    (B) boxing

    (C) the Boxer Rebellion

    (D) the siege of Beijing

12. According to the professor, the Boxers thought that training in martial arts and eating correctly would

    (A) make them bulletproof

    (B) make them peasants

    (C) make them missionaries

    (D) defeat the royal army

13. The lecture states that the Eight-Nation Alliance

    (A) maintained the cease-fire between the missionaries and the Boxers

    (B) defeated the Boxers and the royal army

    (C) defeated the missionaries and foreigners

    (D) were financed by the royal army

Listen to audio track 19.6 on idiotsguides.com/toefl.

14. What does the professor mean when she says this?

    (A) There were twice as many Chinese people as there were missionaries, and this angered the Chinese.

    (B) The Chinese people could not live up to the expectations of the missionaries and felt bad about it.

    (C) The missionaries only wanted friendship with the Chinese, but the Chinese rejected them.

    (D) The foreigners were not subject to the same laws and rules the Chinese people were, and that made the Chinese people angry.

15. How does the professor show what caused the Boxer Rebellion?

    (A) by detailing the Boxers' training methods and philosophy

    (B) by discussing the conditions in China when the missionaries arrived to explain the Boxers' motivations

    (C) by asking why the droughts and floods happened so that students could understand the unfairness of these conditions

    (D) by explaining why the missionaries came to China and what they planned to accomplish there

16. The lecture implies that

    (A) racial tension was part of the cause of the Boxer Rebellion

    (B) the Empress Dowager had no power

    (C) the drought caused the missionaries to come to China

    (D) the end of the Boxer Rebellion brought stability

Lecture 4

Listen to audio track 19.7 on idiotsguides.com/toefl.

17. What is the topic of the lecture?

    (A) government-owned television channels

    (B) the influence of television on language development

    (C) how the Norwegian language developed

    (D) the evolution of four Scandinavian languages

18. According to the lecture, why were pockets of Norwegian people speaking an old-fashioned form of Norwegian?

    (A) They did not understand any other languages.

    (B) They are a small island nation without access to external languages.

    (C) They were isolated by mountains and did not hear others speaking more modern versions of the language.

    (D) They did not want to speak anything that was close to Swedish or Danish.

19. The professor states that because Iceland is so isolated

    (A) Icelandic is closer to Swedish and Danish than Norwegian

    (B) Icelandic is closer to Old Norse than the other three languages

    (C) Icelandic people all speak English

    (D) Iceland is not part of Scandinavia

Listen to audio track 19.8 on idiotsguides.com/toefl.

20. What does the professor mean when she says this?

    (A) Iceland has an opposite situation from the situations of Sweden and Denmark.

    (B) Iceland has had extremely rapid language change.

    (C) Iceland is far away from the rest of Scandinavia.

    (D) Icelandic people do not understand Swedish or Danish.

21. How does the professor show the way governments use technology to influence language?
    (A) She describes the Icelandic government's use of island culture to influence language.
    (B) She describes the Norwegian government's use of television to promote nynorsk to citizens.
    (C) She describes the Swedish government's use of flat lands to encourage interaction with other Swedes.
    (D) She describes the Danish government's use of the internet to promote the Danish language to other countries.
22. You can infer from the lecture that the professor
    (A) does not like Finnish
    (B) does not consider Finland part of Scandinavia
    (C) thinks Iceland should become more modern
    (D) thinks technology facilitates language evolution

Lecture 5

Listen to audio track 19.9 on idiotsguides.com/toefl.

23. What is the topic of the lecture?
    (A) pricing products and dead weight loss
    (B) calculating dead weight loss
    (C) operating in a monopolistic environment
    (D) making widgets
24. According to the lecture, a competitive environment means that
    (A) there is one firm selling one product
    (B) there is one firm selling multiple products
    (C) there are multiple firms selling the same product
    (D) there are multiple firms selling different products
25. The lecture says that dead weight loss is a loss to society because
    (A) the product should be priced lower to attract more customers
    (B) the customer is not willing to spend more money to buy the product, and this is anticapitalistic
    (C) the product is not worth the money the customer is willing to purchase it for
    (D) the money the customer would have spent on the product is now not spent at all

Listen to audio track 19.10 on idiotsguides.com/toefl.

26. What does the professor mean when she says this?

    (A) The UltraWidget cannot be manufactured by any firm, so customers cannot have it.

    (B) The UltraWidget is a special product that only one firm makes, and some customers are only satisfied with this product.

    (C) The UltraWidget is a regular widget, just with the name "ultra" on it.

    (D) The UltraWidget is sold in a competitive environment at marginal cost.

27. How does the professor show that the optimal price in a monopoly can be calculated?

    (A) The professor gives examples of the number of customers that will buy at different prices.

    (B) The professor shows the social good that is lost from dead weight loss.

    (C) The professor discusses the logistics of the manufacturing process.

    (D) The professor explains why marginal cost equals marginal revenue in a competitive environment.

28. The lecture implies that a monopolistic firm can charge what it wants to for a product because

    (A) no other firm has lower production costs

    (B) other firms are price-makers, while the monopolistic firm is a price-taker

    (C) it is the only firm making that product, so customers cannot get a lower price from another firm

    (D) customers do not actually need that product and are satisfied with other products as substitutes

Lecture 6

Listen to audio track 19.11 on idiotsguides.com/toefl.

29. What is the topic of the lecture?

    (A) the four types of LEED certification

    (B) new buildings versus old buildings

    (C) different types of construction materials

    (D) LEED certification of buildings

30. According to the lecture, LEED certification levels are based on

    (A) earning points for compliance with different requirements

    (B) making a favorable impression on the LEED judges

    (C) following the proper procedures for submitting a portfolio

    (D) constructing a building from one standardized blueprint

31. According to the professor, old buildings can be

    (A) improved but never completely efficient

    (B) as environmentally efficient as new buildings

    (C) modified but will not be as efficient as new buildings

    (D) less stable than newer buildings

Listen to audio track 19.12 on idiotsguides.com/toefl.

32. What does the professor mean when he says this?

    (A) Have you submitted your paper on LEED certification yet?

    (B) Have you already taken this class?

    (C) I don't know what LEED certification is.

    (D) I'm going to talk about LEED certification now.

33. Why does the professor discuss old buildings' thicker walls and smaller plots of land?

    (A) to demonstrate that old buildings will never earn all the points required for LEED certification

    (B) to explain how to build newer buildings

    (C) to show how they can be more efficient than new buildings

    (D) to discuss why they are less efficient than new buildings

34. The lecture implies that

    (A) while old buildings can be made more efficient, if they are not rehabilitated completely, they will not be as efficient as new buildings

    (B) a building that is certified while it is empty might not be certified once it is filled with tenants or residents

    (C) the selection of a site is the most important factor in obtaining LEED certification

    (D) LEED certification is primarily used for residential housing

Speaking Section

Give yourself 20 minutes to complete this section.

Question 1

Read the prompt and give yourself 15 seconds to prep and write notes. Then take 45 seconds to record your response.

1. Describe a person who has been a good influence on your life. Please include specific examples and details of this influence.

Question 2

Read the prompt and give yourself 15 seconds to prep and write notes. Then take 45 seconds to record your response.

2. Some students work to pay for their university studies, while others borrow money they will pay back later when they have jobs after graduation. Which method of financing university studies makes the most sense, and why?

Question 3

The university has changed the prices for parking passes for parking lots on campus. Read the email that has been sent to all parking pass holders. You will have 45 seconds to read the email. Begin reading now.

Email

To: Parking pass holders

From: University Parking Services

Subject: Parking Pass Prices to Increase in May

To all parking pass holders:

The university parking garage system has been redesigned to allocate more parking spots to faculty and staff who need to park close to their departments. As a result of this restructuring, the cost of parking passes for regular full-time students will increase according to the following schedule:

Green Pass (all lots, 24/7 access): Increase from $700 to $880

Blue Pass (limited lots, 24/7 access): Increase from $350 to $390

Yellow Pass (limited lots, 24/7 access): Increase from $320 to $360

Brown Pass (limited lots, 3 P.M. through 7 A.M. M-F access and weekends): Increase from $190 to $240

The price increase will take effect on the official renewal date, May 28. If you have a prorated pass for this year, it will be reset then to follow the official schedule. If you have any questions, please contact the Parking Services office.

Listen to audio track 19.13 on idiotsguides.com/toefl.

Now get ready to answer the question. Give yourself 30 seconds to create notes for your response. Then take 60 seconds to speak your response.

3. The woman has a problem stemming from the information in the email. State what the problem is and what she decides to do about that problem.

Question 4

In this question, you will read a short passage on an academic subject and then listen to a talk on the same topic. You will then answer a question using information from both the reading passage and the talk. After you hear the question, you will have 30 seconds to prepare your response and 60 seconds to speak.

Read the passage about the creation of labor unions. You will have 45 seconds to read the passage. Begin reading now.

The Industrial Revolution began a new era in the history of labor relations across the world and in the United States. As owners and managers began to see workers as increasingly interchangeable, because each worker only performed one small part of the manufacturing process, workers themselves became increasingly concerned with wages and working conditions. The Triangle Shirtwaist fire, in which workers at the Triangle Shirtwaist factory burned to death when a fire broke out—and they were locked in, so they could not leave their posts—galvanized a generation of workers and sparked protests that ultimately led to the creation of labor unions. Those unions advocated for workers to ensure that management was providing safe and humane working conditions.

Listen to audio track 19.14 on idiotsguides.com/toefl.

Now get ready to answer the question. Give yourself 30 seconds to create notes for your response. Then take 60 seconds to speak your response.

4. The professor describes the achievements of the unions and some problems with some unions. Explain how these achievements and problems relate to and contrast with each other.

Question 5

In this question, you will hear a conversation. Then you will be asked to talk about the conversation and give your opinion about the subject of the conversation. You will be given 20 seconds to prepare. Then you will be given 60 seconds to speak.

Listen to audio track 19.15 on idiotsguides.com/toefl.

Give yourself 20 seconds to create notes for your response. Then take 60 seconds to speak your response.

5. The students discuss how to print a document and what the woman's options are for printing. Describe the two options. Then explain which option you think she should pursue, and why.

Question 6

Listen to audio track 19.16 on idiotsguides.com/toefl.

Give yourself 20 seconds to create notes for your response. Then take 60 seconds to speak your response.

6. Using data and examples from the lecture, explain how the Babylonians expanded on existing astronomical study.

Writing Section

Give yourself 20 minutes for the first writing task and 30 minutes for the second writing task.

Integrated Writing Task

Reading:

> Plagiarism refers to the practice of copying or appropriating another's writing or other intellectual or artistic work as one's own. While it is considered a serious breach of ethics and can ruin careers and cause expulsion from academic programs today, plagiarism was not always seen as negative. In fact, centuries ago, students were encouraged to copy directly from the writers or artists they were studying as a way of training or apprenticing. It was thought that only by retracing the exact steps of the acknowledged masters could people learn creative skills. Students of painting practiced for hours to be able to emulate the exact brushstrokes of a revered artist, and the artists who were copied were aggrandized by all the copies of their work.
>
> In writing, form was considered at least as important, if not more so, than originality of thought. Students were taught to follow the forms of established writers and to prize eloquence and elegant turn of phrase over innovation of thought. For this reason, budding writers copied passages word for word to learn the phrasing and tone of the masters. Writers who copied the works of those they emulated did so to perfect their own craft, not to pass off the master's work as their own. Now, however, originality of thought is prized more highly even than eloquence is, so copying another's work is a serious intellectual crime.

Lecture: Listen to audio track 19.17 on idiotsguides.com/toefl.

1. Summarize the points made in the lecture, being sure to explain how they differ from the view in the reading passage.

Independent Writing Task

2. Do you agree or disagree with the following statement? Use specific details and examples to support your answer.

   It is better to be a good team player than to work individually.

Chapter 20

Practice Test 1 Answer Keys and Explanations

Here are the answer keys and explanations for the first practice test.

Reading Section Answer Key

1. C
2. C
3. A
4. D
5. A
6. D
7. B
8. A
9. B
10. 2, 6, 5
11. D
12. B
13. A
14. B
15. C
16. A
17. D
18. A
19. D
20. A
21. B
22. D
23. A
24. C
25. D
26. A
27. C
28. A
29. C
30. B

31. D
32. B
33. C
34. D
35. A
36. D

Reading Section Explanations

1. What is the main idea of the passage?

   (A) The two main types of muscle are skeletal and smooth.

   (B) Skeletal and smooth muscles are known as Type I and Type II muscles, respectively.

   (C) The two types of skeletal muscles, slow-twitch and fast-twitch, have different functions and uses.

   (D) Slow-twitch and fast-twitch muscles can be trained with different exercises.

   The answer is C. The passage talks about slow-twitch and fast-twitch muscles and the differences between them. Eliminate A, B, and D because they are all small parts of the passage but not the main point.

2. The word *anaerobic* in the passage is closest in meaning to

   (A) cardio

   (B) using oxygen

   (C) not using oxygen

   (D) fast

   The answer is C. *Aerobic* means "using oxygen," so *anaerobic* means "not using oxygen." Eliminate A and B because they both mean the opposite of anaerobic. Eliminate D because it is out of the scope of this lecture.

3. The word *twitch* in the passage is closest in meaning to

   (A) shake

   (B) freeze

   (C) run

   (D) fiber

   The answer is A. The passage states that *twitch* means "contract," which is similar to "shake." Eliminate B because it has the opposite meaning. Eliminate C and D because they do not mean "contract."

4. The phrase *two types* in the passage refers to

   (A) smooth and skeletal

   (B) voluntary and involuntary

   (C) Type IIa and Type IIb

   (D) slow-twitch and fast-twitch

   The answer is D. The sentence previous to this phrase refers to slow-twitch and fast-twitch muscles. Eliminate A and B because they are referenced only briefly and are not referred to by that phrase. Eliminate C because it is not mentioned until the next paragraph.

5. In the second paragraph, why does the author include the information about the length of contractions?

   (A) to explain how slow-twitch muscles provide endurance

   (B) to give evidence that slow-twitch muscles are red

   (C) to show why capillaries carry oxygen

   (D) to describe why strength training is necessary

   The answer is A. The author includes information about the length of contractions to show that these muscles provide endurance, not strength. Eliminate B and C because they refer to each other, not to the reason contractions are mentioned. Eliminate D because it is a misrepresentation of the information in the passage.

6. Which of the following can be inferred from the fourth paragraph about the color of fast-twitch muscles?

   (A) The color of fast-twitch muscles is determined by the strength of their contractions.

   (B) The color of fast-twitch muscles varies from person to person.

   (C) The color of fast-twitch muscles is red.

   (D) The color of fast-twitch muscles is determined by not carrying oxygen.

   The answer is D. There is a connection between carrying oxygen or not and being red or not. Eliminate A because it is not implied. Eliminate B because there is no evidence to support this in the passage. Eliminate C because the opposite is true.

7. According to the passage, sprinters use more fast-twitch muscles than slow-twitch muscles because

   (A) sprinting involves endurance more than speed and strength

   (B) sprinting involves speed and strength more than endurance

   (C) sprinters are born with more fast-twitch muscles

   (D) sprinters use more oxygen than long-distance runners

The answer is B. Sprinting requires speed and strength to run short distances quickly, and this uses fast-twitch muscles. Eliminate A because it is the opposite of the answer. Eliminate C because it misrepresents the information in the passage—some people are born with more fast-twitch muscles, but an athlete can develop the muscles they do have in the sport they participate in. Eliminate D because it does not have anything to do with the types of muscles.

8. The author implies in the eighth paragraph that understanding the differences between fast-twitch and slow-twitch muscles can

   (A) help athletes prevent injury and heal faster

   (B) cause genetic changes in athletes

   (C) inspire more athletes to become sprinters

   (D) increase the oxygen processed by the two types of muscles

   The answer is A. The passage states that understanding how different types of muscles work helps with performance and leads to fewer injuries, and that this knowledge in medicine is helping patients heal faster. Eliminate B because there is no indication in the passage that people can cause genetic changes in muscle. Eliminate C because there is no evidence of this in the passage. Eliminate D because this misrepresents information in the passage.

9. According to the passage, all of the following are true about fast-twitch and slow-twitch muscles EXCEPT

   (A) Each person has a mix of slow-twitch and fast-twitch muscles.

   (B) A person can change the mix of fast-twitch and slow-twitch muscles in the body.

   (C) Athletes can train both fast-twitch and slow-twitch muscles.

   (D) Working one type of muscle strengthens that type of muscle.

   The answer is B. The passage specifically states that a person's mix is determined genetically. Eliminate A, C, and D because they are all found in the passage.

10. Sum up the passage by choosing three of the six sentences below and putting them in the correct order following the introductory sentence. The incorrect sentences will express information that was not in the passage or were minor ideas in the passage. This question is worth 2 points.

    There are two types of skeletal muscle in the human body: fast-twitch muscle and slow-twitch muscle.

    *

    *

    *

    1. Fast-twitch muscle is responsible for endurance, while slow-twitch muscle is responsible for speed and strength.
    2. Fast-twitch muscle is responsible for speed and strength, while slow-twitch muscle is responsible for endurance.
    3. Long-distance runners must train for more hours a day than sprinters, because the slow-twitch muscles take longer to become fully developed than fast-twitch muscles.
    4. Fast-twitch muscles and slow-twitch muscles can be identified by the color they are.
    5. By understanding the differences between the two types of muscle, athletes, trainers, and doctors can help athletes perform better and can heal patients with muscle injuries.
    6. Humans all have both types of muscle, but athletes strengthen the type of muscle they use more in training and performance.

    The answer is 2, 6, 5. This sequence tells the function of each type of muscle, that those muscles can be strengthened with use, and why understanding the muscles is important. Eliminate 1 because it is the opposite of the function of each type of muscle. Eliminate 3 because it is not in the passage. Eliminate 4 because it is a small detail in the passage.

    This is not to say that elite athletes only focus on one type of muscle and ignore the other type. Even endurance athletes need well-developed fast-twitch muscles, and sprint and weight athletes need well-developed slow-twitch muscles. Many athletes focus on working both types of muscles specifically, through different forms of athletic training, to maintain balance and support for their sports. They also support the development of balanced muscle types through diet, as the two types of muscle are fueled by different nutrients.

11. Which of the following choices best expresses the essential meaning of the highlighted sentence in the passage? Incorrect choices will change the meaning or leave out important details.

    (A) The type of muscle athletes work with primarily will be the type of muscle they work on almost exclusively, although some athletes may choose to balance their muscles by working the other type occasionally.

    (B) The type of muscle an athlete works primarily will determine how much success that athlete has in a chosen sport.

    (C) Athletes who use one type of muscle primarily do not need to focus on the other type of muscle, although they will be better balanced if they do.

    (D) Athletes who use one type of muscle primarily still need to work on the other type of muscle for balance and to stay in condition for their chosen sport.

    The answer is D. It summarizes the highlighted section appropriately. Eliminate A and C because they shift the focus from the need to work both types of muscles. Eliminate B because this is a detail from an earlier part of the passage, not the highlighted section addressed here.

12. The passage implies that

    (A) athletes have more muscles than nonathletes

    (B) there is a connection between athletic performance and medicine

    (C) athletes cannot train for their sports if they do not understand the differences between fast-twitch and slow-twitch muscles

    (D) the genetic preset a person has of the mix of fast-twitch muscles and slow-twitch muscles can be changed with enough work

    The answer is B. The last paragraph draws a connection between performance and medicine. Eliminate A because this is not indicated in the passage. Eliminate C because this is a misrepresentation of the passage. Eliminate D because it is contradicted in the passage.

13. What is the main idea of the passage?

    (A) to describe the rise and fall of Carthage

    (B) to explain who Dido was

    (C) to detail Hannibal's contribution to military strategy

    (D) to question the importance of Carthage in history

    The answer is A. The passage describes Dido's creation of Carthage, major battles of Carthage, and the fall of Carthage. Eliminate B and C because Dido and Hannibal were only details in the passage. Eliminate D because the passage does the opposite by attempting to establish that Carthage was important in history.

14. The word *locals* in the passage is closest in meaning to

    (A) generals

    (B) residents

    (C) cities

    (D) houses

    The answer is B. *Locals* in the passage means "people who reside in the local area." This is closest in meaning to *residents.* Eliminate A, as it is a false opposite of the word. Eliminate C and D, as they refer to places instead of people.

15. The word *fleet* in the passage is closest in meaning to

    (A) swift and easy

    (B) lightweight vessel

    (C) group of ships

    (D) army battalion

    The answer is C. In the passage, *fleet* describes Carthage's group of ships. Eliminate A because it is a meaning for *fleet,* but not the meaning in the passage. Eliminate B because *fleet* describes a group of vessels, not one. Eliminate D because *fleet* describes boats, not something army-related.

16. The word *crescent* in the passage is closest in meaning to

    (A) half-moon shape

    (B) cylindrical shape

    (C) oval shape

    (D) cross shape

    The answer is A. A crescent is shaped like a half-moon, or a circle with a disc cut out of it. Eliminate B and C because they do not describe a crescent. Eliminate D because while *crescent* sounds similar to *cross,* the two shapes are not the same.

17. In the fifth paragraph, the word *them* refers to

    (A) horns

    (B) crescents

    (C) Carthaginians

    (D) Romans

    The answer is D. The formation of the Carthaginian army encouraged the Romans, who then went into the Carthaginians' trap. Eliminate A and B because they refer to part of the Carthaginian formation, not humans who could be encouraged. Eliminate C because *them* does not refer to the Carthaginians.

18. In the fourth paragraph, the author mentions elephants and African soldiers in order to

    (A) give examples of Hannibal's military genius

    (B) question the authenticity of Hannibal's methods

    (C) deny claims that the Roman army was superior

    (D) maintain an antimilitary stance

    The answer is A. The author mentions elephants and African soldiers, along with other items, as examples of Hannibal's leadership and genius. Eliminate B because there is no questioning in the passage. Eliminate C because it is too extreme. Eliminate D because it is out of the scope of the passage.

19. It can be inferred from the passage that

    (A) Carthage would have survived if Hannibal had not been its military leader

    (B) naval power is less important than army power

    (C) Carthage was not as great as Rome

    (D) a larger army can be defeated by a smaller army if the larger army is trapped

    The answer is D. Hannibal's crescent formation allowed the smaller army to defeat the larger army. Eliminate A because this is not implied in the passage at all. Eliminate B and C because they are too far of a reach from the information in the passage.

20. Which of the following can be inferred from the passage about Rome's military power?

    (A) Rome's larger army did not defeat Carthage in every battle.

    (B) Rome's larger army provided a rapid defeat of Carthage.

    (C) Rome's military power was earned through battling Carthage.

    (D) Rome's military power was no match for Hannibal's strategy.

    The answer is A. The passage details a battle in which Carthage defeated Rome. Eliminate B because Carthage's defeat was not rapid. Eliminate C, as it misrepresents the sequence of events in the passage. Eliminate D, as Rome eventually beat Carthage despite Hannibal.

21. The passage states that Carthage obtained most of its territory

    (A) by defeating Rome at sea

    (B) by trading along the Mediterranean

    (C) by battling African soldiers

    (D) by marking out an area with cow hide

    The answer is B. The passage says that Carthage expanded its territory through sea trade. Eliminate A because the passage does not discuss battles with Rome at sea. Eliminate C because Carthage did not battle against African soldiers. Eliminate D because this was how Carthage was established by Dido, but not how it was expanded.

22. The author of the passage mentions the order that salt be sprinkled on the grounds of Carthage in order to

    (A) build a case against Rome's military superiority

    (B) explain why Hannibal used the crescent formation

    (C) describe the environmental conditions at Carthage

    (D) indicate how final Carthage's defeat was

    The answer is D. This detail indicates how completely Carthage had been wiped away. Eliminate A because this has nothing to do with the detail mentioned. Eliminate B because the detail is from a different battle than the battle involving the crescent formation. Eliminate C because there is no description of environmental conditions in Carthage in the passage.

Outnumbered, Hannibal engineered a plan to ambush the Romans, in which he killed 40,000 Romans for the loss of only 5,000 Carthaginians. He deployed his infantry in a crescent formation, horns to the rear, and the Romans advanced right into it. The crescent reversed itself, horns to the enemy, so to the Romans it looked like the Carthaginian front line was crumbling. This encouraged them, and they had their entire army attack the Carthaginian "front line." At that time, Hannibal gave the signal. Thousands of fresh Carthaginian forces swooped in from behind hills and surrounded the Romans on three sides. Then Hannibal gave another signal. The Spanish cavalry swung around and surrounded the Romans again. Roman morale was dashed. They fought to the last man, with no Roman survivors. All that remained of an entire generation of Roman young men was a heap of corpses.

23. Which of the following choices best expresses the essential meaning of the highlighted sentence in the passage? Incorrect choices will change the meaning or leave out important details.

    (A) Hannibal gave two signals to tell two different armies to advance, trapping the Roman army in the middle and killing all the Roman soldiers.

    (B) Hannibal gave two different signals to two different armies to advance, trapping the Roman army in the middle, and the Roman army surrendered.

    (C) First Hannibal gave a signal to the Carthaginian army, then to the Spanish army. After the signals, the Roman army admitted defeat.

    (D) First Hannibal gave a signal to the Spanish army, then to the Carthaginian army. After the signals, the Roman army was defeated.

    The answer is A. This covers the two signals to two armies, the army movement that trapped the Romans, and the killing of the Roman soldiers. Eliminate B because it indicates that the Roman army surrendered instead of fighting. Eliminate C and D because they both skip any movement of the two armies.

24. According to the passage, which of the following was responsible for the Carthaginian win at Cannae?

    (A) the Spanish cavalry

    (B) Scipio Aemilianus

    (C) Hannibal's strategy

    (D) sea trade on the Mediterranean

    The answer is C. Hannibal's strategy and crescent formation allowed the smaller Carthaginian army to defeat the larger Roman army at Cannae. Eliminate A because the Spanish cavalry was only part of the victory. Eliminate B because he appeared later in Carthage's history. Eliminate D because sea trade had nothing to do with Cannae.

25. The main idea of the passage is

    (A) to discuss the Senate majority leader

    (B) to explain the U.S. bicameral legislature

    (C) to determine which party has the majority in the U.S. Senate

    (D) to describe the hierarchy of the U.S. Senate

    The answer is D. The passage describes the different hierarchies of the U.S. Senate. Eliminate A and B, as they are details of the passage, not the main idea. Eliminate C, as this is out of the scope of the passage.

26. The word *majority* in the passage is closest in meaning to

    (A) larger

    (B) smaller

    (C) older

    (D) newer

    The answer is A. *Majority* means the party with the larger number of members. Eliminate B because it is the opposite of the correct answer. Eliminate C and D because they refer to the length of time a party has been in office, not the size.

27. The word *bloc* in the passage is closest in meaning to

    (A) government

    (B) prevent

    (C) unit

    (D) achievement

    The answer is C. A voting bloc is a unit of members that all vote together. Eliminate A and D because they do not mean *bloc*. Eliminate B because one meaning of *block* is to prevent, but that is not the meaning of *bloc*.

28. The word *voice* in the passage is closest in meaning to

    (A) spokesperson

    (B) singer

    (C) secretary

    (D) president

    The answer is A. The voice of the party is the person who speaks for the party, or the spokesperson. Eliminate B because it has nothing to do with the Senate. Eliminate C and D because they do not mean *spokesperson*.

29. The phrase *these honorifics* in the passage refers to

    (A) Senate majority leader and Senate minority leader

    (B) senator and representative

    (C) senior senator and junior senator

    (D) president pro tempore and vice president

    The answer is C. In the highlighted passage, the phrase *these honorifics* directly follows the mention of the terms "senior senator" and "junior senator." Eliminate A and B because they are mentioned in earlier sections of the passage. Eliminate D because those honorifics are not specific to the Senate.

30. The author mentions the titles "junior senator" and "senior senator" in the paragraph in order to

    (A) list the two most important positions in the Senate

    (B) give an example of hierarchies that have little practical effect

    (C) explain the process of becoming president pro tempore of the Senate

    (D) reject the assertion that the Senate majority leader has the most power in the Senate

    The answer is B. Junior senator and senior senator are differentiating titles, but they have little practical effect. Eliminate A because those are not the two most important positions in the Senate. Eliminate C because there is no explanation of process in that part of the passage. Eliminate D because these titles are not mentioned to reject any assertions.

31. Which of the following can be inferred from the passage about the Senate minority leader?

    (A) The Senate minority leader is a senior senator.

    (B) The Senate minority leader gets paid less than the Senate majority leader.

    (C) The Senate minority leader only speaks once the Senate majority leader has spoken.

    (D) The Senate minority leader has less power to influence votes than the Senate majority leader.

The answer is D. The Senate minority leader has less power to influence votes because the minority party has fewer votes than the majority party. Eliminate A because that does not have to be true. Eliminate B because there is no information about salaries in the passage. Eliminate C because there is no information about speaking order in the passage.

32. You can infer from the passage that

    (A) larger states have more senators than smaller states

    (B) states all have the same number of senators, no matter the size or population

    (C) population size determines the number of senators a state has, not physical size

    (D) states with senior senators have more senators than states with only junior senators

    The answer is B. All states have two senators, no matter what the size or population of the state. Eliminate A, C, and D because they say that the number of senators vary.

33. All of the following can be inferred from the passage EXCEPT

    (A) The Senate majority leader and Senate minority leader are chosen by their respective parties.

    (B) A voting bloc means that all members of the bloc vote the same way on an issue.

    (C) The junior senator gets to choose an office before the senior senator.

    (D) The Senate majority leader does not run voting procedures in the Senate.

    The answer is C. The opposite can be inferred from the passage. Eliminate A because the passage says that the Senate majority and minority leaders are chosen by their respective parties. Eliminate B because a bloc indicates that all members vote the same way. Eliminate D because the leader of the Senate (vice president or president pro tempore) runs voting procedures in the Senate.

34. According to the third paragraph, the majority party has more power because

    (A) it has the title "majority party"

    (B) it has a bigger budget than the minority party

    (C) it has a stronger leader than the minority party

    (D) it has more votes than the minority party

    The answer is D. The majority party can win because it has more votes than the minority party if both parties vote as blocs. Eliminate A because the title alone has no power. Eliminate B because you have no information about budgets in the passage. Eliminate C because the leader is not necessarily stronger than the minority party leader.

The leader of the majority party within the Senate is called the Senate majority leader, and the leader of the minority party within the Senate is called the Senate minority leader. Together they are called floor leaders. The Democrats began the practice of electing a floor leader in 1920 when they were the minority party, and the Republicans soon followed suit. Thus, electing floor leaders is a tradition in the Senate but not written into the Senate rules. The floor leaders speak as the official representatives of their party within the Senate and externally.

35. Which of the following choices best expresses the essential meaning of the highlighted sentence in the passage? Incorrect choices will change the meaning or leave out important details.

    (A) The floor leaders, also called the Senate majority leader and the Senate minority leader, are the leaders of their respective parties in the Senate.

    (B) The Senate majority leader is one of the floor leaders who leads his or her respective party in the Senate.

    (C) The Senate majority leader and Senate minority leader are elected by their parties by tradition but not by a rule.

    (D) The Senate floor leaders are elected through a process dating back to 1920.

    The answer is A. This covers the two leaders and that they lead their respective parties. Eliminate B because it omits the Senate minority leader. Eliminate C because the tradition is not included in the highlighted section of text. Eliminate D because the information about 1920 is not included in the highlighted section of text.

36. Look at the four bullets in the passage and indicate where the sentence below should be inserted.

    The senior senator has no official power over the junior senator, and the junior senator does not need to defer to the senior senator.

    (A) The senior senator has no official power over the junior senator, and the junior senator does not need to defer to the senior senator. •The two senators for each state also have an official hierarchy. •The senator who has been in office for longer is called the senior senator, while the senator who has been in office for less time is called the junior senator. •As these honorifics have no relationship to the ages of the senators, it is possible for a junior senator to be older than a senior senator. These titles are merely a tradition, however, and do not serve a practical purpose. •The only privilege the senior senator has over the junior senator is in the choosing of physical offices.

    (B) •The two senators for each state also have an official hierarchy. The senior senator has no official power over the junior senator, and the junior senator does not need to defer to the senior senator. •The senator who has been in office for longer is called the senior senator, while the senator who has been in office for less time is called the junior senator. •As these honorifics have no relationship to the ages of the senators, it is possible for a junior senator to be older than a senior senator. These titles are merely a tradition, however, and do not serve a practical purpose. •The only privilege the senior senator has over the junior senator is in the choosing of physical offices.

(C) •The two senators for each state also have an official hierarchy. •The senator who has been in office for longer is called the senior senator, while the senator who has been in office for less time is called the junior senator. The senior senator has no official power over the junior senator, and the junior senator does not need to defer to the senior senator. •As these honorifics have no relationship to the ages of the senators, it is possible for a junior senator to be older than a senior senator. These titles are merely a tradition, however, and do not serve a practical purpose. •The only privilege the senior senator has over the junior senator is in the choosing of physical offices.

(D) •The two senators for each state also have an official hierarchy. •The senator who has been in office for longer is called the senior senator, while the senator who has been in office for less time is called the junior senator. •As these honorifics have no relationship to the ages of the senators, it is possible for a junior senator to be older than a senior senator. These titles are merely a tradition, however, and do not serve a practical purpose. The senior senator has no official power over the junior senator, and the junior senator does not need to defer to the senior senator. •The only privilege the senior senator has over the junior senator is in the choosing of physical offices.

The answer is D. The inserted sentence reiterates that there is no official power relationship between the junior and senior senators, and this placement expresses that. Eliminate A and B because they refer to the positions before they are explained. Eliminate C because it indicates a lack of power before that idea is introduced.

Listening Section Answer Key

1. C
2. D
3. C
4. B
5. A
6. A
7. A
8. D
9. C
10. B
11. C
12. A
13. B
14. D
15. B
16. A
17. D
18. C
19. B
20. A
21. B
22. D
23. A
24. C
25. D
26. B
27. A
28. C
29. D
30. A

31. B
32. D
33. C
34. B

Listening Section Explanations

Lecture 1

The following is a transcript of the conversation you heard.

Librarian: Good morning, can I help you?

Student: Hi. Um, yeah. I need the reference desk, or where the copy packs are.

Librarian: You need to pick up a copy pack for one of your classes?

Student: Yes. For my political theories class. Do I need to know the number of the class?

Librarian: No. We have the copy packs sorted by student ID number. Can I have your ID?

Student: Sure. [pause] Here it is.

[pause]

Librarian: The system is saying the copy pack hasn't been paid for yet. Did you order and pay for it through the link your professor sent you?

Student: I have to pay for it? I thought I could just come pick it up like a library book.

Librarian: No, a copy pack is copies of relevant articles and papers, and it's yours to keep like a textbook, and you have to pay for it like a textbook. Would you like me to look in the system and see how much this one costs?

Student: Yes, please. I have my credit card and can pay you for it.

Librarian: The system says your copy pack is $56.48. I just re-sent you the email with the link to buy it online. Once you click through the link and buy it with a credit card, it gets released and I can give it to you. You said you have your credit card with you?

Student: Yes, I do.

Librarian: Good. Then go to one of the student computers along that wall, log in, open the email, and click through the link to buy it right now. When you're done and you get the confirmation of payment received, come back over to me and I can give you the copy pack.

Student: I can't just give you my credit card and have you run it?

Librarian: We don't do any financial transactions at this desk, so no.

Student: Oh. But I can use my credit card to buy it online at one of those computers?

Librarian: Yes, and the link walks you through it step by step. It should only take you two or three minutes to pay for it online. Here's your ID back. I'll need it again when you come back to pick up the copy pack, so don't put it too far down in your backpack.

Student: Okay, thank you. I'll be back to get the copy pack in a few minutes.

1. Why does the student visit the library?

   (A) to check out a book

   (B) to ask for help with research

   (C) to pick up material for a class

   (D) to use the internet

   The answer is C. The student comes to pick up a course pack of readings for a class. Eliminate A because the student isn't picking up a book. Eliminate B because the student is not doing research. Eliminate D because the student ends up using the internet after the conversation, but that is not why the student comes to the library.

2. Why could the librarian not give the student the course pack?

   (A) The librarian could not find the student's account in the system.

   (B) The student needed to print the course pack on a computer.

   (C) The internet was down.

   (D) The student had not paid for the course pack yet.

   The answer is D. The student hadn't paid for the course pack. Eliminate A because the librarian found the student's account. Eliminate B because the student did not need to print the course pack. Eliminate C because the internet was not down.

3. How can the student pay for the course pack?

   (A) by giving the librarian cash

   (B) by giving the librarian a credit card

   (C) by using a credit card on the internet

   (D) by giving cash to the professor

   The answer is C. The student can order the course pack and pay for it with a credit card on the internet. Eliminate A and B because the librarian cannot take any payments. Eliminate D because the professor cannot take payments.

We don't do any financial transactions at this desk, so no.

4. What did the librarian mean?

    (A) Everything at her desk is free.

    (B) She can't process a credit card at that desk.

    (C) The course pack is too expensive.

    (D) The student does not need to pay for the course pack.

    The answer is B. The librarian cannot run a credit card at that desk. Eliminate A and D because the course pack is not free. Eliminate C because the librarian does not have an opinion about the cost of the course pack.

5. What will the student do now?

    (A) Use a credit card to order the course pack on a computer in the library.

    (B) Give the librarian his credit card to pay for the course pack.

    (C) Email his professor to ask about buying the course pack.

    (D) Make copies of important readings for a political theories class.

    The answer is A. The student will use one of the computers in the library to order the course pack with his credit card. Eliminate B because the librarian can't process a payment. Eliminate C, as the student already has the information about buying the course pack. Eliminate D because the course pack is the copied readings.

Lecture 2

The following is a transcript of the conversation you heard.

Health worker: Hi there. Do you have an appointment?

Student: No. I think I have the flu, and my roommate told me to come here.

Health worker: Okay. We're backed up this afternoon—you're not the only one with the flu. But I'll get you in; you just might have to wait a bit.

Student: Oh. Thank you.

Health worker: Have you been to Health Services before?

Student: No. I never get sick.

Health worker: Okay, then I need you to fill out this form. Here's a pen. Do you have your student ID with you?

Student: No … but I know my ID number. Does that help?

Health worker: Yes, that's great. You'll need to write down your student ID number on the forms. Health Services is free to full-time students, so I'll just run your number to make sure you qualify.

Student: I'm full time. What happens to people who aren't full time, though?

Health worker: If they have outside insurance, we bill their insurance for our services like a regular clinic or doctor's office. And if they don't have insurance, we charge them a sliding-scale fee.

Student: I'm glad I'm full time, then!

Health worker: Well, you're paying for us through your tuition and fees anyway, so we're not actually free. But it does make it nice that you don't have to pay us anything now. Let me look at the schedule again while you're filling out the form.

[pause]

Health worker: Okay, I can give you an actual 20-minute appointment three hours from now, or if you want to sit here and wait, I can squeeze you in for five minutes in about half an hour. Can you describe your symptoms?

Student: My head hurts and my whole body aches and I'm dizzy and my stomach hurts.

Health worker: That sounds a lot like everything else we're seeing today. If I were you, I'd wait for half an hour and then I'll squeeze you in. The nurse practitioner won't need much time to diagnose you, and then we can write you a prescription and get you on your way back to your room. What part of campus do you live on?

Student: I'm over in West Quad, in the new extension of the dorm behind the Social Work building.

Health worker: Ah, okay. That means it'll actually be easier for you to fill the prescription at the pharmacy on West University than to go over to the university pharmacy. Do you know the one I mean? It's right between the coffee shop and the T-shirt store.

Student: Yeah, I go in there all the time. It's right across the street from my dorm.

Health worker: Good. When we get your prescription, I can call it in, and it should be ready for you to pick up by the time you walk back over there, and it won't cost you anything.

Student: Wow. Thank you.

Health worker: You're welcome. I'll take your form and put it in the computer, and I'll let you know when I can get you in to the nurse practitioner.

6. Why does the student visit Health Services?

   (A) The student is feeling sick.

   (B) The student needs to buy insurance.

   (C) The student needs to pay the doctor.

   (D) The student needs to enroll as a full-time student.

   The answer is A. The student thinks she has the flu and wants to see the nurse practitioner. Eliminate B, as the student's health care is covered by enrollment fees. Eliminate C, as the student will not need to pay out of pocket. Eliminate D, as the student is already enrolled.

7. How much does the student have to pay for the visit to Health Services?

   (A) nothing, as she is a full-time student

   (B) nothing, because she will be billed later

   (C) twenty dollars, and insurance will cover the rest

   (D) a fee determined by a sliding scale

   The answer is A. Full-time students do not have to pay to visit Health Services. Eliminate B because she will not be billed later. Eliminate C and D because she does not have to pay to use Health Services.

8. According to the health worker, why will the prescription be filled at the pharmacy on West University?

   (A) The pharmacy is in the Social Work building.

   (B) The pharmacy may not have the prescription the student needs.

   (C) The pharmacy is part of the university health system.

   (D) The pharmacy is close to the student's room.

   The answer is D. The prescription will be at the pharmacy near the student's room so the student doesn't have to go all over campus to get the prescription filled. Eliminate A because the pharmacy is not in the Social Work building. Eliminate B because there is no indication that the pharmacy won't have the prescription. Eliminate C because the pharmacy is not part of the university health care system.

   If you want to sit here and wait, I can squeeze you in for five minutes in about half an hour.

9. What did the health worker mean?

   (A) The student needs to wait in a crowded waiting room with no room to sit down.

   (B) The student should wait, but may not get to see a nurse practitioner.

   (C) She could get the student a short appointment in 30 minutes.

   (D) She could get the student an appointment that lasts 30 minutes in three hours.

   The answer is C. The health worker can get the student a short appointment with the nurse practitioner half an hour from when the conversation takes place. Eliminate A because you don't know anything about the waiting room. Eliminate B because the health worker says she can get the student an appointment. Eliminate D because the appointment the health worker could give the student in three hours would last for 20 minutes.

10. What will the student do in half an hour?

    (A) go to the pharmacy

    (B) be examined by the nurse practitioner

    (C) pay an office visit fee

    (D) go to class

    The answer is B. The student will see the nurse practitioner for five minutes in half an hour. Eliminate A because the student will go to the pharmacy after being seen by the nurse practitioner to get a prescription. Eliminate C because the student does not need to pay anything. Eliminate D because the student is sick.

Lecture 3

The following is a transcript of the lecture you heard.

Professor: Thanks for the papers. I'll grade them this weekend and have them back to you by next Wednesday. So let's get down to it today, and talk about the Boxer Rebellion. The Boxer Rebellion came out of antiforeign sentiment in China in 1900.

Let's back up and talk about what was going on in China at the time. The Empress Dowager was in power at the time, and the country was still very largely rural, with a feudal system and peasants who were in very poor conditions. I mean, they were peasants! It wasn't a good life. And while things were industrializing in other parts of the world, things were still very rural in China and that was causing some tension, because the peasants weren't very happy, but at the same time they didn't want things to change, you know? There was a huge drought and people starved, and that was followed by some floods, and the countryside was ruined, so many of the independent farmers had to move to the cities to find work, which was disorienting and disruptive. The whole country was a mess economically, and it was behind the rest of the world, but because of instability the people were relying even more heavily on traditions and the Chinese way.

So into the middle of that comes this influx of foreigners. And some of them were merchants trying to make money in the Chinese market. But a lot of them were missionaries trying to bring Christianity to China. The missionaries were white and from the United States or Europe, and they came in and really wanted to make changes. Their hearts were in the right place, and they wanted to help the peasants, but they just barreled in and tried to change things with no respect for traditional Chinese culture or the contemporary society. And they weren't subject to local laws, so they could essentially do whatever they wanted to. And even the ones who were trying to do the right thing still did highly offensive things, and the ones who didn't have good motives were able to get away with all sorts of crimes that the Chinese people couldn't get away with. There was a big double-standard, and the Chinese people were getting angry about it.

So in 1898, a movement started of peasants who basically formed a militia, but with martial arts instead of weapons. They were against foreigners and were very pro-China, and their goal was to defend China and get rid of the missionaries and other foreigners. They started training and began calling themselves the Society of Righteous and Harmonious Fists. They were really into the spiritual side of martial arts and believed that if they trained hard enough and ate right, they could basically turn themselves into super-human fighting machines that would be impervious to bullets! So some of that was a bit fantastical, but they were very hard-core and disciplined. Because they were focused on hand-to-hand combat, foreigners started referring to them as "Boxers." The Boxers continued to train and became more and more nationalistic and more anti-Christian and antiforeigner. As the movement developed steam, they decided to take action, so they moved in on Beijing.

They came into Beijing and started attacking foreigners, and forced them into a section of the city called the Legation Quarter. Because the Boxers were sure that they were physically impervious to bullets and other weapons, they had no fear and were fueled by the desire to save China from the foreigners. At first the Empress Dowager was concerned for the foreigners, but the conservatives in the royal court urged her to support the Boxers. In June 1900, she ordered war on foreigners in China. At that point, the royal army of China joined the Boxers in attacking foreigners.

In response to this, over 20,000 troops from different countries, called the Eight-Nation Alliance, rushed into Beijing and defeated the royal army. On August 21, 1900, the Eight-Nation Alliance officially took over Beijing and stopped the Boxer Rebellion. The whole country at that point went into chaos, with looting all over the country and a witch hunt of anyone suspected of being a Boxer being hunted down and killed.

11. What is the topic of the lecture?

    (A) martial arts

    (B) boxing

    (C) the Boxer Rebellion

    (D) the siege of Beijing

    The answer is C. The lecture is about the Boxer Rebellion. Eliminate A, B, and D because they are small parts of the lecture.

12. According to the professor, the Boxers thought that training in martial arts and eating correctly would

    (A) make them bulletproof

    (B) make them peasants

    (C) make them missionaries

    (D) defeat the royal army

    The answer is A. The Boxers thought that intense training regimens would make them impervious to bullets and other weapons. Eliminate B because they were already peasants. Eliminate C because they did not want to be missionaries. Eliminate D because they did not want to defeat the royal army.

13. The lecture states that the Eight-Nation Alliance

    (A) maintained the cease-fire between the missionaries and the Boxers

    (B) defeated the Boxers and the royal army

    (C) defeated the missionaries and foreigners

    (D) were financed by the royal army

    The answer is B. The Eight-Nation Alliance defeated the Boxers and royal army and took over Beijing. Eliminate A because there was no cease-fire. Eliminate C because the Eight-Nation Alliance came to defend the foreigners and missionaries. Eliminate D because they were fighting against the royal army.

There was a big double-standard, and the Chinese people were getting angry about it.

14. What does the professor mean when she says this?

    (A) There were twice as many Chinese people as there were missionaries, and this angered the Chinese.

    (B) The Chinese people could not live up to the expectations of the missionaries and felt bad about it.

    (C) The missionaries only wanted friendship with the Chinese, but the Chinese rejected them.

    (D) The foreigners were not subject to the same laws and rules the Chinese people were, and that made the Chinese people angry.

    The answer is D. A double-standard is when different sets of rules are applied to different groups. Eliminate A because there were not twice as many Chinese people as missionaries. Eliminate B because this is a misrepresentation of the lecture. Eliminate C because the missionaries did not only want friendship with the Chinese people.

15. How does the professor show what caused the Boxer Rebellion?

    (A) by detailing the Boxers' training methods and philosophy

    (B) by discussing the conditions in China when the missionaries arrived to explain the Boxers' motivations

    (C) by asking why the droughts and floods happened so that students could understand the unfairness of these conditions

    (D) by explaining why the missionaries came to China and what they planned to accomplish there

    The answer is B. The professor explained the conditions in China so that the Boxers' anger at the missionaries made sense. Eliminate A because this did not explain what caused the rebellion. Eliminate C because the professor did not ask why the drought or floods happened. Eliminate D because the professor did not explain why the missionaries came and what they planned to accomplish.

16. The lecture implies that

    (A) racial tension was part of the cause of the Boxer Rebellion

    (B) the Empress Dowager had no power

    (C) the drought caused the missionaries to come to China

    (D) the end of the Boxer Rebellion brought stability

    The answer is A. The Chinese peasants were angry at the white American and European missionaries. Eliminate B because the lecture states that the Empress Dowager ordered a war against foreigners. Eliminate C because there is no direct connection between the drought and the missionaries' arrival. Eliminate D because the end of the Boxer Rebellion brought looting and executions, not stability.

Lecture 4

The following is a transcript of the lecture you heard.

Professor: Today's topic is the evolution of modern Scandinavian languages with a common origin, by which I mean Swedish, Danish, Norwegian, and Icelandic. We're not going to talk about Finnish today, because even though Finland is part of Scandinavia, the language doesn't have the same roots as those other languages. The evolution of modern Scandinavian languages has been largely a result of geography. Does anyone have an idea of what I mean by that?

Student: It means that all the geographic features like mountains and oceans have formed the languages, right?

Professor: Exactly. If you look at these four languages, they are segmented by country, but even more they're segmented by region. Swedish is largely uniform because the country is easy to navigate and not so mountainous, whereas there are pockets of Norway in which the dialect spoken is very old-fashioned and very similar to Old Norse. That's a function of the fact that Norway as a country is so mountainous, so that there is little movement from one region to another, and even sometimes from one town to another!

As far as modernization, Danish and Swedish have undergone the most change, and that's a function of their easy access to each other and to other countries, and inter-country access. Because the people were able to move around inside the country while interacting with external forces at the same time, the language evolved. At the other extreme is Iceland. Because it is so isolated—an island nation that is not close to any big land mass—and has such a small population, Icelandic has remained remarkably close to Old Norse. Norwegian was sort of a mix, with easy access to foreigners from the seaport cities but difficult intra-country access. So Norwegian is very different regionally.

Now, of course, other factors have affected language development. Some of them have been intentional and some unintentional. The most obvious change agent is television, which has been around for 60 years. Scandinavian governments have had varying levels of intervention in programming the television channels their citizens can see and have used television to unify language. In the 1980s, the government of Norway decided to try to standardize the

Norwegian all citizens spoke and created a streamlined form of Norwegian called nynorsk (which was not the same as bokmaal, which was the form of Norwegian taught in school). Nynorsk was more similar to modern Swedish than to Old Norse. The government used television to try to promote nynorsk. The government had varied success with this because of political and ideological movements, but the use of television did begin to even out the Norwegian that isolated Norwegian people understood, even if they didn't start using it in daily conversation.

Student: Wait, the government decides what's on TV?

Professor: Yes. In the Scandinavian countries (and most European countries, in fact), the government controls at least one television channel. So the government runs news programming and public interest programs, as well as some entertainment programming. When television first came out, those were the only channels people could get, but now that people have cable and satellite television, private and commercial channels have developed, and people can get channels from other countries as well. So people in Denmark can watch the Danish government channel, and commercial Danish channels, and channels from Norway and Sweden and England and other countries. That has created a bigger mix, because if you're watching the news in Danish but you're watching a fiction show in Swedish, then you begin to understand both of those languages and they eventually will become more similar.

So the way language has evolved and is evolving is fascinating, because those countries are all so similar but have so many differences, too. And as technology has evolved and is evolving more constantly, the languages are becoming more similar—at least Norwegian and Danish and Swedish. Icelandic is still the outlier because it isn't geographically close to the other three, so Icelandic has still remained relatively steady while the Icelandic people communicate with the rest of the world in English.

17. What is the topic of the lecture?

    (A) government-owned television channels

    (B) the influence of television on language development

    (C) how the Norwegian language developed

    (D) the evolution of four Scandinavian languages

    The answer is D. The lecture describes many factors influencing the evolution of Norwegian, Danish, Swedish, and Icelandic. Eliminate A, B, and C because they are small details in the lecture, not the topic.

18. According to the lecture, why were pockets of Norwegian people speaking an old-fashioned form of Norwegian?

    (A) They did not understand any other languages.

    (B) They are a small island nation without access to external languages.

    (C) They were isolated by mountains and did not hear others speaking more modern versions of the language.

    (D) They did not want to speak anything that was close to Swedish or Danish.

The answer is C. The Norwegians who were isolated by mountains did not get to mix with others who spoke more modern forms of Norwegian. Eliminate A because other languages are not relevant. Eliminate B because Iceland is a small island nation, not Norway. Eliminate D because the Norwegians were speaking Norwegian, not Swedish or Danish.

19. The professor states that because Iceland is so isolated

    (A) Icelandic is closer to Swedish and Danish than Norwegian

    (B) Icelandic is closer to Old Norse than the other three languages

    (C) Icelandic people all speak English

    (D) Iceland is not part of Scandinavia

    The answer is B. Icelandic has stayed close to Old Norse because of lack of contact with other languages. Eliminate A because this is not stated in the lecture. Eliminate C because this is true, but not a result of Iceland being isolated. Eliminate D because Iceland is considered part of Scandinavia.

    At the other extreme is Iceland.

20. What does the professor mean when she says this?

    (A) Iceland has an opposite situation from the situations of Sweden and Denmark.

    (B) Iceland has had extremely rapid language change.

    (C) Iceland is far away from the rest of Scandinavia.

    (D) Icelandic people do not understand Swedish or Danish.

    The answer is A. Iceland has a different situation from Sweden and Denmark in terms of language exposure. Eliminate B because it is the opposite of what is stated in the lecture. Eliminate C because it is true but is not what the professor means by this sentence. Eliminate D because you do not have any information on this.

21. How does the professor show the way governments use technology to influence language?

    (A) She describes the Icelandic government's use of island culture to influence language.

    (B) She describes the Norwegian government's use of television to promote nynorsk to citizens.

    (C) She describes the Swedish government's use of flat lands to encourage interaction with other Swedes.

    (D) She describes the Danish government's use of the internet to promote the Danish language to other countries.

    The answer is B. The professor gives the example of the promotion of nynorsk to the Norwegian people on television. Eliminate A and C because these are topographical features, not technology. Eliminate D because this was not in the lecture.

22. You can infer from the lecture that the professor

    (A) does not like Finnish

    (B) does not consider Finland part of Scandinavia

    (C) thinks Iceland should become more modern

    (D) thinks technology facilitates language evolution

    The answer is D. The professor indicates that she sees technology as useful for evolving language. Eliminate A because it is out of the scope of the lecture. Eliminate B because it contradicts what the professor says. Eliminate C because there is no information about this in the lecture.

Lecture 5

The following is a transcript of the lecture you heard.

Professor: I'm going to continue discussing the supply and demand curve today. We're going to start at pricing and end up at dead weight loss. Are any of you familiar with dead weight loss?

Student: It's what happens when the producer charges more for a product than the buyer is willing to pay, so it's money that's just lost because no one buys or sells the product at that price.

Professor: Exactly. Let me go back to review a bit before we jump into this. Remember from before that we agreed that marginal cost equals marginal revenue. In other words, when a firm is operating in a competitive environment—which means that there are several firms making and selling the same products, so buyers have a choice of who they buy from—the amount it costs a firm to make a product is called marginal cost. Because it's the cost, and *marginal* means "for each extra unit." The reason we're figuring in how much it costs for each extra unit is that we don't care about how much we've already spent, for things like building our factory and buying the machines we use. Those are sunk costs. We're only looking at how much it costs us to make each extra widget we make on our assembly line. Got that?

Student: Yes.

Professor: So marginal cost is how much it costs us to make each additional widget. What does marginal revenue mean?

Student: How much revenue we make on each additional widget?

Professor: Exactly! Marginal revenue is the revenue, or dollars we get from selling, each additional unit. I'm calling them widgets just because I don't want to come up with a specific example. Anyway, when a firm is only one of several firms all making the same widget to sell to people, then the environment is competitive, because all these firms are competing against each other for customers. So they can't just price their widgets sky-high—they have to price their widgets as low as they can without losing money on each one they sell. That means that the marginal revenue they earn from each widget is going to be exactly the same as the marginal cost it takes them to make that widget. If the marginal cost is bigger than marginal revenue, they lose money and go out of business. If marginal revenue is bigger than marginal cost, then they make money, but one of the other firms will be able to price lower and take away their customers, so they won't sell anything. So marginal cost equals marginal revenue because that's the balance point.

Now, this all assumes a competitive environment. What happens, though, if a firm is the only firm in the whole world, or at least that customers can get to, making and selling this one thing? Let's call it a super-widget. Let's call it the UltraWidget. And you are the only company in the whole world that makes the UltraWidget. Now, plenty of companies make a regular widget, and some customers are very happy with a regular widget and will buy those. But your UltraWidget is so ultra that you're the only one making it, and there are customers who only want the UltraWidget. Since you are the only company making it, you are a monopoly. This is called a monopolistic environment instead of a competitive environment. In a monopoly, the firm can charge whatever it wants, in theory. The only limit is that customers will only pay a certain amount of money for your UltraWidget.

That amount is different from customer to customer, though. Some customers will only pay $5 for your UltraWidget, but some will pay $7 and some will even pay $12. So where do you price it? Let's say it costs you $3 to make your UltraWidget. In a competitive environment, you would price your UltraWidget at $3, because that's what you'd have to price it at. In a monopolistic environment, however, marginal cost does not equal marginal revenue, and you can price higher. If you price at $5, then all of your customers will buy it. If you price it above $12, then none of your customers will buy it. But if you price it higher than $5 but lower than $12, some of your customers but not all of them will buy it.

You can determine by calculating what price to sell the UltraWidget at. If 999 people will buy it at $5 but only one customer will buy it at $6, it's pretty easy to decide. At the same time, if 70 people will buy it at $10 and only 74 will buy it at $9, that's also easy to decide. So you just run the numbers and figure out how to maximize your profit by selling to the combo of the most people at the highest price.

But we're talking about dead weight loss today. So when you, a monopolist, price your widget at a higher price than even one customer is willing to buy it at, you create dead weight loss. That loss is the value that's lost to society because your customer did not spend money to buy your product. Remember that we're assuming that commerce is good for society, so buying and selling helps society. So if a customer does not buy something because you priced it higher than the value it has to the customer, something is lost. It's called dead weight loss. The dead weight loss is calculated as the difference between the price the firm charges and the amount the customer is willing to pay. So there are different amounts of dead weight loss for different customers and different price points. Remember that when we go into the exam and I ask you to calculate the dead weight loss, that you need to know the specific price, and you also need to know which customer so you know which price they will be willing to pay.

23. What is the topic of the lecture?

    (A) pricing products and dead weight loss

    (B) calculating dead weight loss

    (C) operating in a monopolistic environment

    (D) making widgets

    The answer is A. The lecture covers marginal cost and revenue, pricing in competitive and monopolistic environments, and dead weight loss. Eliminate B because calculating dead weight loss is a small part of the lecture. Eliminate C because only half the lecture is about monopolies. Eliminate D because making widgets is not the topic of the lecture.

24. According to the lecture, a competitive environment means that

    (A) there is one firm selling one product

    (B) there is one firm selling multiple products

    (C) there are multiple firms selling the same product

    (D) there are multiple firms selling different products

    The answer is C. In a competitive environment, multiple firms sell the same product and compete for customers. Eliminate A and B because an environment with only one firm is a monopolistic environment. Eliminate D because a competitive environment means the firms compete selling the same product, so it doesn't matter if any of the firms sell multiple products as long as they compete with each other selling a given product.

25. The lecture says that dead weight loss is a loss to society because

    (A) the product should be priced lower to attract more customers

    (B) the customer is not willing to spend more money to buy the product, and this is anticapitalistic

    (C) the product is not worth the money the customer is willing to purchase it for

    (D) the money the customer would have spent on the product is now not spent at all

    The answer is D. The theory of dead weight loss relies on the assumption that commerce is good for society, so not spending money to purchase an object is a loss to society. Eliminate A and B because there is no judgment about which side should change their price when describing dead weight loss. Eliminate C because the assumption is that the product is worth—to the customer—what the customer is willing to pay for it.

But your UltraWidget is so ultra that you're the only one making it, and there are customers who only want the UltraWidget.

26. What does the professor mean when she says this?

    (A) The UltraWidget cannot be manufactured by any firm, so customers cannot have it.

    (B) The UltraWidget is a special product that only one firm makes, and some customers are only satisfied with this product.

    (C) The UltraWidget is a regular widget, just with the name "ultra" on it.

    (D) The UltraWidget is sold in a competitive environment at marginal cost.

    The answer is B. The professor means that the UltraWidget is better than a regular widget, so some customers want the UltraWidget and will not substitute a regular widget, and you are the only manufacturer of the UltraWidget. Eliminate A because you are manufacturing it. Eliminate C because the UltraWidget is not a regular widget. Eliminate D because you are the only manufacturer of the UltraWidget, so you are a monopoly.

27. How does the professor show that the optimal price in a monopoly can be calculated?

    (A) The professor gives examples of the number of customers that will buy at different prices.

    (B) The professor shows the social good that is lost from dead weight loss.

    (C) The professor discusses the logistics of the manufacturing process.

    (D) The professor explains why marginal cost equals marginal revenue in a competitive environment.

    The answer is A. The professor gives examples of the number of customers that will buy at different prices to show that the optimal price for maximum profit can be calculated. Eliminate B because the social good is not directly related to optimal pricing. Eliminate C because the manufacturing process is out of the scope of this lecture. Eliminate D because a competitive environment is not related to monopolistic pricing.

28. The lecture implies that a monopolistic firm can charge what it wants to for a product because

    (A) no other firm has lower production costs

    (B) other firms are price-makers, while the monopolistic firm is a price-taker

    (C) it is the only firm making that product, so customers cannot get a lower price from another firm

    (D) customers do not actually need that product and are satisfied with other products as substitutes

    The answer is C. The customers cannot get a lower price on the product, so they either buy it or don't—so price is less sensitive. Eliminate A because other firms don't matter in a monopoly. Eliminate B because price-takers and price-makers are not discussed in the passage. Eliminate D because if customers do not need the product, it is irrelevant.

Lecture 6

The following is a transcript of the lecture you heard.

Professor: Have any of you noticed the special features of the building we're in now? The windows, and the materials it's built with, and the special features in the bathrooms?

Student: Oh, like the low-flow toilets and sinks?

Professor: Yes. This building was built specifically to be LEED certified. Have you heard of LEED certification? LEED is a program that certifies buildings as being environmentally friendly. LEED stands for Leadership in Energy and Environmental Design, and it is a system of rules and standards created by a group of architects and environmentalists to be an objective standard to which new buildings can be built and existing buildings can be modified to have the least negative impact on the environment. A building that is LEED certified is a building that meets certain standards for energy efficiency, safety of building materials, and consumption of resources. This building that we're in right now is LEED gold-certified, which is the second highest level of certification that can be achieved.

LEED certification consists of achieving points across a number of different measures. The criteria are published in easily accessible documents so that anyone who wants to build or modify buildings—whether they're commercial buildings, private homes, or other buildings like schools and hospitals—can use the checklists for planning purposes to make sure they'll be in compliance. The document with the rules for compliance for new construction is 100 pages long, and it covers everything from "Site Selection" and "Development Density and Community Connectivity" to "Innovative Wastewater Technologies" to "Green Power" to "Increased Ventilation." Different categories have different possible point values. There are 100 possible points. For basic certification, a building must earn 40 points. For Silver certification 50 points, for Gold certification 60 points, and for Platinum certification 80 points.

Because of these certification standards for new construction, many developers have begun to construct new buildings that meet at least the minimum standards for certification. One problem with the system of certifying new construction, however, is that the rating is earned while the building is being constructed, before there are any people using the building. In the case of a residential building, such as an apartment building, the residents may use vastly larger amounts of water, electricity, and heat than was originally accounted for during the certification process. For a commercial building that will house commercial tenants, depending on the nature of the businesses that inhabit the spaces, enormous amounts of energy and electricity may be consumed, much more than the architects and developers planned for and were rated for.

On the other hand, existing buildings are sometimes assumed to be environmentally bad just because they were built back before anyone designing or constructing buildings knew about environmental concerns, but they can end up achieving higher LEED ratings than new buildings built specifically to LEED standards do. The existing buildings need to be modified according to LEED standards, of course—they are usually not environmentally compliant just as they have been operating. But with modifications, these buildings can be far more efficient than newer buildings are, because they have thicker walls, are built on smaller plots of land, and generally cause much less impact on the communities around them.

LEED certification is very worth the effort for the environment and for the positive challenge it provides for the architects, designers, and builders who build and modify buildings to meet LEED standards. The fact that it is a voluntary program, so no one is forced to participate, means that those who do participate are doing so because they feel they have something to gain. And they do, whether it's knowledge or a higher rental or sale value, or a bigger return on investment, or investing in higher-quality materials and hiring workers who do better-quality work. LEED certification is good for the environment, the economy, and the communities in which these buildings are located.

29. What is the topic of the lecture?

    (A) the four types of LEED certification

    (B) new buildings versus old buildings

    (C) different types of construction materials

    (D) LEED certification of buildings

    The answer is D. The lecture is about all kinds of LEED certification of buildings, new and old. Eliminate A because the four types of certification are a detail, not the topic. Eliminate B because this is not the focus of the lecture. Eliminate C because this is not covered in the lecture.

30. According to the lecture, LEED certification levels are based on

    (A) earning points for compliance with different requirements

    (B) making a favorable impression on the LEED judges

    (C) following the proper procedures for submitting a portfolio

    (D) constructing a building from one standardized blueprint

    The answer is A. The level of certification a building earns is determined by the number of points it earns. Eliminate B because there are no judges. Eliminate C because there is no portfolio involved. Eliminate D because there is no standardized blueprint involved.

31. According to the professor, old buildings can be

    (A) improved but never completely efficient

    (B) as environmentally efficient as new buildings

    (C) modified but will not be as efficient as new buildings

    (D) less stable than newer buildings

    The answer is B. Old buildings can be modified and can be as efficient or more than new buildings. Eliminate A and C because they contradict what the professor says. Eliminate D because there is nothing about stability in the lecture.

Have you heard of LEED certification?

32. What does the professor mean when he says this?

    (A) Have you submitted your paper on LEED certification yet?

    (B) Have you already taken this class?

    (C) I don't know what LEED certification is.

    (D) I'm going to talk about LEED certification now.

    The answer is D. The professor introduces the lecture topic of LEED certification by asking if the students have heard of it. Eliminate A and B because the professor's question is rhetorical and not meant to be answered. Eliminate C because the professor does know what LEED certification is.

33. Why does the professor discuss old buildings' thicker walls and smaller plots of land?

    (A) to demonstrate that old buildings will never earn all the points required for LEED certification

    (B) to explain how to build newer buildings

    (C) to show how they can be more efficient than new buildings

    (D) to discuss why they are less efficient than new buildings

    The answer is C. Eliminate A because old buildings can earn enough points for LEED certification. Eliminate B because this describes old buildings, not how to build new buildings. Eliminate D because this description shows why old buildings can be more efficient, not the opposite.

34. The lecture implies that

    (A) while old buildings can be made more efficient, if they are not rehabilitated completely, they will not be as efficient as new buildings

    (B) a building that is certified while it is empty might not be certified once it is filled with tenants or residents

    (C) the selection of a site is the most important factor in obtaining LEED certification

    (D) LEED certification is primarily used for residential housing

    The answer is B. The lecture states that a building may earn more points while empty than it would when full. Therefore, it would be possible for a building to go below the requirement for LEED certification once it is full. Eliminate A because there is nothing in the passage about full rehabilitation. Eliminate C because while "Site Selection" is first, there is nothing to indicate that it is most important. Eliminate D because there is no indication that LEED certification is primarily for residential housing.

Speaking Section Explanations

Question 1

Read the prompt and give yourself 15 seconds to prep and write notes. Then take 45 seconds to record your response.

1. Describe a person who has been a good influence on your life. Please include specific examples and details of this influence as you describe the person.

   An excellent response will discuss the person who has been a good influence, including at least two separate details or incidents that explain how the person has influenced you positively. It will contain a solid opening statement and a solid closing statement.

Question 2

Read the prompt and give yourself 15 seconds to prep and write notes. Then take 45 seconds to record your response.

2. Some students work to pay for their university studies, while others borrow money they will pay back later when they have jobs after graduation. Which method of financing university studies makes the most sense, and why?

   An excellent response will pick one side of the question and not argue both sides. It will use at least two strong reasons for the opinion expressed in the response and support those reasons with facts or examples.

Question 3

The university has changed the prices for parking passes for parking lots on campus. Read the email that has been sent to all parking pass holders. You will have 45 seconds to read the email. Begin reading now.

Email

To: Parking pass holders

From: University Parking Services

Subject: Parking Pass Prices to Increase in May

To all parking pass holders:

The university parking garage system has been redesigned to allocate more parking spots to faculty and staff who need to park close to their departments. As a result of this restructuring, the cost of parking passes for regular full-time students will increase according to the following schedule:

Green Pass (all lots, 24/7 access): Increase from $700 to $880

Blue Pass (limited lots, 24/7 access): Increase from $350 to $390

Yellow Pass (limited lots, 24/7 access): Increase from $320 to $360

Brown Pass (limited lots, 3 P.M. through 7 A.M. M–F access and weekends): Increase from $190 to $240

The price increase will take effect on the official renewal date, May 28. If you have a prorated pass for this year it will be reset then to follow the official schedule. If you have any questions, please contact the Parking Services office.

The following is a transcript of the conversation you heard.

Woman: Did you read that email about the parking passes?

Man: I know! No warning, just bam! The price is going up!

Women: I'm not sure what to do. I really can't afford to pay an extra $180.

Man: You have a Green Pass? I only have a Blue Pass, because all my classes are in the same three buildings, all right near one parking garage.

Woman: You're lucky. I'm all over the place all of the time. I diagrammed out where I have to be in the course of a week and neither Blue nor Yellow worked for me, so I had to get a Green Pass. I'm not sure what I'm going to do now.

Man: How far do you drive in to campus?

Woman: About 2 miles. It's not horrible. Maybe I could walk it? If I were on a bus line it would be easier, but I'm nowhere near a bus that comes to campus.

Man: Do you have a bike? Two miles on a bike is no big deal, and you could bike around campus during the day, too.

Woman: I haven't ridden a bike in years, but I bet I could now. That might work. I wonder how much a bike costs, if it would be cheaper than the parking.

Man: One of my roommates has a bike that she never uses. It's been in our garage for a year. Let me ask her if she'll just let you use it next year. Then you won't have to pay for a new bike or for parking.

Woman: Wow! If she'd let me borrow her bike that would save me a lot of money. Thank you so much for asking her.

Now get ready to answer the question. Give yourself 30 seconds to create notes for your response. Then take 60 seconds to speak your response.

3. The woman has a problem stemming from the information in the email. State what the problem is and what she decides to do about that problem.

   An excellent response will sum up the email about the price increase and say that the woman cannot afford to pay the parking increase, nor can she buy a cheaper parking pass. The response will conclude that she is going to begin biking to campus, and that the man will ask his roommate if the woman can borrow her bicycle.

Question 4

In this question, you will read a short passage on an academic subject and then listen to a talk on the same topic. You will then answer a question using information from both the reading passage and the talk. After you hear the question, you will have 30 seconds to prepare your response and 60 seconds to speak.

Read the passage about the creation of labor unions. You will have 45 seconds to read the passage. Begin reading now.

> The Industrial Revolution began a new era in the history of labor relations across the world and in the United States. As owners and managers began to see workers as increasingly interchangeable, because each worker only performed one small part of the manufacturing process, workers themselves became increasingly concerned with wages and working conditions. The Triangle Shirtwaist fire, in which workers at the Triangle Shirtwaist factory burned to death when a fire broke out—and they were locked in, so they could not leave their posts—galvanized a generation of workers and sparked protests that ultimately led to the creation of labor unions. Those unions advocated for workers to ensure that management was providing safe and humane working conditions.

The following is a transcript of the lecture you heard.

> Professor: We've been talking about labor relations and how the unions arose out of a need to protect workers from dangerous and demoralizing conditions. Originally unions fought for workers' rights to things like bathroom breaks and meal breaks, and to be able to enter and leave a factory at will instead of being locked in or locked out. Unions employed methods like picketing and strikes to force management to negotiate with them. As they began to have more power, they advocated for other things, like shorter working hours. The "standard" 40-hour work week we enjoy here in the United States only came about because of union efforts—before that it was commonplace for factory workers to work 12 to 14 hours a day, six days a week, even children. The unions are also responsible for our child labor laws and the minimum working age.
>
> As unions grew in power, some of them were taken over by corruption, so that they began to negotiate in bad faith. Some union bosses achieved so much power that they stopped advocating in the best interests of their members, but to increase their own power and wealth. Corrupt union bosses have negotiated deals that don't benefit members simply so that they could get kickbacks or preferential treatment from management. In addition, corruption in some unions has damaged the reputation and level of popular support for unions in general, which harms all workers. It is ironic that the organizations that grew out of a need to protect workers have, in some cases, hurt their workers.

Now get ready to answer the question. Give yourself 30 seconds to create notes for your response. Then take 60 seconds to speak your response.

4. The professor describes the achievements of the unions and some problems with some unions. Explain how these achievements and problems relate to and contrast with each other.

   An excellent response will describe the advances unions gained, such as safety measures and hour reductions, and the power of corruption in the unions arising from the power the unions gained. It will explain that corrupt unions have hurt their workers, even while unions as a whole have improved working conditions and helped workers.

Question 5

In this question, you will hear a conversation. Then you will be asked to talk about the conversation and give your opinion about the subject of the conversation. You will be given 20 seconds to prepare. Then you will be given 60 seconds to speak.

The following is a transcript of the conversation you heard.

> Woman: Excuse me, do you know where the printer is that prints from this computer?
>
> Man: This computer can print to any printer in the building. Have you ever printed before here?
>
> Woman: No, this is my first time. How do I print to a specific printer?
>
> Man: You don't have to. The way it works is that when you click "Print" on your document, it defaults to the printer pool, but stores it on the network under your account. Then, you walk up to the printer you want to use and type in your username and password, and it pulls up your account, and any document you sent to the printer pool is there and you can print it off on that printer.
>
> Woman: Hmm. Now I can't decide if I should print it now. If I print it now, I'll be late for class. But if I wait to print after class, none of the printers might be free, and I might have to wait to print and be late to my next class.
>
> Man: Good point. There's usually a line for this printer, and I know the printers up on 3 are always swamped. I'm surprised this printer is free right now.
>
> Woman: I'll send the paper to the network right now, but I really don't know if I should print now and be late for sure, or take a chance on a free printer later.

Give yourself 20 seconds to create notes for your response. Then take 60 seconds to speak your response.

5. The students discuss how to print a document and what the woman's options are for printing. Describe the two options. Then explain which option you think she should pursue, and why.

   An excellent response will describe the woman's option to print the document now and be late for her class, or the option to print later and risk being much later for another class if she has to wait for a free printer. The response will choose one of the options and give a reason for choosing that option.

Question 6

The following is a transcript of the lecture you heard.

> Professor: Today we're talking about the very beginnings of astronomy as a science. Astronomy has been called the first science, and I'm inclined to agree with that assessment. Early peoples always looked up at the sky and tried to figure out what was above them, and why the landscape of stars changed from season to season. Some of the earliest writings available were essentially lab reports about stars and planets and their positions.
>
> Very very early peoples associated the things in the sky—the sun, stars, and planets—with gods and goddesses and other spirits. They associated the objects in the sky with physical events on Earth such as droughts and floods and earthquakes and assumed that a heavenly being was causing those events on purpose. The first people to begin serious scientific astronomy work were from Mesopotamia. The Sumerians named the stars and began a system of astral theology, which assigned stars and planets places is the Sumerian system of religion. The Babylonians understood that events in the sky happened on a cycle and used mathematics to predict and document those cycles. They documented the movement of planets in the sky, sunrise and sunset times as they varied during the year, and the difference in the Earth's distance from the Sun during different seasons based on length of shadows. Not only did they begin to use mathematics and observation to document phenomena, they applied it to daily life.
>
> The Babylonians began even more significant, regular study of astronomy when the king Nabonassar came into power in the year 747 B.C.E., and the records from this period of study have been used by astronomers throughout the ages as references and guides. This period of serious Babylonian study of astronomy lasted from 747 B.C.E. all the way through 60 B.C.E. and the end of the Seleucid Empire. By the end of this period, the Babylonians had developed models based on centuries of data that allowed them to predict the movement of the planets.

Give yourself 20 seconds to create notes for your response. Then take 60 seconds to speak your response.

6. Using data and examples from the lecture, explain how the Babylonians expanded on existing astronomical study.

   An excellent response will explain that Babylonians took the existing observations of the Sumerians and applied mathematics to them to observe patterns, describe the patterns, and eventually make models for predictions.

Writing Section Explanations

Integrated Writing Task

Reading:

Plagiarism refers to the practice of copying or appropriating another's writing or other intellectual or artistic work as one's own. While it is considered a serious breach of ethics and can ruin careers and cause expulsion from academic programs today, plagiarism was not always seen as negative. In fact, centuries ago, students were encouraged to copy directly from the writers or artists they were studying as a way of training or apprenticing. It was thought that only by retracing the exact steps of the acknowledged masters could people learn creative skills. Students of painting practiced for hours to be able to emulate the exact brushstrokes of a revered artist, and the artists who were copied were aggrandized by all the copies of their work.

In writing, form was considered at least as important, if not more so, than originality of thought. Students were taught to follow the forms of established writers and to prize eloquence and elegant turn of phrase over innovation of thought. For this reason, budding writers copied passages word for word to learn the phrasing and tone of the masters. Writers who copied the works of those they emulated did so to perfect their own craft, not to pass off the master's work as their own. Now, however, originality of thought is prized more highly even than eloquence is, so copying another's work is a serious intellectual crime.

Lecture:

I'm sorry we're having this discussion today, but I've been asked by the dean of standards to talk to you all about plagiarism. As you should already know, plagiarism consists of copying another's work directly or significantly and passing it off as your own work. This is a serious offense, and can result in your expulsion from the department and from the university. We admitted you to this program because of your records as scholars, and we expect you to be able to do your own work, using your own thoughts and research, and writing everything in your own words.

Now we understand that some of you may be having problems understanding what is plagiarism and what isn't, in terms of citing references and quoting others' words in your papers. In general, if you write anything that someone else said, and you write it in the same words they used, you need to put quotation marks around it and give that person credit, but in the body of the paper and in your footnotes or endnotes or references cited section at the end. If you take what someone else has written and put it into your own words, you don't need to use the quotes, but you still need to give that person credit for the idea and research in your paper. Those are the basics, and we're going to have one of the directors of the Writing Center do an hour-long class on avoiding plagiarism for us next Friday at 3 P.M. I am hoping you will all attend.

1. Summarize the points made in the lecture, being sure to explain how they differ from the view in the reading passage.

   Sample essay that would score a 5:

   The speaker in the lecture discusses the seriousness of plagiarism. She explains why it is considered a serious offense, then discusses what constitutes plagiarism, ways to

avoid plagiarism, and an upcoming event about plagiarism. The content of the lecture contrasts with the information about plagiarism in the passage.

First, she states that she has been asked to discuss plagiarism because it is a serious offense that can lead to being dropped from the program. This is a contrast with the historical views of plagiarism expressed in the reading passage, in which plagiarism was considered a form of flattery to the original writer and a way for the copier to learn.

Then, she discusses what constitutes plagiarism, and gives ways to cite references correctly to avoid plagiarism. She gives details of what to include in a paper to make sure that the original author of the idea is given credit correctly. Again, this is a contrast with historical views of plagiarism that felt that imitation was a form of flattery. In the past, there would have been no reason to cite the original author, because the act of copying was a way to honor the original.

Finally, the lecturer gives the details about a special class with in-depth information on writing papers correctly without plagiarizing. She finishes by saying that she hopes the listeners will attend this special class.

Independent Writing Task

2. Do you agree or disagree with the following statement? Use specific details and examples to support your answer.

   It is better to be a good team player than to work individually.

Sample essay that would score a 5:

While some feel that it is better to be a team player than to work individually, others prefer to work alone. While both sides make sense logically, the argument for working individually is more compelling.

First, people must feel motivation internally to be able to do good work. If all they focus on is working well with a team, then they will not develop a competitive spirit to push themselves to do better work. They won't have ambition to do more and be better, because they will always just be part of a team, so there won't be motivation to reach for more.

Second, it can be too easy to hide in a team and not contribute your best work. While teams are supposed to function well and be supportive and efficient, many teams don't have members who all contribute equally. Because more than one person is working on a task, people on the team can hide and not contribute their best work because they know the rest of the team will carry them. A person can focus on getting along with other team members to make the team function socially, but not develop the ability to do quality work.

Finally, people are ultimately responsible for themselves, and will succeed or fail based on their own efforts. It is dangerous to rely on the ability to work well in a team, because people are not hired and fired in teams, but individually. To have a long, successful career, you need to be able to do your own work well.

In conclusion, being able to work well individually is more important than working well in a team. While it is useful to be able to work in a team, it does not make up for the ability to do good quality work individually.

Chapter 21

Practice Test 2

Now that you have studied and worked through the practice sections for all four sections of the TOEFL, it's time to take the second full-length practice test. Set aside four hours in a quiet place near a computer, with a clean surface to work on. You should circle your answers to the multiple-choice questions in the Reading and Listening sections in the book. For the Speaking section, speak your response into your phone or a computer with voice-recoding software. For the Writing section, type your responses into a blank document on your computer. Make sure you have several pieces of blank paper to use for note-taking.

Be sure to give yourself a 10-minute break after the Listening section and before the Speaking section. Stay focused and keep going.

Good luck!

Reading Section

Give yourself 60 minutes to complete this section. Circle your answers to the questions in the book. You may take notes on your blank paper.

Passage 1

Natural Gas Conversions

A new trend in vehicle technology is to design systems that run on natural gas instead of gasoline or diesel. Compressed natural gas (CNG) is far better for the environment than either gasoline or diesel because it burns cleaner, vehicles that run on natural gas instead of gasoline or diesel are more fuel efficient, and CNG is less expensive than more traditional options. Auto and truck manufacturers are rushing to bring new engines to market that run on natural gas and to modify existing engines to run on natural gas.

There is a growing market for fuel-efficient vehicles in the United States and around the world, and vehicles that run on natural gas are at the forefront of meeting this demand. Most of the market for fuel-efficient vehicles that run on natural gas are companies with large fleets of trucks, specifically energy companies, field service companies, telecom companies, and government fleets. They are making the decision to switch to CNG vehicles primarily because of the fuel savings, but also for the environmental benefits and the push toward supporting a domestic fuel source that creates economic growth in the United States. Compressed natural gas is produced in the United States as well as around the world, so using CNG gives American companies a way to use a local fuel source that is not subject to fluctuations in the international market or external factors affecting the price of gasoline, such as conflicts in oil-producing regions, OPEC, or other political maneuverings. Increasing CNG use and production in the United States also contributes to the country's gross domestic product (GDP), a number that indicates the health and strength of the country's economy overall. Using CNG is good for the economy.

In addition, because of the political visibility of the vast benefits of CNG, many states are implementing tax incentives that further reduce the cost of converting current vehicles from using gasoline to using CNG. At the same time, vehicles are being designed to use either CNG alone or to have duel-combustion systems that can run on either gasoline or compressed natural gas. Because of rapid industry growth and the increased availability of CNG technology, companies producing CNG or developing CNG conversion technology are investing in the development of infrastructure (CNG fueling stations) needed to support the rising number of CNG vehicles on the road.

Converting a vehicle that currently runs on gasoline or diesel to run on CNG is a simple process consisting of installing a converter unit to the existing engine. These units are produced by companies that have obtained certification from environmental agencies that have determined the parameters for considering a CNG engine conversion "clean" enough to be environmentally friendly. The companies that produce these conversion units install them into existing vehicles owned by the companies that request them, or to new vehicles delivered straight from the vehicle manufacturer to the CNG conversion company. Technicians install the CNG converter units, test the installation, and deliver them to the customer company, which can begin using the vehicles immediately.

Because of the simplicity and relatively low cost of converting engines to using CNG, it makes solid financial sense for companies running large fleets of trucks to convert them. Once the tax savings and incentives to these companies are figured in, the conversion process is a negligible expense that pays for itself almost immediately. As more and more companies running fleets of trucks discover the financial benefits of running their trucks on CNG instead of gasoline, the market for CNG conversions and CNG-native engines will continue to increase.

1. What is the main idea of the passage?

   (A) what compressed natural gas is

   (B) why companies are becoming more environmentally friendly

   (C) compressed natural gas as a fuel source that is good for the environment and for companies that convert to it

   (D) how CNG conversion is performed on a truck that runs on gasoline

2. The word *modify* in the passage is closest in meaning to

   (A) substitute

   (B) make less intense

   (C) change

   (D) reduce

3. The word *factors* in the passage is closest in meaning to

   (A) issues

   (B) disasters

   (C) products

   (D) benefits

4. The phrase *these units* in the passage refers to

   (A) CNG fueling stations

   (B) gasoline engines

   (C) CNG engines

   (D) CNG engine conversion units

5. In the second paragraph, why does the author include information about the types of companies that are the market for compressed natural gas vehicles?

   (A) to give examples of companies that use fleets of trucks so the reader understands the economics for the company

   (B) to question whether the market is so narrow that the technology is not worth pursuing

   (C) to examine the motivations for these companies to make such a radical choice for fuel

   (D) to describe the process of converting a gasoline engine to a CNG engine

6. Which of the following can be inferred from the second paragraph about the gasoline used to run fleet vehicles in the United States?

   (A) It is more difficult to refine than CNG.

   (B) It has the same environmental impact as CNG.

   (C) It is cheaper to use than CNG.

   (D) It is not produced in the United States.

7. According to the passage, it is easy to convert truck engines using gasoline to CNG because

   (A) the conversion is financed by environmental groups

   (B) the conversion simply requires installing one premade unit onto the engine

   (C) the conversion can be done by the driver of the truck

   (D) the conversion is done when the truck is manufactured in the factory

8. The author implies in the last paragraph that the cost of installing a CNG converter into a truck already in a company's fleet

   (A) pays for itself in savings in fuel costs

   (B) is greater than the cost of buying a truck that already runs on CNG

   (C) is equal to the cost of running a truck on diesel fuel

   (D) may be paid for by special-interest groups

9. According to the passage, all of the following are true of trucks that run on CNG EXCEPT

   (A) They are cheaper to run than trucks that run on gasoline.

   (B) The conversion process makes them more difficult to drive than trucks that run on gasoline.

   (C) They have a smaller environmental impact than trucks that run on gasoline.

   (D) Companies can have them converted to run CNG before taking delivery of them from the factory.

10. Sum up the passage by choosing three of the six sentences below and putting them in the correct order following the introductory sentence. The incorrect sentences will express information that was not in the passage or were minor ideas in the passage. This question is worth 2 points.

    Many companies are converting the trucks in their fleets to run on compressed natural gas (CNG) instead of gasoline or diesel.

    *

    *

    *

    1. Although CNG is more expensive than gasoline, many companies are switching to CNG for the environmental benefits.
    2. CNG is better for the environment than gasoline, as well as less expensive, and the cost savings for a fleet can be significant.
    3. CNG is refined primarily in the United States, which will now export CNG to other countries.
    4. After a technician installs the CNG conversion unit in a truck engine, the technician tests the installation to make sure it is working properly.
    5. Since the process of converting a truck that runs on gasoline to CNG is so simple, many companies are choosing to convert their fleets.
    6. There are significant financial incentives for a company to convert its fleet to run on CNG instead of gasoline.

In addition, because of the political visibility of the vast benefits of CNG, many states are implementing tax incentives that further reduce the cost of converting current vehicles from using gasoline to using CNG. At the same time, vehicles are being designed to use either CNG alone or to have duel-combustion systems that can run on either gasoline or compressed natural gas. Because of rapid industry growth and the increased availability of CNG technology, companies producing CNG or developing CNG conversion technology are investing in the development of infrastructure (CNG fueling stations) needed to support the rising number of CNG vehicles on the road.

11. Which of the following choices best expresses the essential meaning of the highlighted sentence in the passage? Incorrect choices will change the meaning or leave out important details.

    (A) CNG producers would like to see more CNG fueling stations available for users of CNG and companies that convert trucks to using CNG.

    (B) Companies that install CNG converters do not know where to refuel on CNG because there are still very few CNG fueling stations.

    (C) CNG producers are investing in CNG fueling stations to support the companies that perform CNG conversions on trucks.

    (D) CNG producers and companies that sell truck conversions are investing in building CNG fuel stations to support growth in the use of CNG.

12. The passage implies that
    (A) trucks that run on CNG have more cargo space than trucks that run gasoline
    (B) more trucks will run on CNG in the future
    (C) CNG fueling stations will be subsidized by CNG producers
    (D) the long-term environmental benefits of running a truck on CNG do not outweigh the significant costs of converting the truck

Passage 2

The Stages of Grief

In 1969, in her book *On Death and Dying*, psychologist Elisabeth Kübler-Ross introduced the idea that there are several distinct stages of grief. The book, which was based on her work with terminally ill and dying patients, posited that people who were going through the grieving process went through unique and separate stages. These stages are as follows: denial, anger, bargaining, depression, and acceptance.

While there are five commonly accepted stages in the Kübler-Ross model, other interpretations of her model use seven stages of grief, which are shock and denial, pain and guilt, anger and bargaining, depression and loneliness, beginning to heal, reconstruction, and acceptance and hope. The main differences are that the five stages model considers anger and bargaining to be two separate stages, does not include guilt, and considers the final three stages of the seven stages model to be one stage.

The five stages of the Kübler-Ross model can be summarized and applied to a wide variety of grief situations. The first stage, denial, consists of a phase in which the victim can't believe that something bad is happening. It takes time for the victim to process that the bad event is actually happening, and this stage may be lengthened by the unfolding of the news of the situation.

The second stage, anger, consists of a phase in which the victim becomes upset and filled with rage and jealousy of those outside of the bad situation. While the victim may feel justified in having these feelings, this stage can isolate the victim from people who would care for him or her by pushing them away.

In bargaining, the third stage, the victim feels a temporary hope that something they can do, give, or sacrifice will stop the bad situation from occurring or make the bad situation that has already happened (such as the death of a loved one or a divorce) go away. While this is rarely true, the hope provides the victim with a brief respite from the negative feelings of the anger stage, and can cause a temporary positive outlook. While this makes the victim easier to be around, those around the victim who know that the bad situation will continue also know that the victim's negative feelings will return as soon as it is discovered that no bargain can be struck that will end the bad situation.

The fourth stage of grief, depression, consists of the victim's realization that the bad situation is not going to end, and that he or she will not be able to escape it. Some victims become so mired in the sadness and other negative feelings of this stage that they lose interest in maintaining their lives and relationships. Ironically, the sadness and other negative feelings of the depression stage show that the victim is finally realizing that the bad situation is real and beginning to process that reality.

The fifth stage, acceptance, is when the victim begins to find peace with the bad situation and his or her place in it. While acceptance contains sadness, it is not the paralyzing sadness of the depression stage that makes the victim lose interest in others or in maintaining daily activities. Acceptance is the stage referred to as "coming out the other side."

Thousands of counselors around the world have used Kübler-Ross's model of the five stages of grief since she published the book. In the last few years, however, it has been suggested by psychologists and researchers that this model may be limited and too simplistic. Those who feel this say that grief is not a linear process, so distinct and separate stages cannot be assigned. Instead, it may be more useful to think of these five stages as common stages that victims of grief flow through in a nonlinear fashion, so that a victim can experience several stages at the same time, or over a short time period, and may flow back and forth through the model and return to earlier stages. Even if this new theory is correct, there is no doubt that Kübler-Ross's contribution to the theory of grieving is significant, as it has allowed humans to discuss grief in a way that shows both compassion and understanding of those who grieve.

13. What is the main idea of the passage?

    (A) to describe the stages of grief

    (B) to explain who Elisabeth Kübler-Ross was

    (C) to detail the differences in the five stages versus the seven stages of grief

    (D) to question the importance of the stages of grief theory

14. The word *grief* in the passage is closest in meaning to

    (A) sadness

    (B) mourning

    (C) theory

    (D) death

15. The word *stage* in the passage is closest in meaning to

    (A) theory

    (B) theater

    (C) phase

    (D) denial

16. The word *ire* in the passage is closest in meaning to
    (A) anger
    (B) denial
    (C) bargaining
    (D) grief
17. In the sixth paragraph, the word *it* refers to
    (A) the theory
    (B) Kübler-Ross
    (C) the victim
    (D) the bad situation
18. In the last paragraph, the author mentions psychologists and researchers in order to
    (A) show that those who question the theory are qualified to question it
    (B) question the credentials of those who debate the theory
    (C) deny claims that Kübler-Ross's theory is incorrect
    (D) maintain a sense of common usage
19. It can be inferred from the passage that
    (A) people who are dying will not survive to reach the acceptance stage
    (B) the seven stages model is more robust than the five stages model
    (C) Kübler-Ross's critics have more experience with grief than she did
    (D) the grieving person is not always dying
20. Which of the following can be inferred from the passage about the denial stage?
    (A) It results from information received by the victim.
    (B) It is the shortest stage.
    (C) It always lasts from a few days to a week.
    (D) It is combined with guilt.
21. The passage states that Kübler-Ross based her theory on her experience
    (A) working with children whose parents were divorcing
    (B) working with people who were dying
    (C) working with researchers who had a theory of seven stages of grief
    (D) working with the author of the book On Death and Dying

22. The author of the passage mentions the idea that some people disagree with Kübler-Ross's theory in order to

    (A) build a case that the theory is incorrect

    (B) establish that those people are the true experts

    (C) describe the credentials of those who support Kübler-Ross's work

    (D) show that there may be room for more work on this theory

In bargaining, the third stage, the victim feels a temporary hope that something they can do, give, or sacrifice will stop the bad situation from occurring. While this is rarely true, the hope provides the victim with a brief respite from the negative feelings of the anger stage, and can cause a temporary positive outlook. While this makes the victim easier to be around, those around the victim who know that the bad situation will continue also know that the victim's negative feelings will return as soon as it is discovered that no bargain can be struck that will end the bad situation.

23. Which of the following choices best expresses the essential meaning of the highlighted sentence in the passage? Incorrect choices will change the meaning or leave out important details.

    (A) Although nothing the victim does can affect the outcome of the situation, he or she may temporarily have hope that something can and become happy.

    (B) The victim may become very happy that something he or she does can change the outcome of the situation.

    (C) The victim may become very happy to think that something he or she does can change the outcome of the situation.

    (D) Nothing the victim does can change the outcome of the situation positively or negatively.

24. According to the passage, which of the following is characteristic of the acceptance stage?

    (A) feeling jealous

    (B) feeling guilty

    (C) feeling peaceful

    (D) feeling angry

Passage 3

Currency Exchange Rates

As different countries have different currencies of money, an international market exists for these currencies. This means, simply, that governments, private citizens, banks, and other organizations often desire to purchase the currency of a country they do not reside in and sell the currency they own of the country in which they reside. "Exchange rates" refers to the formulas used to determine how much any one country's currency can be bought or sold for relative to another country's currency. Some currencies, including the U.S. dollar, the

European euro, and the Japanese yen, are considered standard currencies, so the prices of other less-popular currencies are often expressed by exchange rates compared to the U.S. dollar, euro, and yen.

Exchange rates are determined primarily by the movement of the markets, which means that when there is more demand for one particular currency, the price of that currency will go up, and when there is less demand for a currency, the price of that currency will go down. If, for some reason, many organizations and people around the world want to buy the Mexican peso, the exchange rate will show that it costs more of other currencies to buy one peso. At the same time, 1 peso will be able to buy more of another currency should someone holding pesos want to sell those pesos to buy another currency.

Because exchange rates fluctuate, companies that do business internationally need to be mindful of the way they structure purchases and sales and what currency they use. For example, if an American company is selling something to a Japanese company, both companies need to think carefully about whether the sale should be transacted in U.S. dollars or Japanese yen (or some other currency entirely). It can be very costly for a company to make the wrong decision. In general, the company whose currency is being used for the transaction bears less risk than the company which is converting their currency for the sale. So if the two companies agree that the Japanese company will pay the U.S. company 500,000 U.S. dollars, the U.S. company will still receive that sum whether the exchange rate for yen to U.S. dollars goes up or down. In contrast, the Japanese company has to buy U.S. dollars to pay the bill. If the price of yen goes up between the time the contract is signed and the money is due, the Japanese company can buy more dollars with fewer yen and gets a deal. However, if the price of the yen to the U.S. dollar goes down, the Japanese company can end up owing much more money than initially thought.

The risks of doing transactions across currencies is called exposure. There are three types of exposure companies doing business internationally must contend with. The first, translation exposure, is simply a matter of the risk involved in converting one currency to another and how that is reflected in a company's statement of profits and losses. For example, a company that sells many of its products in U.S. dollars but has to report its earnings to shareholders in Euros will look like it has made less money simply because the dollar is weaker than the euro.

The second type of exposure, transaction exposure, is described in the example above of the Japanese company and the American company making a sale. Transaction exposure is really a time problem. Between the time you agree to the deal and the time you have to pay for or receive money for the deal, what will happen to the exchange rate? Will you receive or give more money, less money, or the same amount of money you thought you would have to pay? There are numerous ways for companies to attempt to protect themselves from the risk of exchange rate fluctuations that would hurt them, but these protections, called hedges, are merely insulation from risk, not any ability to get a favorable exchange rate when payment is due.

The third type of exposure is called economic exposure. This refers to the decisions a company makes about how to structure their business to take advantage of exchange rates. For instance, a company that sells its products in a country with a stronger currency but manufactures them in a country with a weaker currency benefits from the exchange rates on both sides of the transaction. However, there is always the risk that the stronger currency will get weaker, which means the sales revenue will go down or the weaker currency will get stronger, which in turn means that the manufacturing costs will go up. Understanding how currencies and exchange rates fluctuate, and the three types of exposure, is essential for companies that operate internationally.

25. The main idea of the passage is
    (A) how exchange rates are determined
    (B) transaction exposure for companies
    (C) purchasing power parity and interest rate parity
    (D) to describe the concepts of exchange rates for currency and how that affects international business
26. The word *currency* in the passage is closest in meaning to
    (A) kind of money
    (B) exchange rate
    (C) exposure
    (D) interest
27. The word *standard* in the passage is closest in meaning to
    (A) European
    (B) foreign
    (C) common
    (D) inflated
28. The word *fluctuate* in the passage is closest in meaning to
    (A) go up and down
    (B) cross international borders
    (C) be indecisive
    (D) stay at one level
29. The phrase *that currency* in the passage refers to
    (A) the U.S. dollar
    (B) an undetermined amount
    (C) the currency in greater demand
    (D) the currency in less demand

30. The author mentions the words *translation exposure*, *transaction exposure*, and *economic exposure* in the passage in order to

    (A) give an example of what can happen when the exchange rate goes up unexpectedly

    (B) list the three types of exposure a company doing business internationally faces

    (C) explain the process of causing exchange rates to fluctuate

    (D) question the assumption that there is no risk in doing business internationally

31. Which of the following can be inferred from the example of the Japanese company doing business with the U.S. company in dollars in the third paragraph?

    (A) In this example, the U.S. company is buying something from the Japanese company in dollars.

    (B) In this example, the U.S. company is buying something from the Japanese company in yen.

    (C) In this example, the Japanese company is buying something from the U.S. company in yen.

    (D) In this example, the Japanese company is buying something from the U.S. company in dollars.

32. You can infer from the passage that

    (A) things made in the United States are paid for in U.S. dollars

    (B) companies that are not located in the United States may need to purchase things in dollars

    (C) companies can minimize translation exposure by purchasing in U.S. dollars

    (D) using hedges to protect from exchange rate risk is illegal

33. All of the following can be inferred from the passage EXCEPT

    (A) Currencies that are purchased more often will be stronger than currencies that are not in demand.

    (B) Some currencies tend to be stronger than others.

    (C) The U.S. dollar is stronger than the Canadian dollar.

    (D) There is no one universal currency used by all countries worldwide.

34. According to the third paragraph, the company whose home currency is the currency chosen for payment bears

    (A) more risk, because there is no way to determine what the final payment will be

    (B) more risk, because the other company will get a better exchange rate

    (C) less risk, because the other company controls how much it will pay

    (D) less risk, because that company will receive the exact amount of money specified in the deal

The second type of exposure, transaction exposure, is described in the example above of the Japanese company and the American company making a sale. Transaction exposure is really a time problem. Between the time you agree to the deal and the time you have to pay for or receive money for the deal, what will happen to the exchange rate? Will you receive or give more money, less money, or the same amount of money you thought you would have to pay?

35. Which of the following choices best expresses the essential meaning of the highlighted sentence in the passage? Incorrect choices will change the meaning or leave out important details.

    (A) During the lag between when the deal is signed and the payment is due, the exchange rate may have changed, so the actual amount being paid or received may be higher or lower than initially anticipated.

    (B) Between when the deal is signed and payment is due, one or the other of the parties to the deal may change the terms of payment.

    (C) Even once a deal is signed, there is no way to guarantee how much money will be received from the deal.

    (D) Who will pay more or less money than they thought they would?

36. Look at the four bullets in the passage and indicate where the sentence below should be inserted.

    If either the amount of money received from sales or the amount of money required to produce products changes, the company's profits are affected.

    (A) The third type of exposure is called economic exposure. •If either the amount of money received from sales or the amount of money required to produce products changes, the company's profits are affected. This refers to the decisions a company makes about how to structure their business to take advantage of exchange rates. •For instance, a company that sells its products in a country with a stronger currency but manufactures them in a country with a weaker currency benefits from the exchange rates on both sides of the transaction. •However, there is always the risk that the stronger currency will get weaker, which means the sales revenue will go down or the weaker currency will get stronger, which in turn means that the manufacturing costs will go up. •Understanding how currencies and exchange rates fluctuate, and the three types of exposure, is essential for companies that operate internationally.

    (B) The third type of exposure is called economic exposure. •This refers to the decisions a company makes about how to structure their business to take advantage of exchange rates. •If either the amount of money received from sales or the amount of money required to produce products changes, the company's profits are affected. For instance, a company that sells its products in a country with a stronger currency but manufactures them in a country with a weaker currency benefits from the exchange rates on both sides of the transaction. •However, there is always the risk that the stronger currency will get weaker, which means the sales revenue will go down or the weaker currency will get stronger, which in turn means that the manufacturing costs will go up. •Understanding how currencies and exchange rates fluctuate, and the three types of exposure, is essential for companies that operate internationally.

(C) The third type of exposure is called economic exposure. •This refers to the decisions a company makes about how to structure their business to take advantage of exchange rates. •For instance, a company that sells its products in a country with a stronger currency but manufactures them in a country with a weaker currency benefits from the exchange rates on both sides of the transaction. •If either the amount of money received from sales or the amount of money required to produce products changes, the company's profits are affected. However, there is always the risk that the stronger currency will get weaker, which means the sales revenue will go down or the weaker currency will get stronger, which in turn means that the manufacturing costs will go up. •Understanding how currencies and exchange rates fluctuate, and the three types of exposure, is essential for companies that operate internationally.

(D) The third type of exposure is called economic exposure. •This refers to the decisions a company makes about how to structure their business to take advantage of exchange rates. •For instance, a company that sells its products in a country with a stronger currency but manufactures them in a country with a weaker currency benefits from the exchange rates on both sides of the transaction. •However, there is always the risk that the stronger currency will get weaker, which means the sales revenue will go down or the weaker currency will get stronger, which in turn means that the manufacturing costs will go up. •If either the amount of money received from sales or the amount of money required to produce products changes, the company's profits are affected. Understanding how currencies and exchange rates fluctuate, and the three types of exposure, is essential for companies that operate internationally.

Listening Section

Give yourself 60 minutes to complete this section.

Lecture 1

Listen to audio track 21.1 on idiotsguides.com/toefl.

1. Why does the student visit the registrar's office?
   (A) to request a copy of her transcript
   (B) to find out where she is on the waitlist
   (C) to find out why she can't register for a class
   (D) to ask the registrar about financial aid
2. Why was the student not able to register for the class?
   (A) The registrar could not find the class from last semester.
   (B) The student does not have a computer.
   (C) The waitlist was too long.
   (D) The class was already filled with other students.
3. Why must the student register for a philosophy class?
   (A) The registrar cannot find the student's account in the system.
   (B) The student does not have room in her schedule for a philosophy class.
   (C) The student needs to be registered for a minimum number of classes to continue to receive financial aid.
   (D) The student can take a later philosophy class than 8 a.m.

Listen to audio track 21.2 on idiotsguides.com/toefl

4. What did the registrar mean?
   (A) If three people get sick and stop coming to the class, the woman will be able to register for the class.
   (B) If three people who are registered for the class drop the class next week, they free up three spaces for the student and the two people already on the waitlist.
   (C) There are still three spots open in the class, but they are first come first served.
   (D) The registrar has no idea if the woman will be able to get into the class by looking at the size of the waitlist.

5. What will the student do now?

   (A) Attend the classes the registrar has signed her up for.

   (B) Send an email to find out if she has gotten off the waitlist.

   (C) Attend the 8 a.m. session of the philosophy class.

   (D) Register for financial aid.

Lecture 2

Listen to audio track 21.3 on idiotsguides.com/toefl.

6. Why does the student ask the other student to borrow money?

   (A) The student has run out of money on her meal plan card.

   (B) The student needs to buy soup.

   (C) The student needs to take the bus to the Dining Services office.

   (D) The student does not have a debit card.

7. How much does the student have left on her meal plan card account?

   (A) nothing, as she just spent everything left on the card

   (B) nothing, which is why she is not eating lunch

   (C) enough to last the rest of the semester

   (D) one dollar and fifty cents

8. According to the male student, which of the following is true?

   (A) The Dining Services office is the large building next to the law library.

   (B) Once the money in the meal plan is used, there is no way to add more money to the account.

   (C) The Dining Services office can only take cash.

   (D) A payment can be made to the meal plan card account with a debit card.

Listen to audio track 21.4 on idiotsguides.com/toefl.

9. What did the female student mean?

   (A) She is not sure she can do it.

   (B) She thinks it is not a challenging-enough task for her to attempt.

   (C) She thinks she can do it without much effort.

   (D) She doesn't want to do it because it is too much of a challenge.

10. What will the student do immediately after this conversation?
    (A) buy some soup
    (B) go to the Dining Services office
    (C) go to dinner
    (D) study for a quiz online

Lecture 3

Listen to audio track 21.5 on idiotsguides.com/toefl.

11. What is the topic of the lecture?
    (A) hierarchical structures
    (B) summer internships
    (C) organizational dynamics
    (D) flat structures
12. According to the professor, the field of organizational dynamics is
    (A) a mixture of several other disciplines
    (B) an older discipline
    (C) needed to understand compensation schemes for most organizations
    (D) not yet proven by research
13. The lecture states that
    (A) organizational dynamics consists of the study of the way organizations are structured
    (B) there are different ways an organization can be structured
    (C) hierarchical structures are preferred over flat structures
    (D) the opposite of a flat structure is a matrix structure

Listen to audio track 21.6 on idiotsguides.com/toefl.

14. What does the professor mean when she says this?
    (A) The chain of command at a flat structure is very informal and cannot be understood by employees at that organization.
    (B) A flat structure cannot induce employees to show respect to each other.
    (C) A flat structure does not have to do with the military chain of command.
    (D) The structure of the organization is described visually, so a flat structure has no strong hierarchy or vertical chain of command.

15. How does the professor show how structure affects employee behavior?
    (A) by detailing the different structures an organization can have with diagrams
    (B) by asking a student details of how he behaved on a job he had
    (C) by showing that a student who worked in an internship had not been subject to the structure of the company he had worked at
    (D) by explaining why a flat structure is the best structure for cooperation
16. The lecture implies that
    (A) there are other areas of study in organizational dynamics than structures of organizations
    (B) a hierarchical structure creates more opportunities for interaction across job functions
    (C) organizational dynamics is not accepted as a valid field of study by all managers
    (D) flat structures only work in fields in which employees have creative skills

Lecture 4

Listen to audio track 21.7 on idiotsguides.com/toefl.

17. What is the topic of the lecture?
    (A) the four dialects of Szechuanese
    (B) why Mandarin is increasing in use in China
    (C) how Szechuanese is different from Mandarin
    (D) the two most commonly spoken Chinese languages
18. According to the lecture, when did Szechuanese begin to develop?
    (A) Szechuanese began to develop when other, non-Chinese languages began to rise in Europe.
    (B) Szechuanese developed in the southern provinces of China.
    (C) Szechuanese began to develop right around the time that Mandarin became the official language of China.
    (D) Szechuanese is a dialect of Mandarin.
19. The professor states that Mandarin
    (A) was in use from the year 1000 through the fourteenth century
    (B) began developing in the year 1000 and is still in use today
    (C) continues to increase in use in China because the other dialects are considered frivolous
    (D) is considered a dialect of Szechuanese

Listen to audio track 21.8 on idiotsguides.com/toefl.

20. What does the professor mean when she says this?

    (A) Those other dialects and languages are not flourishing anymore.

    (B) Mandarin is no longer the official language of China.

    (C) Not everyone in China speaks Mandarin.

    (D) Mandarin is spoken by more people in Hong Kong than any other language.

21. How does the professor show the relationship of Szechuanese to Mandarin?

    (A) She describes the history of the development of Standard Chinese.

    (B) She describes the ways the two languages are similar and dissimilar to each other.

    (C) She describes the Chinese government's concern with preserving Szechuanese.

    (D) She describes the way broadcast media is increasing the spread of Mandarin.

22. You can infer from the lecture that the professor

    (A) has not been to the parts of China that speak one of the four Szechuanese dialects

    (B) speaks Szechuanese but not Mandarin

    (C) speaks Mandarin but not Szechuanese

    (D) knows more about dialects of Mandarin than she is able to discuss in this short lecture

Lecture 5

Listen to audio track 21.9 on idiotsguides.com/toefl.

23. What is the topic of the lecture?

    (A) natural features of Puerto Rico

    (B) bioluminescent bays

    (C) El Yunque rainforest

    (D) conservation of rainforest land

24. According to the lecture, the dry season in El Yunque

    (A) begins after the hurricane season

    (B) lasts for six months

    (C) does not exist; it rains every day

    (D) does not exist; it is dry every day

25. The lecture says that the bioluminescence of the bay is caused by
    (A) vitamin B_{12}
    (B) lights that have been placed on the bottom of the bay
    (C) special coral that reflect the light of the moon
    (D) tiny plankton that glow

Listen to audio track 21.10 on idiotsguides.com/toefl.

26. What does the professor mean when she says this?
    (A) No reporters have seen a chupacabra.
    (B) The stories are just stories, because the details in them cannot be confirmed.
    (C) If the chupacabra exists, it does not live in El Yunque.
    (D) Only native Puerto Ricans can see the chupacabra.
27. How does the professor show that the chupacabra stories are not official, verified information?
    (A) The professor says, "As an aside" and tells the chupacabra stories as an unofficial note.
    (B) The professor asks the students to prove the chupacabra stories.
    (C) The professor discusses the reasons a chupacabra cannot exist.
    (D) The professor explains why no one has been able to verify the existence of a chupacabra.
28. The lecture implies that
    (A) U.S. forest rangers consider El Yunque not officially part of the national system
    (B) the bioluminescent bay will disappear soon because of pollution
    (C) no other national forests in the U.S. system have the same climate as El Yunque
    (D) a rainforest and a bioluminescent bay exist only in Puerto Rico

Lecture 6

Listen to audio track 21.11 on idiotsguides.com/toefl.

29. What is the topic of the lecture?
    (A) Lars Magnus Ericsson's original mobile telephone
    (B) cellular technology
    (C) the differences between the generations of mobile telephony
    (D) the development of mobile telephones

30. According to the lecture, sound is transmitted
    (A) as waves through wires or the air
    (B) from cars to base stations
    (C) from a cell receiver to a transmitter
    (D) more slowly than data
31. According to the professor, 2G technology is
    (A) analog transmission of sound
    (B) digital transmission of sound
    (C) digital transmission of sound and data
    (D) broadband digital transmission of sound and data

Listen to audio track 21.12 on idiotsguides.com/toefl.

32. What does the professor mean when he says this?
    (A) Ericsson hadn't dreamed of putting a telephone into a car.
    (B) Ericsson had designed his car along with the telephone in it.
    (C) Ericsson had a better car than anyone else at the time.
    (D) Ericsson's mobile phone was ahead of the rest of technology at the time.
33. Why does the professor discuss the lack of available radio spectrum for Ericsson?
    (A) to demonstrate the need for more radio spectrum to be opened up by the Swedish government
    (B) to show that Ericsson was an anomaly
    (C) to explain why it took so many years from his first mobile phone to develop mobile phone technology
    (D) to discuss radio receivers at the time
34. The lecture implies that
    (A) Bell Labs took Ericsson's ideas and claimed them as their own
    (B) as transmission technology improves, phones will have increasing capabilities
    (C) the Japanese were more interested in car phones than Americans
    (D) newer phones will no longer transmit data digitally

Speaking Section

Give yourself 20 minutes to complete this section.

Question 1

Read the prompt and give yourself 15 seconds to prep and write notes. Then take 45 seconds to record your response.

1. Describe a song that is meaningful to you. Please include specific examples and reasons why the song is meaningful.

Question 2

Read the prompt and give yourself 15 seconds to prep and write notes. Then take 45 seconds to record your response.

2. Some students finish their university studies as quickly as possible so they can graduate and begin working. Other students work while they go to university, which means they take longer to finish university but have been working during that time. Which method of sequencing university studies and work makes the most sense, and why?

Question 3

The university has changed the hours during which students can use the gymnasium facilities. Read the notice posted on the door of the gym. You will have 45 seconds to read the notice. Begin reading now.

Notice

Effective May 5, the gym hours will be extended to 5 A.M. to midnight Monday through Friday, 5 A.M. to 8 P.M. Saturday, and 9 A.M. to 8 P.M. Sunday. Pool open swim hours will be from 5 A.M. to 9 A.M. and 8 P.M. to midnight Monday through Friday, 6 A.M. to 8 P.M. Saturday, and 10 A.M. to 8 P.M. Sunday. Open gym hours will be 7 A.M. to 10 P.M. Monday through Friday, 7 A.M. to 7 P.M. Saturday, and 10 A.M. to 7 P.M. Sunday. All class times will be posted in the course catalog as soon as they are scheduled.

Listen to audio track 21.13 on idiotsguides.com/toefl.

Now get ready to answer the question. Give yourself 30 seconds to create notes for your response. Then take 60 seconds to speak your response.

3. The man has a problem related to the information in the notice. State what the problem is and what he decides to do about that problem.

Question 4

In this question, you will read a short passage on an academic subject and then listen to a talk on the same topic. You will then answer a question using information from both the reading passage and the talk. After you hear the question, you will have 30 seconds to prepare your response and 60 seconds to speak.

Read the passage about climate change. You will have 45 seconds to read the passage. Begin reading now.

> Climate change caused by pollution and other human intervention in the natural workings of the planet Earth has accelerated in the last 20 years. Before this point, only scientists were noticing symptoms of climate change, but in the last few decades, the change has become noticeable even to the common person. Changes in average temperature, an increase in lethal climate events around the world, and changing weather patterns have begun to catch the attention of the popular press and have entered into the international discourse. Unfortunately, there has been little agreement on how to stop or slow this climate change, so the awareness is not leading to productive steps to manage or end climate change.

Listen to audio track 21.14 on idiotsguides.com/toefl.

Now get ready to answer the question. Give yourself 30 seconds to create notes for your response. Then take 60 seconds to speak your response.

4. The professor describes some of the effects of climate change and the problems we have implementing solutions to climate change. Explain how these effects and problems relate to and contrast with each other.

Question 5

In this question, you will hear a conversation. Then you will be asked to talk about the conversation and give your opinion about the subject of the conversation. You will be given 20 seconds to prepare. Then you will be given 60 seconds to speak.

Listen to audio track 21.15 on idiotsguides.com/toefl.

Give yourself 20 seconds to create notes for your response. Then take 60 seconds to speak your response.

5. The students discuss two housing options for the woman's living situation in the coming year. Describe the two options. Then explain which option you think she should pursue, and why.

Question 6

Listen to audio track 21.16 on idiotsguides.com/toefl.

Give yourself 20 seconds to create notes for your response. Then take 60 seconds to speak your response.

6. Using facts and examples from the lecture, explain how frostbite can occur and what the different degrees of frostbite are.

Writing Section

Give yourself 20 minutes for the first writing task and 30 minutes for the second writing task.

Integrated Writing Task

Reading:

On August 28, 1963, the Reverend Martin Luther King Jr. delivered a speech to a crowd of 200,000 civil rights activists from the steps of the Lincoln Memorial in Washington, D.C., as part of a march on Washington for civil rights. The speech, which became known as the "I Have a Dream" speech, lasted 17 minutes and left a lasting legacy for Dr. King.

The march, called the March on Washington for Jobs and Freedom, was designed to be a peaceful march which would appeal to a large segment of the American population. The march's organizers wanted the march to show a peaceful side of the civil rights movement, which had been characterized up to that point by civil disobedience. Civil disobedience is the act of actively refusing to comply with rules or laws that violate civil rights. Civil disobedience is often called nonviolent resistance, but those who practice civil disobedience have historically been victims of violence against them by citizens and authorities who have an interest in maintaining the status quo.

The peaceful nature of the march was designed to appeal to average Americans who may not have been engaged with the civil rights movement up to that point. Dr. King's speech echoed the peaceful nature of the march. He began by referencing Abraham Lincoln's Emancipation Proclamation and built a case for national unity, not division, and equal rights for all. The speech achieved its purpose by inspiring many who had never identified with the civil rights movement to support equal rights for all Americans.

Lecture: Listen to audio track 21.17 on idiotsguides.com/toefl.

1. Summarize the points made in the lecture, being sure to explain how they differ from the view in the reading passage.

Independent Writing Task

Do you agree or disagree with the following statement? Use specific details and examples to support your answer.

2. It is more important to exercise your mind than it is to exercise your body.

Chapter 22

Practice Test 2 Answer Keys and Explanations

Here are the answer keys and explanations for the second practice test.

Reading Section Answer Key

1. C
2. C
3. A
4. D
5. A
6. D
7. B
8. A
9. B
10. 2, 6, 5
11. D
12. B
13. A
14. B
15. C
16. A
17. D
18. A
19. D
20. A
21. B
22. D
23. A
24. C
25. D
26. A
27. C
28. A
29. C
30. B

31. D
32. B
33. C
34. D
35. A
36. D

Reading Section Explanations

1. What is the main idea of the passage?

   (A) what compressed natural gas is

   (B) why companies are becoming more environmentally friendly

   (C) compressed natural gas as a fuel source that is good for the environment and for companies that convert to it

   (D) how CNG conversion is performed on a truck that runs on gasoline

   The answer is C. The passage discusses compressed natural gas and why it is good for business and the environment. Eliminate A, B, and D because they are all small parts of the passage but not the main point.

2. The word *modify* in the passage is closest in meaning to

   (A) substitute

   (B) make less intense

   (C) change

   (D) reduce

   The answer is C. *Modify* means "to alter or change." Eliminate A, B, and D because they are not the meanings of *modify*.

3. The word *factors* in the passage is closest in meaning to

   (A) issues

   (B) disasters

   (C) products

   (D) benefits

   The answer is A. The passage gives examples of factors, which shows that it means "issues or events." Eliminate B because it goes too far. Eliminate C because products and factors are terms from mathematics but do not have anything to do with the topic of this passage. Eliminate D because it goes too far.

4. The phrase *these units* in the passage refers to

(A) CNG fueling stations

(B) gasoline engines

(C) CNG engines

(D) CNG engine conversion units

The answer is D. The sentence previous to this phrase refers to units to convert gasoline engines to run on CNG. Eliminate A and C because they are referenced only briefly and are not referred to by that phrase. Eliminate B because it would contradict the meaning of the passage.

5. In the second paragraph, why does the author include information about the types of companies that are the market for compressed natural gas vehicles?

(A) to give examples of companies that use fleets of trucks so the reader understands the economics for the company

(B) to question whether the market is so narrow that the technology is not worth pursuing

(C) to examine the motivations for these companies to make such a radical choice for fuel

(D) to describe the process of converting a gasoline engine to a CNG engine

The answer is A. The author includes information about the specific types of companies that convert their fleets to CNG, so the business issues make sense in context. Eliminate B and C because they are misrepresentations of information in the passage. Eliminate D because it is not mentioned until much later in the passage.

6. Which of the following can be inferred from the second paragraph about the gasoline used to run fleet vehicles in the United States?

(A) It is more difficult to refine than CNG.

(B) It has the same environmental impact as CNG.

(C) It is cheaper to use than CNG.

(D) It is not produced in the United States.

The answer is D. The passage states that one benefit to using CNG is that it can be produced domestically, which implies that gasoline is not. Eliminate A because it is not implied. Eliminate B because there is no evidence to support this in the passage. Eliminate C because the opposite is true.

7. According to the passage, it is easy to convert truck engines using gasoline to CNG because

   (A) the conversion is financed by environmental groups

   (B) the conversion simply requires installing one premade unit onto the engine

   (C) the conversion can be done by the driver of the truck

   (D) the conversion is done when the truck is manufactured in the factory

   The answer is B. The passage states that conversion is simple because the process only requires installing one premade unit. Eliminate A and C because there is no evidence for either one of them in the passage. Eliminate D because the passage states that this is not true.

8. The author implies in the last paragraph that the cost of installing a CNG converter into a truck already in a company's fleet

   (A) pays for itself in savings in fuel costs

   (B) is greater than the cost of buying a truck that already runs on CNG

   (C) is equal to the cost of running a truck on diesel fuel

   (D) may be paid for by special-interest groups

   The answer is A. The passage states that the cost of the conversion will be offset by savings in fuel costs. Eliminate B because the opposite is true. Eliminate C because there was no comparison to diesel fuel. Eliminate D because this is not stated in the passage.

9. According to the passage, all of the following are true of trucks that run on CNG EXCEPT

   (A) They are cheaper to run than trucks that run on gasoline.

   (B) The conversion process makes them more difficult to drive than trucks that run on gasoline.

   (C) They have a smaller environmental impact than trucks that run on gasoline.

   (D) Companies can have them converted to run CNG before taking delivery of them from the factory.

   The answer is B. The passage does not discuss the difficulty of driving trucks that have been converted to run CNG. Eliminate A, C, and D because they are all found in the passage.

10. Sum up the passage by choosing three of the six sentences below and putting them in the correct order following the introductory sentence. The incorrect sentences will express information that was not in the passage or were minor ideas in the passage. This question is worth 2 points.

Many companies are converting the trucks in their fleets to run on compressed natural gas (CNG) instead of gasoline or diesel.

*

*

*

1. Although CNG is more expensive than gasoline, many companies are switching to CNG for the environmental benefits.
2. CNG is better for the environment than gasoline, as well as less expensive, and the cost savings for a fleet can be significant.
3. CNG is refined primarily in the United States, which will now export CNG to other countries.
4. After a technician installs the CNG conversion unit in a truck engine, the technician tests the installation to make sure it is working properly.
5. Since the process of converting a truck that runs on gasoline to CNG is so simple, many companies are choosing to convert their fleets.
6. There are significant financial incentives for a company to convert its fleet to run on CNG instead of gasoline.

The answer is 2, 6, 5. This sequence tells why companies are interested in CNG, what the main reason for switching to CNG is for these companies, and how simple the conversion process is. Eliminate 1 because it is the opposite of the information in the passage. Eliminate 3 because it is not in the passage. Eliminate 4 because it is a small detail in the passage.

In addition, because of the political visibility of the vast benefits of CNG, many states are implementing tax incentives that further reduce the cost of converting current vehicles from using gasoline to using CNG. At the same time, vehicles are being designed to use either CNG alone or to have duel combustion systems that can run on either gasoline or compressed natural gas. Because of rapid industry growth and the increased availability of CNG technology, companies producing CNG or developing CNG conversion technology are investing in the development of infrastructure (CNG fueling stations) needed to support the rising number of CNG vehicles on the road.

11. Which of the following choices best expresses the essential meaning of the highlighted sentence in the passage? Incorrect choices will change the meaning or leave out important details.

    (A) CNG producers would like to see more CNG fueling stations available for users of CNG and companies that convert trucks to using CNG.

    (B) Companies that install CNG converters do not know where to refuel on CNG because there are still very few CNG fueling stations.

    (C) CNG producers are investing in CNG fueling stations to support the companies that perform CNG conversions on trucks.

    (D) CNG producers and companies that sell truck conversions are investing in building CNG fuel stations to support growth in the use of CNG.

    The answer is D. It summarizes the highlighted section appropriately. Eliminate A and C because they discuss the CNG producers' desire for more CNG fueling stations without discussion of the companies that do conversions to CNG. Eliminate B because this is never mentioned in the passage.

12. The passage implies that

    (A) trucks that run on CNG have more cargo space than trucks that run gasoline

    (B) more trucks will run on CNG in the future

    (C) CNG fueling stations will be subsidized by CNG producers

    (D) the long-term environmental benefits of running a truck on CNG do not outweigh the significant costs of converting the truck

    The answer is B. The last paragraph discusses the increase in the number of trucks running on CNG and how this trend is continuing. Eliminate A because this is not indicated in the passage. Eliminate C because this is a misrepresentation of the passage. Eliminate D because it is contradicted in the passage.

13. What is the main idea of the passage?

    (A) to describe the stages of grief

    (B) to explain who Elisabeth Kübler-Ross was

    (C) to detail the differences in the five stages versus the seven stages of grief

    (D) to question the importance of the stages of grief theory

The answer is A. The passage describes Kübler-Ross's stages of grief theory. Eliminate B, C, and D because they are details in the passage, not the main idea.

14. The word *grief* in the passage is closest in meaning to

    (A) sadness

    (B) mourning

    (C) theory

    (D) death

    The answer is B. Grief is the process of mourning. Eliminate A, as *sadness* is close but not correct. Eliminate C because it has nothing to do with grief. Eliminate D, as grief can accompany death but is not the same thing.

15. The word *stage* in the passage is closest in meaning to

    (A) theory

    (B) theater

    (C) phase

    (D) denial

    The answer is C. The word *stage* in the passage means "step or phase." Eliminate A, as it does not mean *stage.* Eliminate B because it is a different meaning of *stage* not used in the passage. Eliminate D because *denial* is a stage but does not mean *stage.*

16. The word *ire* in the passage is closest in meaning to

    (A) anger

    (B) denial

    (C) bargaining

    (D) grief

    The answer is A. The word *ire* is a synonym for *rage* and *anger.* Eliminate B, C, and D, as they come from different stages than the anger stage, which contains the word *ire.*

17. In the sixth paragraph, the word *it* refers to

    (A) the theory

    (B) Kübler-Ross

    (C) the victim

    (D) the bad situation

    The answer is D. The word *it* refers to the phrase "the bad situation" earlier in the sentence. Eliminate A because the theory is not referred to earlier in the sentence. Eliminate B and C because *it* is not used to refer to people.

18. In the last paragraph, the author mentions psychologists and researchers in order to

    (A) show that those who question the theory are qualified to question it

    (B) question the credentials of those who debate the theory

    (C) deny claims that Kübler-Ross's theory is incorrect

    (D) maintain a sense of common usage

    The answer is A. The author mentions psychologists and researchers to show that those who question Kübler-Ross's theory are experts who are qualified to question it. Eliminate B and C because they are opposite of what the passage is trying to say. Eliminate D because it does not follow the passage.

19. It can be inferred from the passage that

    (A) people who are dying will not survive to reach the Acceptance stage

    (B) the seven stages model is more robust than the five stages model

    (C) Kübler-Ross's critics have more experience with grief than she did

    (D) the grieving person is not always dying

    The answer is D. The passage states that the theory can be used for people in any grief situation. Eliminate A because this is not implied in the passage at all. Eliminate B and C because they are too far of a reach from the information in the passage.

20. Which of the following can be inferred from the passage about the Denial stage?

    (A) It results from information received by the victim.

    (B) It is the shortest stage.

    (C) It always lasts from a few days to a week.

    (D) It is combined with guilt.

    The answer is A. The passage says that denial can be affected by the length of time it takes for the victim to receive full information. Eliminate B and C because there is no information about them in the passage. Eliminate D because it is a misrepresentation of the passage.

21. The passage states that Kübler-Ross based her theory on her experience

    (A) working with children whose parents were divorcing

    (B) working with people who were dying

    (C) working with researchers who had a theory of seven stages of grief

    (D) working with the author of the book *On Death and Dying*

    The answer is B. The passage says that her theory came out of her work with people who were dying. Eliminate A because this is never mentioned in the passage. Eliminate C and D because these are misrepresentations of the information in the passage.

22. The author of the passage mentions the idea that some people disagree with Kübler-Ross's theory in order to

    (A) build a case that the theory is incorrect

    (B) establish that those people are the true experts

    (C) describe the credentials of those who support Kübler-Ross's work

    (D) show that there may be room for more work on this theory

    The answer is D. The author shows that the theory is sound but may need to be refined even more. Eliminate A and B because they go too far. Eliminate C because it misrepresents information in the passage.

In bargaining, the third stage, the victim feels a temporary hope that something they can do, give, or sacrifice will stop the bad situation from occurring. While this is rarely true, the hope provides the victim with a brief respite from the negative feelings of the anger stage, and can cause a temporary positive outlook. While this makes the victim easier to be around, those around the victim who know that the bad situation will continue also know that the victim's negative feelings will return as soon as it is discovered that no bargain can be struck that will end the bad situation.

23. Which of the following choices best expresses the essential meaning of the highlighted sentence in the passage? Incorrect choices will change the meaning or leave out important details.

    (A) Although nothing the victim does can affect the outcome of the situation, he or she may temporarily have hope that something can and become happy.

    (B) The victim may become very happy that something he or she does can change the outcome of the situation.

    (C) The victim may become very happy to think that something he or she does can change the outcome of the situation.

    (D) Nothing the victim does can change the outcome of the situation positively or negatively.

    The answer is A. This covers the idea that the victim's actions can't stop the bad event from happening, but the victim gets hope from thinking that he or she can. Eliminate B and C because they leave out the idea that nothing the victim does can change the outcome. Eliminate D because it leaves out the idea that the victim becomes happy.

24. According to the passage, which of the following is characteristic of the acceptance stage?

    (A) feeling jealous

    (B) feeling guilty

    (C) feeling peaceful

    (D) feeling angry

    The answer is C. The passage states that part of acceptance is coming to peace with the situation. Eliminate A and D because they are from the anger stage. Eliminate B because it is from the seven stages of grief theory.

25. The main idea of the passage is

 (A) how exchange rates are determined

 (B) transaction exposure for companies

 (C) purchasing power parity and interest rate parity

 (D) to describe the concepts of exchange rates for currency and how that affects international business

 The answer is D. The passage describes the concepts of currency exchange rates and how those rates affect businesses in the international market. Eliminate A and B, as they are details of the passage, not the main idea. Eliminate C, as this is out of the scope of the passage.

26. The word *currency* in the passage is closest in meaning to

 (A) kind of money

 (B) exchange rate

 (C) exposure

 (D) interest

 The answer is A. Currency is the type of money used in a country. Eliminate B because currencies are traded by exchange rates. Eliminate C and D because they are not related to the word.

27. The word *standard* in the passage is closest in meaning to

 (A) European

 (B) foreign

 (C) common

 (D) inflated

 The answer is C. The most commonly traded currencies are common. Eliminate A and B because *standard* does not have anything to do with *origin*. Eliminate D because inflation is out of the scope of the passage.

28. The word *fluctuate* in the passage is closest in meaning to

 (A) go up and down

 (B) cross international borders

 (C) be indecisive

 (D) stay at one level

 The answer is A. *Fluctuate* means "to go up and down." Eliminate B and C because they have nothing to do with the word. Eliminate D because it is the opposite in meaning to the word.

29. The phrase *that currency* in the passage refers to

    (A) the U.S. dollar

    (B) an undetermined amount

    (C) the currency in greater demand

    (D) the currency in less demand

    The answer is C. In the highlighted passage, the phrase *that currency* directly follows the mention of the phrase "more demand for one particular currency." Eliminate A because it is an assumption. Eliminate B because it is not indicated in the passage. Eliminate D because it is the opposite of the correct answer.

30. The author mentions the words *translation exposure*, *transaction exposure*, and *economic exposure* in the passage in order to

    (A) give an example of what can happen when the exchange rate goes up unexpectedly

    (B) list the three types of exposure a company doing business internationally faces

    (C) explain the process of causing exchange rates to fluctuate

    (D) question the assumption that there is no risk in doing business internationally

    The answer is B. Those are the three types of exposure for an international company. Eliminate A because it misrepresents information in the passage. Eliminate C because those phrases do not cause fluctuation. Eliminate D because no assumption is presented that says there is no risk to doing business internationally.

31. Which of the following can be inferred from the example of the Japanese company doing business with the U.S. company in dollars in the third paragraph?

    (A) In this example, the U.S. company is buying something from the Japanese company in dollars.

    (B) In this example, the U.S. company is buying something from the Japanese company in yen.

    (C) In this example, the Japanese company is buying something from the U.S. company in yen.

    (D) In this example, the Japanese company is buying something from the U.S. company in dollars.

    The answer is D. The Japanese company is buying something from the U.S. company because the Japanese company is paying money, and it is paying in dollars. Eliminate A and B because the Japanese company is buying something, not selling something. Eliminate C because the Japanese company is paying in dollars.

32. You can infer from the passage that

    (A) things made in the United States are paid for in U.S. dollars

    (B) companies that are not located in the United States may need to purchase things in dollars

    (C) companies can minimize translation exposure by purchasing in U.S. dollars

    (D) using hedges to protect from exchange rate risk is illegal

    The answer is B. The example in the passage illustrates this answer choice by showing a situation in which a foreign company purchased something in U.S. dollars. Eliminate A because it is stated that the companies choose what currency to use for a transaction. Eliminate C because this would not help translation exposure at all. Eliminate D because this is not implied in the passage.

33. All of the following can be inferred from the passage EXCEPT

    (A) Currencies that are purchased more often will be stronger than currencies that are not in demand.

    (B) Some currencies tend to be stronger than others.

    (C) The U.S. dollar is stronger than the Canadian dollar.

    (D) There is no one universal currency used by all countries worldwide.

    The answer is C. The passage contains no information about the U.S. dollar relative to the Canadian dollar. Eliminate A, B, and D because they are all referenced in the passage.

34. According to the third paragraph, the company whose home currency is the currency chosen for payment bears

    (A) more risk, because there is no way to determine what the final payment will be

    (B) more risk, because the other company will get a better exchange rate

    (C) less risk, because the other company controls how much it will pay

    (D) less risk, because that company will receive the exact amount of money specified in the deal

    The answer is D. The company that uses the currency in which the deal is written will receive exactly the amount in the contract. Eliminate A and B because that company bears less risk. Eliminate C because the other company does not control how much it will pay because of exchange rates.

The second type of exposure, transaction exposure, is described in the example above of the Japanese company and the American company making a sale. Transaction exposure is really a time problem. Between the time you agree to the deal and the time you have to pay for or receive money for the deal, what will happen to the exchange rate? Will you receive or give more money, less money, or the same amount of money you thought you would have to pay?

35. Which of the following choices best expresses the essential meaning of the highlighted sentence in the passage? Incorrect choices will change the meaning or leave out important details.

    (A) During the lag between when the deal is signed and the payment is due, the exchange rate may have changed so the actual amount being paid or received may be higher or lower than initially anticipated.

    (B) Between when the deal is signed and payment is due, one or the other of the parties to the deal may change the terms of payment.

    (C) Even once a deal is signed, there is no way to guarantee how much money will be received from the deal.

    (D) Who will pay more or less money than they thought they would?

    The answer is A. This covers the concept of time allowing the exchange rate to fluctuate to change the payment amount. Eliminate B because it is not true. Eliminate C because it omits the concept of exchange rate. Eliminate D because it omits the concepts of time and exchange rate.

36. Look at the four bullets in the passage and indicate where the sentence below should be inserted.

    If either the amount of money received from sales or the amount of money required to produce products changes, the company's profits are affected.

    (A) The third type of exposure is called economic exposure. •If either the amount of money received from sales or the amount of money required to produce products changes, the company's profits are affected. This refers to the decisions a company makes about how to structure their business to take advantage of exchange rates. •For instance, a company that sells its products in a country with a stronger currency but manufactures them in a country with a weaker currency benefits from the exchange rates on both sides of the transaction. •However, there is always the risk that the stronger currency will get weaker, which means the sales revenue will go down or the weaker currency will get stronger, which in turn means that the manufacturing costs will go up. •Understanding how currencies and exchange rates fluctuate, and the three types of exposure, is essential for companies that operate internationally.

    (B) The third type of exposure is called economic exposure. •This refers to the decisions a company makes about how to structure their business to take advantage of exchange rates. •If either the amount of money received from sales or the amount of money required to produce products changes, the company's profits are affected. For instance, a company that sells its products in a country with a stronger currency but manufactures them in a country with a weaker currency benefits from the exchange rates on both sides of the transaction. •However, there is always the risk that the stronger currency will get weaker, which means the sales revenue will go down or the weaker currency will get stronger, which in turn means that the manufacturing costs will go up. •Understanding how currencies and exchange rates fluctuate, and the three types of exposure, is essential for companies that operate internationally.

(C) The third type of exposure is called economic exposure. •This refers to the decisions a company makes about how to structure their business to take advantage of exchange rates. •For instance, a company that sells its products in a country with a stronger currency but manufactures them in a country with a weaker currency benefits from the exchange rates on both sides of the transaction. •If either the amount of money received from sales or the amount of money required to produce products changes, the company's profits are affected. However, there is always the risk that the stronger currency will get weaker, which means the sales revenue will go down or the weaker currency will get stronger, which in turn means that the manufacturing costs will go up. •Understanding how currencies and exchange rates fluctuate, and the three types of exposure, is essential for companies that operate internationally.

(D) The third type of exposure is called economic exposure. •This refers to the decisions a company makes about how to structure their business to take advantage of exchange rates. •For instance, a company that sells its products in a country with a stronger currency but manufactures them in a country with a weaker currency benefits from the exchange rates on both sides of the transaction. •However, there is always the risk that the stronger currency will get weaker, which means the sales revenue will go down or the weaker currency will get stronger, which in turn means that the manufacturing costs will go up. •If either the amount of money received from sales or the amount of money required to produce products changes, the company's profits are affected. Understanding how currencies and exchange rates fluctuate, and the three types of exposure, is essential for companies that operate internationally.

The answer is D. The inserted sentence explains why the information in the sentence right before it—about fluctuations in currency—is important, because currency fluctuations can affect profits. Eliminate A, B, and C because they refer to the positions before they are explained.

Listening Section Answer Key

1. C
2. D
3. C
4. B
5. A
6. A
7. A
8. D
9. C
10. B
11. C
12. A
13. B
14. D
15. B
16. A
17. D
18. C
19. B
20. A
21. B
22. D
23. A
24. C
25. D
26. B
27. A
28. C
29. D
30. A

31. B
32. D
33. C
34. B

Listening Section Explanations

Lecture 1

The following is a transcript of the conversation you heard.

Registrar: Can I help you?

Student: Um, yeah. I need to find out how to get into a class that the registration website won't let me into.

Registrar: The website won't let you into a class? What is it saying about the class? Have you taken all the prerequisite classes to get in? If you haven't, the site won't let you register.

Student: No, it's telling me the class is full.

Registrar: Ah, okay. If the class is full, you'll need to get on the waitlist. Then if one of the students who is registered for the class drops it after the drop/add period is over, you might get a seat in the class. There are no guarantees, but it's your only option, really.

Student: Wait, people will register for the class and then drop it after a week?

Registrar: Oh, yes. Plenty of students register for multiple classes and go to them the first week with the intention of choosing a few they need or enjoy the most and dropping the others. We specifically design the drop/add process so students can see the professor and get a taste of how difficult the class will be for them before they're committed to the class.

Student: That's a good idea. I guess I never thought about that before. So does that mean that I'll definitely make it into the class?

Registrar: There's no way to know. What I can do is check the waitlist to see how many people are already on it. And then I can check the professor's classes from last semester to see if they filled up. What class is it?

Student: The Sociology of Urban Education with Whatner.

Registrar: Okay, give me a second. [pause] Okay, it looks like there are only two people on the waitlist ahead of you, and there are 40 seats in the class. So if three people drop next week, you're in. Tell me your student ID number so I can put you on the waitlist before anyone else hops onto it.

Student: 49581684.

Registrar: Got it. Okay, you're third on the waitlist. Now let me look at Whatner's classes from last semester. Hmmm. It looks like one of them didn't fill completely, but the other four were at capacity. Only one of those still had people on a waitlist, though. I can't promise anything, but if I were a betting woman I'd bet you'll get into this class.

Student: That's great!

Registrar: Hold on there, though. Are you getting financial aid?

Student: Yes ...

Registrar: If you're getting financial aid, you need to be enrolled for the correct minimum number of credits per semester. That means you need to register for another class now as a backup, so if you don't end up getting into this class you'll still keep your financial aid. Do you have another class you'll be willing to go to for the next week, and then keep if you don't get into Whatner's class?

Student: Um, yeah. I've never taken a philosophy class and think I probably should.

Registrar: Ah, good. There are at least 10 sections of Philosophy 101 you can take. Let me pull up the rest of your schedule and find one that fits. [pause] Okay, I put you in one on Tuesdays and Thursdays at 10 A.M. There was one at 8 but I didn't think you'd want to get up if you don't have to.

Student: Wow, thanks!

Registrar: You're welcome. If you get off the waitlist, the system will just send you an email. So you should go to the all the classes the first week, even if you don't know you're in, so you won't be behind if you get in.

Student: Okay.

Registrar: Good luck. I hope you get in.

1. Why does the student visit the registrar's office?

   (A) to request a copy of her transcript

   (B) to find out where she is on the waitlist

   (C) to find out why she can't register for a class

   (D) to ask the registrar about financial aid

   The answer is C. The student comes to find out why the website won't allow her to register for a class she wants to take. Eliminate A because it is not mentioned in the lecture. Eliminate B because the student does not know about the waitlist. Eliminate D because the registrar mentioned financial aid to the student, not vice versa.

2. Why was the student not able to register for the class?

   (A) The registrar could not find the class from last semester.

   (B) The student does not have a computer.

   (C) The waitlist was too long.

   (D) The class was already filled with other students.

   The answer is D. The class was already full. Eliminate A because it has no relationship to the question asked. Eliminate B and C because they are not true, according to the lecture.

3. Why must the student register for a philosophy class?

   (A) The registrar cannot find the student's account in the system.

   (B) The student does not have room in her schedule for a philosophy class.

   (C) The student needs to be registered for a minimum number of classes to continue to receive financial aid.

   (D) The student can take a later Philosophy class than 8 a.m.

   The answer is C. The student must register for another class to maintain financial aid in case she does not get into the sociology class. Eliminate A and B because they are not indicated in the lecture and do not answer the question. Eliminate D because it is true but does not answer the question.

   So if three people drop next week, you're in.

4. What did the registrar mean?

   (A) If three people get sick and stop coming to the class, the woman will be able to register for the class.

   (B) If three people who are registered for the class drop the class next week, they free up three spaces for the student and the two people already on the waitlist.

   (C) There are still three spots open in the class, but they are first come first served.

   (D) The registrar has no idea if the woman will be able to get into the class by looking at the size of the waitlist.

   The answer is B. If three people drop the class from their schedules this semester, there will be room in the class for the student. Eliminate A because it misinterprets the word *drop*. Eliminate C and D because they are not supported by the facts of the lecture.

5. What will the student do now?

   (A) Attend the classes the registrar has signed her up for.

   (B) Send an email to find out if she has gotten off the waitlist.

   (C) Attend the 8 a.m. session of the philosophy class.

   (D) Register for financial aid.

   The answer is A. The student will attend the classes she is registered for and wait to find out if she has gotten into the sociology class. Eliminate B because the system will send her an email if she gets off the waitlist, not the other way around. Eliminate C because the registrar put her in the 10 A.M. section, not the 8 A.M. section. Eliminate D because she is already registered for financial aid.

Lecture 2

The following is a transcript of the conversation you heard.

Woman: Hey, can I borrow three dollars?

Man: Sure. Why?

Woman: I just ran my meal plan card through the card reader at checkout and I only had three dollars left on my card! I need the money to pay for the rest of my meal.

Man: Only three dollars? That's bold, letting your balance get so low before you add more money.

Woman: I can add more money to my meal plan card?

Man: Of course. Wait, you mean to tell me that in the two and a half years we've been here you've never needed to add money to your meal plan card?

Woman: No. Last semester I finished the day before we went home with a dollar fifty in my account, but I just thought the money my parents put in at the beginning of the semester was what I had and couldn't spend any more. Besides, I don't eat a lot of expensive stuff. I think I must have gone over this semester because I started eating soup with every meal a couple of weeks ago. So how do I add money to my card?

Man: Well, I add money by going to the meal plan card website and just using my debit card to transfer money into my meal plan card account. But since you've never done it before, I don't think you're in the website system yet. You'll need to go to the Dining Services office and get them to enroll you. You can probably put money in your account while you're at the office, but then definitely enroll in the website so you can just do it from your room if you need to add money again.

Woman: That doesn't sound too challenging. Where's the Dining Services office?

Man: I still can't believe you've never done this before. It's between here and the law library, in a little building that looks like it was built in the '40s.

Woman: That's the Dining Services office? I walk past that building all the time and thought it was something strange because it's so small.

Man: I think they don't have many people working in that actual office because most of the Dining Services employees are in the cafeterias or the catering center. But anyway, now that you know where it is, you should stop in and get everything set up. Do you have a class right after lunch?

Woman: No. I don't have anything this afternoon except studying for a quiz tomorrow. I'll stop in the office after we finish eating. Wait, will I need cash or a debit card?

Man: Good question. I know I use a debit card on the website, so I'm guessing they can take a debit card at the office, too. If not, ask them to set up your website account right away so you can just go back to your room and pay with a debit card before it's time for dinner.

Woman: Good plan. Okay, let's finish up so I can go get this taken care of.

6. Why does the student ask the other student to borrow money?

   (A) The student has run out of money on her meal plan card.

   (B) The student needs to buy soup.

   (C) The student needs to take the bus to the Dining Services office.

   (D) The student does not have a debit card.

   The answer is A. The student has run out of money on her meal plan card and needs to buy her lunch. Eliminate B because you do not know if she is eating soup. Eliminate C and D because they are not mentioned in the lecture.

7. How much does the student have left on her meal plan card account?

   (A) nothing, as she just spent everything left on the card

   (B) nothing, which is why she is not eating lunch

   (C) enough to last the rest of the semester

   (D) one dollar and fifty cents

   The answer is A. The student spent the last three dollars on the card to buy her lunch and still needs to borrow money from the other student. Eliminate B, as she is eating lunch with the male student. Eliminate C because this is not true. Eliminate D because this happened in the past.

8. According to the male student, which of the following is true?

    (A) The Dining Services office is the large building next to the law library.

    (B) Once the money in the meal plan is used, there is no way to add more money to the account.

    (C) The Dining Services office can only take cash.

    (D) A payment can be made to the meal plan card account with a debit card.

    The answer is D. Students can add funds to their meal plan cards with debit cards online or at the Dining Services office. Eliminate A because the Dining Services office is in a small building. Eliminate B and C because these are the opposite of what the student says.

    That doesn't sound too challenging.

9. What did the female student mean?

    (A) She is not sure she can do it.

    (B) She thinks it is not a challenging-enough task for her to attempt.

    (C) She thinks she can do it without much effort.

    (D) She doesn't want to do it because it is too much of a challenge.

    The answer is C. The student thinks she can complete the task easily. Eliminate A, B, and D because they misrepresent the student's attitude in this sentence.

10. What will the student do immediately after this conversation?

    (A) buy some soup

    (B) go to the Dining Services office

    (C) go to dinner

    (D) study for a quiz online

    The answer is B. The student will go to the Dining Services office to get her meal plan card set up for online payments. Eliminate A because it happened in the past. Eliminate C and D because they will happen after the student goes to the Dining Services office.

Lecture 3

The following is a transcript of the lecture you heard.

Professor: I know that organizational dynamics is a broad topic, and some of you have never heard of it before, so let me start at the beginning. Organizational dynamics refers to the study of how people in organizations such as corporations and other similar groups interact within the group and with each other, and how to improve the dynamics of the interactions. Some people joke that organizational dynamics is the study of how people play office politics, or how people kiss up to the boss. And while those are partially true, the field is much broader and takes both a macro and a micro view of interactions in organizations.

Organizational dynamics is a relatively new field of study, as it relies on the acknowledgment that humans are independent actors within the structure of an organization and that their behavior can be predicted, altered, and guided by management practices. It is a hybrid of management, operations, and psychology concepts and theories and relies upon an understanding that companies can be affected as much by the way they organize their employees as by the products they sell.

Let me ask, have any of you ever worked in a large corporation before?

Student: I did an internship downtown last summer for a big investment firm.

Professor: How often did you eat lunch with the head partner of the office?

Student: Um, never. I knew where her office was, but I never even saw her the whole summer.

Professor: That brings me to one area of study in organizational dynamics—the structure and hierarchy of an organization and how the way an organization is organized determines its culture and the way its employees act in the company. Jeff, it sounds like you were in a company with a very formal hierarchy.

Student: Well, we got to wear jeans on Fridays if no clients were coming into the office.

Professor: Ah, not formal in dress. Formal in structure. Very predetermined, with little room for people at different places in the structure to interact. Tell us, who did you spend most of your time with during your internship as part of your daily work?

Student: The other interns. And the assistant of the partner we were working for. We met that partner but didn't see him very often.

Professor: Exactly. You spent the majority of your time with people in the same job function you had, with instruction from the person one level above you acting as your supervisor. That's a hallmark—a primary characteristic, I mean—of a formal hierarchy. In contrast, some organizations are very flat, and by that I mean that there's not really a chain of command, per se. Employees are mostly at the same level, so they interact with people in all different areas of the office, depending on who they need to collaborate with to get their work done. A lot of technology companies are like this, with the CEO being very accessible to the rest of the employees and being more of an official spokesperson for the company than The Boss, so to speak. Some companies are organized on what's called a matrix system, so people interact with their boss and their boss's boss up the chain to the top, and the people below them, but then they also interact with employees at their same levels but in different departments. So they interact up and down and side to side, if that makes sense. I have some slides to show you the graphical representations of these different structures, and I'll talk about some of the pros and cons of organizing in each way, and then will give some examples of companies with those organizational structures. We'll do that after we take a break. Ten minutes. I'll stay in the classroom if anyone has questions.

11. What is the topic of the lecture?

    (A) hierarchical structures

    (B) summer internships

    (C) organizational dynamics

    (D) flat structures

    The answer is C. The lecture is about organizational dynamics. Eliminate A, B, and D because they are small parts of the lecture.

12. According to the professor, the field of organizational dynamics is

    (A) a mixture of several other disciplines

    (B) an older discipline

    (C) needed to understand compensation schemes for most organizations

    (D) not yet proven by research

    The answer is A. The professor states that organizational dynamics is a mixture of management, operations, and psychology. Eliminate B because this is the opposite of what is stated in the lecture. Eliminate C and D because they are not mentioned in the lecture.

13. The lecture states that

    (A) organizational dynamics consists of the study of the way organizations are structured

    (B) there are different ways an organization can be structured

    (C) hierarchical structures are preferred over flat structures

    (D) the opposite of a flat structure is a matrix structure

    The answer is B. The lecture gives examples of several ways an organization can be structured. Eliminate A because it ignores the other areas of organizational dynamics. Eliminate C and D because these are misrepresentations of the information in the lecture.

In contrast, some organizations are very flat, and by that I mean that there's not really a chain of command, per se.

14. What does the professor mean when she says this?

    (A) The chain of command at a flat structure is very informal and cannot be understood by employees at that organization.

    (B) A flat structure cannot induce employees to show respect to each other.

    (C) A flat structure does not have to do with the military chain of command.

    (D) The structure of the organization is described visually, so a flat structure has no strong hierarchy or vertical chain of command.

The answer is D. The word *flat* is used to describe the visual representation of the organization's structure on a diagram. Eliminate A because this is partly true but not supported by the lecture. Eliminate B because this is a misrepresentation of the lecture. Eliminate C because it is true but not what the professor means.

15. How does the professor show how structure affects employee behavior?

(A) by detailing the different structures an organization can have with diagrams

(B) by asking a student details of how he behaved on a job he had

(C) by showing that a student who worked in an internship had not been subject to the structure of the company he had worked at

(D) by explaining why a flat structure is the best structure for cooperation

The answer is B. The professor used a series of questions and answers with a student about the student's experience in a job to show how the student had been influenced by the structure of the organization. Eliminate A because the diagrams came later in the lecture and were only mentioned, not shown. Eliminate C because the professor showed the opposite. Eliminate D because this was not in the lecture.

16. The lecture implies that

(A) there are other areas of study in organizational dynamics than structures of organizations

(B) a hierarchical structure creates more opportunities for interaction across job functions

(C) organizational dynamics is not accepted as a valid field of study by all managers

(D) flat structures only work in fields in which employees have creative skills

The answer is A. The professor says that studying the structures of organizations and how they affect behavior is only one area of study in organizational dynamics. Eliminate B and D because there is nothing to support them in the lecture. Eliminate C because this misrepresents information in the lecture.

Lecture 4

The following is a transcript of the lecture you heard.

Professor: While colloquially people say that a person is "speaking Chinese," this isn't technically correct because there are so many languages and dialects spoken in China that there is no one language called Chinese. The most common languages spoken in mainland China are Mandarin and a dialect of Mandarin called Szechuanese Mandarin or just Szechuanese. One billion people speak Mandarin, and 120 million people speak Szechuanese.

It's not entirely obvious that Szechuanese should be classified as a dialect of Mandarin instead of a separate language, as the vocabulary, grammar, and structure of Szechuanese is different from Mandarin, to the extent that Mandarin speakers and Szechuanese speakers are not guaranteed to understand each other. Mandarin is the national language of China, which means that it is the language in which business is conducted. While Mandarin is an ancient language—with its origins in Old Mandarin, which developed around the year 1000 A.D.E.—it has only been the national language of China since the fourteenth century. In comparison, the Szechuanese dialect began developing in the fourteenth century, when Mandarin was already the national language of China. In this way, Szechuanese could be classified as a dialect of Mandarin, because it developed while Mandarin was a common language. However, it has many distinct features from modern-day Mandarin.

Szechuanese itself can be divided into four dialects. These dialects—Chengdu-Chongqing dialect, Minjiang dialect, Renshou-Fushun dialect, and Ya'an-Shimian dialect—are named after the regions in which they are primarily spoken. Each of these dialects is characterized by differences in tone and pronunciation, but the structure, grammar, and much of the vocabulary is the same across these four dialects.

In contrast, there are hundreds of dialects of Mandarin, including Szechuanese, and while some of these dialects can be understood by speakers of other Mandarin dialects, there are numerous groups of dialects that are incomprehensible to speakers of other groups of dialects. I have diagrams of the relationships of the Mandarin and Szechuanese dialects that I will put up in the course site so that anyone who wants to know more about the dialects can look at them.

While Mandarin has been the national language of China officially for 700 years, other dialects and languages inside China flourished until very recently. With the rise of radio, television, and the internet, more and more Chinese people are being exposed to Mandarin, which is sometimes called Standard Chinese, and this is contributing to the reduction in use of many other languages. While Szechuanese is still spoken by more than a hundred million people and therefore is not in any danger of disappearing as a language, there has been a reduction in its use, particularly in the media, and even for official functions in areas that traditionally used only Szechuanese. Some researchers predict that the use of Szechuanese will continue to decrease unless there is a specific effort made by the Chinese or regional governments to promote its use. The national government of China has little interest in promoting Szechuanese over Standard Chinese, so any revitalization of Szechuanese will come from regional governments or grassroots efforts.

17. What is the topic of the lecture?

    (A) the four dialects of Szechuanese

    (B) why Mandarin is increasing in use in China

    (C) how Szechuanese is different from Mandarin

    (D) the two most commonly spoken Chinese languages

    The answer is D. The lecture describes Mandarin and Szechuanese, including many of their features and their relationship to each other. Eliminate A, B, and C because they are small details in the lecture, not the topic.

18. According to the lecture, when did Szechuanese begin to develop?

    (A) Szechuanese began to develop when other, non-Chinese languages began to rise in Europe.

    (B) Szechuanese developed in the southern provinces of China.

    (C) Szechuanese began to develop right around the time that Mandarin became the official language of China.

    (D) Szechuanese is a dialect of Mandarin.

    The answer is C. Szechuanese began to develop in the fourteenth century, around the time Mandarin became the official language of China. Eliminate A because other languages are not relevant. Eliminate B because this is true but does not answer the question of when it developed. Eliminate D because it is true but does not answer the question.

19. The professor states that Mandarin

    (A) was in use from the year 1000 through the fourteenth century

    (B) began developing in the year 1000 and is still in use today

    (C) continues to increase in use in China because the other dialects are considered frivolous

    (D) is considered a dialect of Szechuanese

    The answer is B. The professor states the Old Mandarin began developing around 1000 and that Mandarin continues to be used today. Eliminate A because this is not stated in the lecture. Eliminate C because it does continue to increase in use, but you do not have information about how the other dialects are seen. Eliminate D because Iceland is considered part of Scandinavia.

While Mandarin has been the national language of China officially for 700 years, other dialects and languages inside China flourished until very recently.

20. What does the professor mean when she says this?

    (A) Those other dialects and languages are not flourishing anymore.

    (B) Mandarin is no longer the official language of China.

    (C) Not everyone in China speaks Mandarin.

    (D) Mandarin is spoken by more people in Hong Kong than any other language.

    The answer is A. Saying that they flourished until recently means that they no longer flourish. Eliminate B because it is the opposite of what is stated in the lecture. Eliminate C because it is true but is not what the professor means by this sentence. Eliminate D because you do not have any information on this.

21. How does the professor show the relationship of Szechuanese to Mandarin?

    (A) She describes the history of the development of Standard Chinese.

    (B) She describes the ways the two languages are similar and dissimilar to each other.

    (C) She describes the Chinese government's concern with preserving Szechuanese.

    (D) She describes the way broadcast media is increasing the spread of Mandarin.

    The answer is B. The professor talks about similar and different features of the two languages to show that they are not very similar to each other. Eliminate A because this is not in the lecture. Eliminate C because this is the opposite of what is in the lecture. Eliminate D because this is not relevant to the question.

22. You can infer from the lecture that the professor

    (A) has not been to the parts of China that speak one of the four Szechuanese dialects

    (B) speaks Szechuanese but not Mandarin

    (C) speaks Mandarin but not Szechuanese

    (D) knows more about dialects of Mandarin than she is able to discuss in this short lecture

    The answer is D. The professor indicates that she has more information about the dialects of Mandarin to show any students who are interested in it. Eliminate A because you have no information about where the professor has been. Eliminate B and C because you have no information about what languages the professor speaks.

Lecture 5

The following is a transcript of the lecture you heard.

Professor: Today I'm going to tell you about the two unique features of the island of Puerto Rico. Puerto Rico is United States territory in the Caribbean, near Cuba and the island of Hispanola, which contains Haiti and the Dominican Republic. The primary language of Puerto Rico is Spanish. Puerto Rico has two unusual features: the rainforest called El Yunque and the bioluminous bay in Vieques.

El Yunque, which was formerly known as the Caribbean National Forest and Luquillo National Forest, is the only tropical rainforest in the United States National Park System. It covers 28,000 acres of land in the mostly mountainous northeast part of Puerto Rico. It is the largest area of public land in Puerto Rico, and as a national forest it is protected from development and open to all to enjoy and explore. Much of El Yunque is unreachable except by the most intrepid hikers. Numerous hiking paths originate at El Portal Rain Forest Center, designed by Puerto Rican architect Aureo Andino. These hiking paths are designed to offer visitors exposure to various areas of El Yunque without having to hike deep into the rainforest.

There are four roads that drive into El Yunque and three rivers in the rainforest—La Mina River, Mameyes River, and Icacos River. In the center of the rainforest is a huge wilderness area, called El Toro. There are four distinct areas of vegetation in El Yunque: Tabonuco Forest,

Palo Colorado Forest, Sierra Palm Forest, and Dwarf Forest. El Yunque contains 13 of the 15 species of coquí, a small frog indigenous to Puerto Rico. There are no seasons in the rainforest, and it rains every day in El Yunque.

As a side note, there have been rumors for hundreds of year about the chupacabra, a mythical creature that attacks and kills livestock. The chupacabra is an important legend in Puerto Rican culture, and there have been numerous reported sightings of the chupacabra in El Yunque. None of these have been confirmed, however, so the stories remain just that.

On the island of Vieques off the main coast of Puerto Rico is a bioluminous bay. Bioluminous means that it glows in the dark for natural reasons. Tiny plankton called dinoflagellates live in the bay and emit light that can be seen from the surface of the water at night. These dinoflagellates live in Vieques bay because of the ideal conditions for their growth. The bay is surrounded by Red Mangrove trees, which emit Vitamin B_{12} through their roots into the bay. The dinoflagellates thrive in this nutrient-rich environment. As Vieques is a sparsely inhabited island, the bioluminescence is particularly strong because it is not overshadowed by lights from human settlements near the bay. The bay is easily accessible by vehicle or on foot, so it is not difficult to visit the bay at night to observe the beautiful glow from the water.

The bioluminescent bay is in danger, of course, because of increasing pollution, but the government of Puerto Rico is making a strong effort to keep Vieques as untouched as possible and to protect the bay.

23. What is the topic of the lecture?

    (A) natural features of Puerto Rico

    (B) bioluminescent bays

    (C) El Yunque rainforest

    (D) conservation of rainforest land

    The answer is A. The lecture covers two natural features of Puerto Rico, El Yunque rainforest and Vieques bioluminescent bay. Eliminate B and C because they are only part of the topic. Eliminate D because it is not the focus of the lecture.

24. According to the lecture, the dry season in El Yunque

    (A) begins after the hurricane season

    (B) lasts for six months

    (C) does not exist; it rains every day

    (D) does not exist; it is dry every day

    The answer is C. The lecture states that there are no seasons in the rainforest and that it rains every day in El Yunque. Eliminate A and B because they are not mentioned in the lecture. Eliminate D because it misrepresents the lecture.

25. The lecture says that the bioluminescence of the bay is caused by

    (A) vitamin B_{12}

    (B) lights that have been placed on the bottom of the bay

    (C) special coral that reflect the light of the moon

    (D) tiny plankton that glow

    The answer is D. The glowing is caused by dinoflagellates, or tiny plankton, that glow. Eliminate A because it is a tiny detail from the lecture. Eliminate B and C because they are not mentioned in the lecture.

None of these have been confirmed, however, so the stories remain just that.

26. What does the professor mean when she says this?

    (A) No reporters have seen a chupacabra.

    (B) The stories are just stories, because the details in them cannot be confirmed.

    (C) If the chupacabra exists, it does not live in El Yunque.

    (D) Only native Puerto Ricans can see the chupacabra.

    The answer is B. The professor means that since none of the chupacabra stories have been verified by other sources, they are just stories, not facts. Eliminate A because reporters are not involved in the information in the lecture. Eliminate C and D because they are not mentioned in the lecture.

27. How does the professor show that the chupacabra stories are not official, verified information?

    (A) The professor says, "As an aside" and tells the chupacabra stories as an unofficial note.

    (B) The professor asks the students to prove the chupacabra stories.

    (C) The professor discusses the reasons a chupacabra cannot exist.

    (D) The professor explains why no one has been able to verify the existence of a chupacabra.

    The answer is A. The professor notes verbally that the stories are not part of the main, fact-based lecture. Eliminate B because the professor does not ask the students to prove anything. Eliminate C and D because these are not in the lecture.

28. The lecture implies that

    (A) U.S. forest rangers consider El Yunque not officially part of the national system

    (B) the bioluminescent bay will disappear soon because of pollution

    (C) no other national forests in the U.S. system have the same climate as El Yunque

    (D) a rainforest and a bioluminescent bay exist only in Puerto Rico

The answer is C. The lecture says that El Yunque is the only tropical rainforest in the U.S. system. Eliminate A because you have no information about park rangers. Eliminate B because this goes too far by giving a time line to the disappearance of the bay. Eliminate D because the lecture does not imply that these features are only found in Puerto Rico.

Lecture 6

The following is a transcript of the lecture you heard.

Professor: How many of you know when the mobile phone, or cell phone, was introduced?

Student: In the 1980s, right?

Professor: Wrong. Good guess, but wrong. The 1980s is when the mobile phone became known to the general public, but the actual origin of the mobile phone was over 100 years ago when a Swedish engineer named Lars Magnus Ericsson put a telephone into his car and then connected the telephone to the telephone lines strung on wires overhead. Can you imagine? But that was a radical thing to do when he did it, in 1910. Think about that—most people didn't even have cars back then, but Ericsson was driving a car with a phone in it!

Now, remember how phones in general work, which is that the voice of the person speaking gets converted into sound waves—just like radio and television broadcasts. The speaker speaks (or sings or makes some other sound) into the microphone, which converts the sound into waves. The waves are invisible and can travel on wires (as in the case of a regular telephone that's wired into a house) or they can travel through the air (as in a radio broadcast). In a radio broadcast, there is one transmitter (where the announcer or DJ is) and multiple receivers (radios). In telephony, each telephone is both a transmitter and a receiver.

This is where Ericsson's car phone had problems, though. It wasn't very successful because he needed to have a radio spectrum to broadcast on, and there wasn't much free spectrum at the time for him to use. Radio stations were broadcasting on most of the available spectrum at the time. But he kept working on the concept in his lab, and others worked on the concept of a phone that could be mobile and not wired in to a house, and almost 40 years later there was a breakthrough at Bell Labs in the United States. They devised a system of cells, each with a transmitter and a receiver, that acted as base stations and would relay sound waves from cell to cell. This meant that the sound didn't have to be transmitted on a radio spectrum, so it could bypass the whole radio system. Because the sound was transmitted from cell to cell, the first phones used cellular technology and became known as cellular telephones, or cell phones.

Bell Labs made their cellular technology discovery in 1947, but it took another few decades to go from the basic technology to a product that could be sold. Different companies worked with the cellular and transmitter-receiver technology Bell Labs and Ericsson Labs had developed to create products. In 1973, Motorola introduced the first portable telephone in the United States, and six years later NTT introduced the first car phone in Japan. Both of these telephones used 1G technology. 1G is short for "first generation," and it means analog transmission of sound. 1G was the standard for most of the 1980s and was advanced technology at the time, even though it had poor sound quality and calls dropped frequently.

Second-generation technology, or 2G, was digital transmission of sound. It became the standard in the 1990s and was a radical improvement over 1G technology in terms of sound quality and lack of interruptions. 3G, or third-generation technology, is digital transmission of sound and data, and has been the standard since the mid-2000s. 4G has been introduced but isn't in all locations. Every time the technology evolves, new telephones need to be designed to capture the benefits of the new technology. A person with a smartphone now can look at the photos of those first 1G phones with their long antennas and think about how primitive they were, but in a few decades our most cutting-edge smartphones will seem primitive by contemporary standards.

29. What is the topic of the lecture?

    (A) Lars Magnus Ericsson's original mobile telephone

    (B) cellular technology

    (C) the differences between the generations of mobile telephony

    (D) the development of mobile telephones

    The answer is D. The lecture is about the origins and development process of mobile telephony. Eliminate A, B, and C because they are all details in the lecture, not the topic.

30. According to the lecture, sound is transmitted

    (A) as waves through wires or the air

    (B) from cars to base stations

    (C) from a cell receiver to a transmitter

    (D) more slowly than data

    The answer is A. Sound is converted to sound waves and transmitted through wires in the case of wired telephones or the air as in radio transmissions. Eliminate B because the cars need to have a transmitter of some sort and the base stations need to have a receiver. Eliminate C because transmission happens the opposite way. Eliminate D because this is not true.

31. According to the professor, 2G technology is

    (A) analog transmission of sound

    (B) digital transmission of sound

    (C) digital transmission of sound and data

    (D) broadband digital transmission of sound and data

    The answer is B. Second-generation technology is digital transmission of sound. Eliminate A because it is 1G technology. Eliminate C because it is 3G technology. Eliminate D because it is 4G technology and is not specified in the lecture.

Think about that—most people didn't even have cars back then, but Ericsson was driving a car with a phone in it!

32. What does the professor mean when he says this?

    (A) Ericsson hadn't dreamed of putting a telephone into a car.

    (B) Ericsson had designed his car along with the telephone in it.

    (C) Ericsson had a better car than anyone else at the time.

    (D) Ericsson's mobile phone was ahead of the rest of technology at the time.

    The answer is D. The professor is showing how advanced Ericsson was over the general public. Eliminate A because it is not true. Eliminate B because Ericsson did not design his own car. Eliminate C because you do not have information about this in the passage.

33. Why does the professor discuss the lack of available radio spectrum for Ericsson?

    (A) to demonstrate the need for more radio spectrum to be opened up by the Swedish government

    (B) to show that Ericsson was an anomaly

    (C) to explain why it took so many years from his first mobile phone to develop mobile phone technology

    (D) to discuss radio receivers at the time

    The answer is C. The lack of radio spectrum meant that Ericsson couldn't develop and test viable mobile phones. Eliminate A because it is out of scope of the lecture. Eliminate B because the whole point of the lecture is that Ericsson was an anomaly. Eliminate D because this is a detail from another part of the lecture.

34. The lecture implies that

    (A) Bell Labs took Ericsson's ideas and claimed them as their own

    (B) as transmission technology improves, phones will have increasing capabilities

    (C) the Japanese were more interested in car phones than Americans

    (D) newer phones will no longer transmit data digitally

    The answer is B. The lecture states that every time technology improves, new phones are made to take advantage of that technology, which implies that these new phones will have increasing capabilities. Eliminate A and D because there is no information about them in the lecture. Eliminate C because this is a misrepresentation of the lecture.

Speaking Section Explanations

Question 1

Read the prompt and give yourself 15 seconds to prep and write notes. Then take 45 seconds to record your response.

1. Describe a song that is meaningful to you. Please include specific examples and reasons why the song is meaningful.

   An excellent response will discuss the song that is meaningful, including at least two separate details or incidents that explain how it is meaningful. It will contain a solid opening statement and a solid closing statement.

Question 2

Read the prompt and give yourself 15 seconds to prep and write notes. Then take 45 seconds to record your response.

2. Some students finish their university studies as quickly as possible so they can graduate and begin working. Other students work while they go to university, which means they take longer to finish university but have been working during that time. Which method of sequencing university studies and work makes the most sense, and why?

   An excellent response will pick one side of the question and will not argue both sides. It will use at least two strong reasons for the opinion expressed in the response and support those reasons with facts or examples.

Question 3

The university has changed the hours during which students can use the gymnasium facilities. Read the notice posted on the door of the gym. You will have 45 seconds to read the notice. Begin reading now.

Notice

Effective May 5, the gym hours will be extended to 5 A.M. to midnight Monday through Friday, 5 A.M. to 8 P.M. Saturday, and 9 A.M. to 8 P.M. Sunday. Pool open swim hours will be from 5 A.M. to 9 A.M. and 8 P.M. to midnight Monday through Friday, 6 A.M. to 8 P.M. Saturday, and 10 A.M. to 8 P.M. Sunday. Open gym hours will be 7 A.M. to 10 P.M. Monday through Friday, 7 A.M. to 7 P.M. Saturday, and 10 A.M. to 7 P.M. Sunday. All class times will be posted in the course catalog as soon as they are scheduled.

The following is a transcript of the discussion you heard.

Woman: Did you see this? The gym hours are changing.

Man: No, what? Oh. I'm not sure I understand how that can work. I'm taking a class in the pool at 8 A.M. on Wednesdays and Fridays, and the class doesn't end until June.

Woman: What do you mean? The pool opens at 5 A.M., so it'll be open for your class.

Man: Yes, but as of May 5, "open swim" hours go until 9. So people are going to be in the pool swimming in the middle of my class.

Woman: Maybe you'll be at one end and the open swim will be at the other.

Man: We use the whole length of the pool. It's a sprint swimming class and we do various lengths across the pool. And the class is full, so we use all the lanes.

Woman: Hmm. That *is* strange. I wonder if your class time is going to change.

Man: I don't think they can do that, because we all took the class because it meets at that time of day. Maybe this sign just has a typo, or the person who made the sign didn't realize that there's a scheduling conflict.

Woman: That makes sense. How are you going to find out?

Man: I think I'll just go in and ask at the front desk and see if they know. If it's a typo, then they can fix it on the sign. And if the schedule is going to change, at least I'll know now instead of later.

Now get ready to answer the question. Give yourself 30 seconds to create notes for your response. Then take 60 seconds to speak your response.

3. The man has a problem related to the information in the notice. State what the problem is and what he decides to do about that problem.

   An excellent response will sum up the notice about the new gym hours and explain the conflict between the man's class and the open swim hours. The response will conclude that the man is going to ask at the front desk if the conflicting hours are a schedule change or a typo.

Question 4

In this question you will read a short passage on an academic subject and then listen to a talk on the same topic. You will then answer a question using information from both the reading passage and the talk. After you hear the question, you will have 30 seconds to prepare your response and 60 seconds to speak.

Read the passage about climate change. You will have 45 seconds to read the passage. Begin reading now.

> Climate change caused by pollution and other human intervention in the natural workings of the planet Earth has accelerated in the last 20 years. Before this point only scientists were noticing symptoms of climate change, but in the last few decades the change has become noticeable even to the common person. Changes in average temperature, an increase in lethal climate events around the world, and changing weather patterns have begun to catch the attention of the popular press, and have entered into the international discourse. Unfortunately, there has been little agreement on how to stop or slow this climate change, so the awareness is not leading to productive steps to manage or end climate change.

The following is a transcript on the lecture you heard.

> Professor: Some of you may be familiar with the concept of climate change from the pictures you see on the internet of polar bear cubs stuck alone on shrinking icebergs with no way to find food. These heartbreaking images are putting a very personal face on the changes that are happening all over the world. It's not just polar bears that are losing their habitats. Animals of all species—from fish to insects to birds to mammals—are losing their homes and are unable to survive the changing temperatures and weather conditions in their environments. We will lose thousands of species of animals over the next few decades because they will not be able to survive the new climate conditions of our planet.
>
> So what can we do about this? At the rate we're going, not that much. Scientists are researching solutions that we could implement to slow the rate at which the climate is changing, but the likelihood that we will actually enact those changes on a wide scale is small. Somehow the ideas behind climate change have become associated with political positions, so instead of being seen as a scientific problem we as humans can solve, climate change is seen as either a moral issue or a conspiracy. Since the topic evokes so much emotion in politicians and government leaders, we have been unable to see it objectively and choose actions to take to slow the change.

Now get ready to answer the question. Give yourself 30 seconds to create notes for your response. Then take 60 seconds to speak your response.

4. The professor describes some of the effects of climate change and the problems we have implementing solutions to climate change. Explain how these effects and problems relate to and contrast with each other.

   An excellent response will describe the loss of animal species and the emotional responses to climate change that prevent scientific solutions to it from being implemented. It will explain how the emotional response relates to the sad effect of losing species.

Question 5

In this question, you will hear a conversation. Then you will be asked to talk about the conversation and give your opinion about the subject of the conversation. You will be given 20 seconds to prepare. Then you will be given 60 seconds to speak.

The following is a transcript of the conversation you heard.

Woman: Have you seen the new dorm they built out behind the psychology building?

Man: I walked past it last week, before they had all the windows in. It's huge!

Woman: I know. I'm trying to figure out if I want to live there next year.

Man: I thought you were going to live down at South Quad with Becky again.

Woman: Becky is going to Scotland for fall semester next year. So if we stay in South Quad, I need to find a roommate to stay in her spot for that semester. I don't know how I'm going to find someone who only needs a roommate for one semester.

Man: Well, I bet there's someone like you whose roommate is going to go abroad fall semester so they need a roommate only for that semester, too.

Woman: Hmmm. I hadn't thought of that. You might be right. But how do I find that person?

Man: Now *that* I don't know. So if you don't stay in South Quad, you're thinking of moving to the new dorm?

Woman: Yes. They have a bunch of singles, so I wouldn't have to worry about finding a roommate, and everything's new, and it's close to all my psych classes.

Man: That sounds ideal. But what will Becky do when she comes back from Scotland?

Woman: That's the problem. I really don't know what to do.

Give yourself 20 seconds to create notes for your response. Then take 60 seconds to speak your response.

5. The students discuss two housing options for the woman's living situation in the coming year. Describe the two options. Then explain which option you think she should pursue, and why.

   An excellent response will describe the woman's option to find a temporary roommate for the fall semester until her current roommate Becky returns from studying in Scotland, and her option to live alone in the new dorm that has just been built. The response will choose one of the options and give a reason or reasons for choosing that option.

Question 6

The following is a transcript of the lecture you heard.

Professor: Congelatio, commonly called frostbite, is a condition in which skin and other tissue is damaged by exposure to cold temperatures. Frostbite is the most severe of three categories of cold damage. There are four degrees of frostbite, but only the third and fourth are what is commonly called frostbite.

The mildest category of cold damage and first degree of frostbite, called frostnip, consists of chilling the skin for enough time to cause pain and itching and some discoloration of the skin, but no lasting damage to anything but the top layer. The second category of cold damage and second degree of frostbite, called chillblains, occurs when there is longer exposure to cold. The skin will itch and hurt as with frostnip, but then the next day blisters will develop. After the blisters heal, the skin may be permanently insensitive to heat and cold. Third- and fourth-degree frostbite is the most severe category of cold-related damage, and it consists of cell damage to skin and tissue. Third- or fourth-degree frostbite occurs when the skin and deeper layers (even down to muscle) freeze. The skin layer gets hard and waxy. The damage may cause infection and gangrene, and if gangrene cannot be stopped, the affected area may need to be amputated.

There are all sorts of ways to get frostbite, but they usually involve a combination of cold and wetness or dampness or cold and a circulation problem that means the patient's skin and tissue isn't as warm as it should be because not enough blood is flowing to the exposed region. Frostbite is a particular concern for patients with chronic circulation problems, especially those who have lost sensation in their limbs. If a patient doesn't have sensation, the patient may not know that a limb is in danger of frostbite because the usual signals—cold and pain—aren't able to be felt. Chronic conditions such as diabetes and nerve damage are big culprits in loss of sensation.

Give yourself 20 seconds to create notes for your response. Then take 60 seconds to speak your response.

6. Using facts and examples from the lecture, explain how frostbite can occur and what the different degrees of frostbite are.

   An excellent response will explain that frostbite occurs when an area becomes overly chilled, sometimes causing a lack of sensation in the area. It will also discuss frostnip, chilblains, and frostbite.

Writing Section Explanations

Integrated Writing Task

Reading:

On August 28, 1963, the Reverend Martin Luther King Jr. delivered a speech to a crowd of 200,000 civil rights activists from the steps of the Lincoln Memorial in Washington, D.C., as part of a march on Washington for civil rights. The speech, which became known as the "I Have a Dream" speech, lasted 17 minutes and left a lasting legacy for Dr. King.

The march, called the March on Washington for Jobs and Freedom, was designed to be a peaceful march which would appeal to a large segment of the American population. The march's organizers wanted the march to show a peaceful side of the civil rights movement, which had been characterized up to that point by civil disobedience. Civil disobedience is the act of actively refusing to comply with rules or laws that violate civil rights. Civil disobedience is often called nonviolent resistance, but those who practice civil disobedience have historically been victims of violence against them by citizens and authorities who have an interest in maintaining the status quo.

The peaceful nature of the march was designed to appeal to average Americans who may not have been engaged with the civil rights movement up to that point. Dr. King's speech echoed the peaceful nature of the march. He began by referencing Abraham Lincoln's Emancipation Proclamation and built a case for national unity, not division, and equal rights for all. The speech achieved its purpose by inspiring many who had never identified with the civil rights movement to support equal rights for all Americans.

Lecture:

I hope you all had a chance to listen to the recording of Dr. Martin Luther King Jr. delivering the "I Have a Dream" speech that I sent you the link to. This speech was probably the most important moment of Dr. King's life in terms of the impact he had on the American public and the way the country started talking about people of different races. And it was an enormous moment for America, for all of us who may or may not have been aware of what the civil rights activists were working for and sometimes being arrested for and physically injured for.

Interestingly, Dr. King's speech didn't start out as emotionally charged as it is perceived now. He started it as an homage to Lincoln's Emancipation Proclamation, which had been a big moment in racial history in the United States. Dr. King referenced the Emancipation Proclamation and then gave a very staid, measured speech about the need for equality. Near the end of the speech, singer Mahalia Jackson, who was present at the march and ceremony, yelled out, "Tell them about the dream, Martin!" At that point, Dr. King began to improvise the most famous part of the speech in which he talks about his dreams for a new future in America. While still sticking to his general outline, Dr. King improvised a more emotional vision for the country, with a dynamic delivery that inspired the audience. This combination of referencing history; beautiful language; and improvised, emotional delivery is what has earned the "I Have a Dream" speech its place in history.

1. Summarize the points made in the lecture, being sure to explain how they differ from the view in the reading passage.

   Sample essay that would score a 5:

   The lecture discusses Martin Luther King, Jr.'s "I Have a Dream" speech. The speaker talks about why the speech was so important, what the content of the speech was, and how it became so emotional. The lecture is different from the passage because the passage focuses more on the context of the march where the speech was given.

   First, the lecture discusses the speech and why it was so important for Dr. King. It talks about how the speech reached many Americans who didn't know about the civil rights movement before, and what civil rights workers sacrificed. This is contrast with the passage, that says that the speech was part of a nonviolent march, because the American public thought the civil rights movement was very violent, so the march and speech were designed to show America that the movement was peaceful.

   Next, the lecture discusses how Dr. King wrote the speech as a tribute to the Emancipation Proclamation and how it was not very emotional the way Dr. King wrote it. The reading passage does not mention the content of the speech of the fact that it was written to echo the Emancipation Proclamation.

   Finally, the speaker talks about how the speech became very emotionally moving after a singer shouted out for Dr. King to "tell them about the dream." After the singer shouted, Dr. King began to improvise, and this made the speech full of emotion that touched the listeners. This is why the speech has become such an important part of American history.

Independent Writing Task

2. Do you agree or disagree with the following statement? Use specific details and examples to support your answer.

   It is more important to exercise your mind than it is to exercise your body.

   Sample essay that would score a 5:

   While some may feel that it is more important to exercise your mind than it is to exercise your body, I feel that the opposite is true. It is useless to exercise your mind if you are not keeping your body in good shape.

   For one thing, your body affects your mind. If you do not exercise your body to stay healthy, you can become so unhealthy that your mind will decline. You could have a stroke or some other disease or condition that would harm your ability to think clearly. It is no good to exercise your mind if you cannot use it because you have gotten sick.

   For another thing, people who exercise their bodies are smarter than those who do not. Recent studies have shown that staying fit through exercise increases IQ, and slows the spread of age-related brain problems such as Alzheimer's disease. This means that by exercising your body you are also helping your mind at the same time.

Finally, no matter how smart you are, you will still be miserable if you don't have your health. If you are in pain or can't move because you haven't exercised and taken care of yourself, you will have a low quality of life. Being mentally fit still won't take away the pain.

In conclusion, it is more important to exercise your body than your mind. There is no doubt that keeping your body in good shape will pay off by keeping you mentally fit as well as allowing you to enjoy your life.

Appendix

Glossary

A

academic lecture The recorded lecture of a professor delivering an academic lecture in the Listening section.

captions Words that run across the bottom of the television or movie screen and tell you what the announcer and characters are saying. Watching videos or television with the captions on will help your English comprehension.

conversation The recorded conversation of two people discussing a topic related to campus life in the Listening section.

eliminate To arrive at the correct answer by finding the answers that are incorrect and ruling them out one by one.

essay A written response to the prompts in the Writing section.

ETS An abbreviation for the Educational Testing Service, the company that writes and administers the TOEFL.

fluency A word that is generally assumed to mean that a person can conduct all daily activities, read, write, listen, and speak well enough in a language to succeed in a university program conducted in that language.

idiom Also known as a figure of speech, an expression that has a different meaning than the literal meaning of the individual words. An example of an idiom is "it's raining cats and dogs" to mean "it's raining very hard."

independent Not reliant or attached to anything else. In the case of the independent writing task, you are given a question and must write a response based only on your own thoughts, not any other information.

integrated Dealing with two or more equal parts. In the case of the integrated writing task, you're looking at the relationship between the lecture and the passage.

jargon Language that has a special meaning in a profession or academic discipline. It is either unknown or has a different meaning outside of that profession or discipline.

lecture The generic name for any recorded passage in the Listening or Speaking sections of the TOEFL.

Listening section The section of the TOEFL that requires listening to recorded lectures and responding to multiple-choice questions.

passage A written piece of text that questions are asked about in the Reading and Speaking sections of the TOEFL.

process of elimination The process for answering multiple-choice questions that involves going through all answer choices and eliminating the ones that are incorrect.

proficiency A word used to indicate that a person can communicate in a language well enough to succeed at daily life tasks. Proficiency may not be enough to succeed in a university program conducted entirely in that language.

prompt A question or short passage that asks a question in the Speaking and Writing sections of the TOEFL.

raters The people who listen to the responses on the Speaking section and read the written responses on the Writing section and give them scores.

Reading section The section of the TOEFL that requires reading written passages and responding to multiple-choice questions.

response A written or spoken reply to a question on the Writing and Speaking sections of the TOEFL.

rhetorical device A tool used in written or spoken language—including similes, metaphors, rhetorical questions, and other ways of expressing ideas—with the intent to provoke an emotional response from the reader.

rubric A standard of performance that tells you what qualities are necessary to achieve a certain level of performance.

score The official grade or rating you are given for each section of the TOEFL. TOEFL scores are reported as raw (absolute) scores and also as a percentage based on how the test-taker did compared to everyone else taking the test.

Speaking section The section of the TOEFL that requires reading written passages, listening to recorded lectures, and giving spoken responses into a recording device.

standardized test A test that has been given to large numbers of people, after which the scores on the test are assigned values on the bell curve. An individual score is given as it compares to the entire group of people who took the test. Standardized test scores are reported as raw scores and also as percentiles.

test center A location that administers the TOEFL exam on designated days.

TOEFL The Test of English as a Foreign Language. This tests English in an academic or university setting.

TOEIC The Test of English for International Communication. Unlike the TOEFL, this tests English in a business setting.

transition words Words or short phrases that connect one idea to another. For example, *consequently*, *therefore*, *in addition*, *first*, and *in conclusion* are all examples of transition words.

vocabulary The group of words you know, understand, and can use. The larger your vocabulary is, the more expressive you can be.

Writing section The section of the TOEFL that requires reading passages and prompts, listening to a lecture, and writing responses to them.

Appendix

Resources

The following are some resources to help you get ready for the TOEFL, including study tools and information on cities that offer it.

TOEFL Study Resources

ETS TOEFL (toefl.org) The official TOEFL site. You can register to take the TOEFL, download practice questions, and get tips on taking the different sections.

Vocabulary.com (vocabulary.com) One of the best free vocabulary study sites on the internet.

Visual Thesaurus (visualthesaurus.com) An interactive thesaurus and dictionary based on an open-source dictionary. It contains close to 55,000 words in English, along with sound files containing pronunciations of all the words in American English. (This site charges $20.00 a year for a subscription.)

Duolingo (duolingo.com) A free language study site that can help with basic up through higher levels of English.

***The Official Guide to the TOEFL Test with CD-ROM* by Educational Testing Service** This is the practice book written by ETS, the company that creates the TOEFL. The tests are excellent practice materials, if you've used all the practice materials in this book and still want to do more.

Tape-a-Talk A free app for Androids and iPhones that allows you to record sound files on your phone and then email them. If you download this app, you can use your phone to record your responses when you practice the Speaking section.

Audacity (audacity.sourceforge.net) A free downloadable program for PCs and Macs that allows you to record onto your computer. If you download this program, you can use your computer to record your responses when you practice the Speaking section.

TOEFL Test Centers in the United States

The following cities, arranged in order by state, offer the iBT version of the TOEFL. Check out ets.org/toefl/ibt/register/centers_dates?WT.ac=toeflhome_centersdates_121127 for test dates and updates on the cities that offer the TOEFL.

Alabama	Gadsen Hunstville Mobile Montgomery Tuscaloosa
Alaska	Anchorage Fairbanks Ketchikan
Arizona	Casa Grande Flagstaff Goodyear Mayer Phoenix Scottsdale Tempe Tucson
Arkansas	Arkadelphia Conway El Dorado Fayetteville Fort Smith Jonesboro Little Rock Magnolia Monticello Russellville Searcy
California	Alameda Anaheim Arcata Bakersfield Berkeley Brea Calexico Camarillo Chico Culver City Cupertino Diamond Bar Downey El Monte

California	Fair Oaks Fresno Fullerton Gardena Glendale Healdsburg Irvine La Verne Lake Forest Los Angeles Northridge Oakland Pasadena Rancho Cucamonga Rosemead San Bruno San Diego San Francisco San Jose San Rafael Santa Barbara Santa Clara Santa Cruz Santa Monica Santa Rosa Sherman Oaks Thousand Oaks Torrance Walnut
Colorado	Boulder Colorado Springs Denver Fort Collins Grand Junction Greenwood Village Littleton Longmont Westminster

continues

continued

Connecticut	Cheshire Glastonbury Hamden Kent Norwalk Salisbury Thompson West Haven Woodbridge
Delaware	Dover New Castle Newark
District of Columbia	Washington
Florida	Boca Raton Celebration Fort Lauderdale Fort Myers Gainesville Hollywood Jacksonville Key West Maitland Melbourne Miami Miami Beach Miami Shores Montverde Orlando Pensacola Pompano Beach Sarasota St. Petersburg Tallahassee Tampa Temple Terrace West Palm Beach
Georgia	Albany Athens Atlanta Augusta Columbus Dahlonega

Georgia	Doraville Macon Marietta Morrow Savannah Smyrna Statesboro Valdosta
Hawaii	Hilo Honolulu
Idaho	Boise Meridian Moscow Pocatello
Illinois	Carbondale Carterville Champaign Charleston Chicago De Kalb Deerfield Joliet Lombard Mount Prospect Peoria River Forest Springfield Sycamore
Indiana	Bloomington Columbus Crown Point Culver Evansville Fort Wayne Indianapolis Lafayette Merrillville Mishawaka Muncie New Albany Saint Mary of the Woods

continues

continued

Iowa	Bettendorf
	Cedar Falls
	Coralville
	Sioux City
	West Des Moines
Kansas	Atchison
	Hays
	Lawrence
	Manhattan
	Overland Park
	Pittsburg
	Topeka
	Wichita
Kentucky	Florence
	Highland Heights
	Lexington
	Louisville
	Murray
Louisiana	Alexandria
	Baton Rouge
	Bossier City
	Lake Charles
	Metairie
	Monroe
	New Orleans
	Ruston
Maine	Bangor
	Bethel
	East Machias
	Farmington
	Fryeburg
	Kents Hill
	Lee
	Pittsfield
	Presque Isle
	South Portland
Maryland	Baltimore
	Bethesda
	College Park
	Columbia
	Landover

Maryland	Salisbury Silver Spring Towson
Massachusetts	Allston Boston Bridgewater Brockton Burlington Cambridge Gill Groton Holyoke Lowell Malden Marlborough Newton North Andover Somerville Waltham West Springfield Worcester
Michigan	Allendale Ann Arbor Auburn Hills Berrien Springs Detroit East Lansing Farmington Hills Flint Grand Rapids Holt Interlochen Kalamazoo Lansing Livonia Mount Pleasant Sault Ste. Marie Troy Wayne

continues

continued

Minnesota	Duluth Edina Faribault Roschester St. Cloud St. Paul Winona Woodbury
Mississippi	Flowood Hattiesburg Jackson Mississippi State Oxford Tupelo
Missouri	Cape Girardeau Columbia Concordia Hannibal Jefferson City Kansas City Kirksville Lee's Summit Rolla St. Louis Springfield Warrensburg
Montana	Billings Bozeman Helena Missoula
Nebraska	Columbus Kearney Lincoln Omaha Scottsbluff
Nevada	Las Vegas Reno
New Hampshire	Andover Concord Lebanon Plymouth Portsmouth Tilton

New Jersey	Clark
	Closter
	East Orange
	Ewing
	Fair Lawn
	Fort Lee
	Hamilton
	Jersey City
	Laurel Spring
	Mercerville
	Mount Laurel
	New Brunswick
	Palisades Park
	Passaic
	Paterson
	Ridgefield
	Rutherford
	Teaneck
	West New York
New Mexico	Albuquerque
	Farmington
	Las Cruces
	Roswell
	Santa Fe
New York	Albany
	Albertson
	Bayside
	Brooklyn
	Buffalo
	East Syracuse
	Elmhurst
	Flushing
	Forest Hills
	Garden City
	Melville
	New York
	Potsdam
	Poughkeepsie
	Purchase
	Queens
	Riverdale

continues

continued

New York	Rochester
	Syracuse
	Vestal
	Westbury
North Carolina	Apex
	Asheville
	Boone
	Cary
	Charlotte
	Cullowhee
	Durham
	Fayetteville
	Greensboro
	Greenville
	Raleigh
	Wilmington
	Winston-Salem
North Dakota	Bismarck
	Devils Lake
	Fargo
	Grand Forks
	Minot
	Wahpeton
Ohio	Akron
	Athens
	Beavercreek
	Cincinnati
	Cleveland
	Columbus
	Dayton
	Maumee
	Mentor
	Niles
	Orville
	Stow
	Strongsville
	Toledo
	Worthington
Oklahoma	Norman
	Oklahoma City
	Stillwater
	Tulsa
	Weatherford

Oregon	Bend Corvallis Eugene La Grande Medford Portland
Pennsylvania	Allentown Clarks Summit Conshohocken Erie Harrisburg Hazleton Indiana Lancaster Mercersburg Millersville Monroeville Pennsburg Philadelphia Pittsburgh Tyrone
Rhode Island	Bristol Cumberland Providence Warwick
South Carolina	Charleston Columbia Conway Florence Greenville North Augusta Rock Hill
South Dakota	Rapid City Sioux Falls
Tennessee	Chattanooga Clarksville Cordova Jackson Johnson City Knoxville Martin Memphis Murfreesboro Nashville

continues

continued

Texas	Abilene
	Amarillo
	Austin
	Beaumont
	Bedford
	Brownsville
	Canyon
	College Station
	Commerce
	Corpus Christi
	Dallas
	Denton
	Edinburg
	El Paso
	Fort Worth
	Houston
	Huntsville
	Kingsville
	Laredo
	Lubbock
	McAllen
	Nacogdoches
	Odessa
	San Antonio
	San Marcos
	Sugar Land
	Texarkana
	Tyler
	Waco
	Wichita Falls
Utah	Blanding
	Cedar City
	Lindon
	Logan
	Mount Pleasant
	Price
	Provo
	St. George
	Salt Lake City
	Taylorsville
Vermont	St. Johnsbury
	Williston

Virginia	Annandale Arlington Blacksburg Bristol Chatham Chesapeake Fairfax Falls Church Fork Union Glen Allen Lynchburg McLean New Market Roanoke Salem Vienna
Washington	Bellevue Bellingham Edmonds Ellensburg Everett Fife Kirkland Lynden Mountlake Terrace Puyallup Renton Seattle Spokane
West Virginia	Bluefield Charleston Huntington Morgantown
Wisconsin	Ashwaubenon Brookfield Delafield Eau Claire La Crosse Madison Milwaukee Oshkosh Stevens Point

continues

continued

Wyoming	Casper
	Cheyenne
	Laramie
	Rock Springs

Index

F

G-H

I

J-K

L

M

N

O

P

Q

R

S

T

U-V

W-X-Y-Z

„The pen is mighter than the Sword."

W. S.

„The pen is mighter than the sword."

W. S.

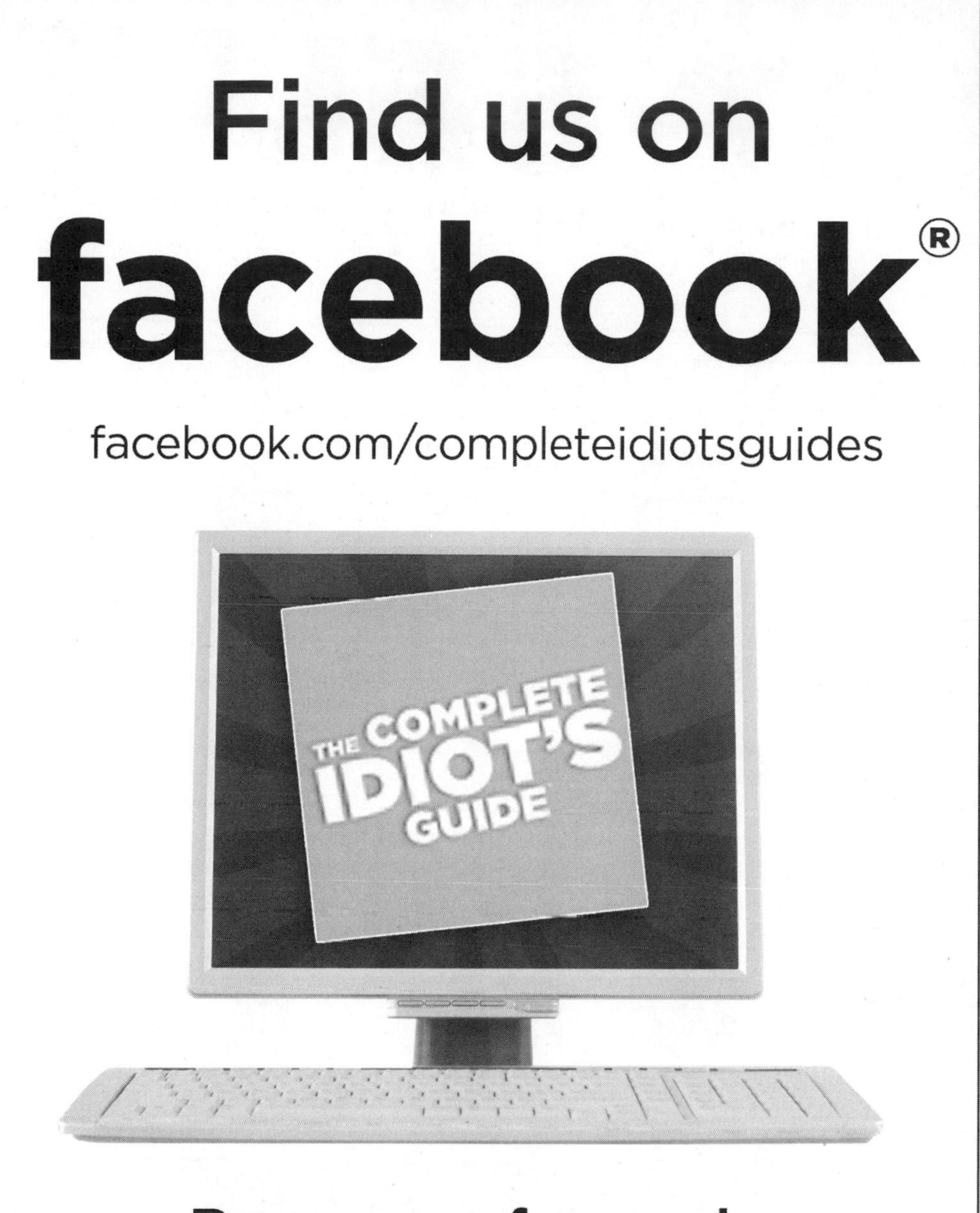
Find us on
facebook®
facebook.com/completeidiotsguides
THE COMPLETE IDIOT'S GUIDE